ON
ROCKY
TOP

ALSO BY CLAY TRAVIS

Dixieland Delight:
A Football Season on the Road in
the Southeastern Conference

ON
ROCKY
TOP

A FRONT-ROW SEAT
TO THE END OF AN ERA

CLAY TRAVIS

itbooks

AN IMPRINT OF HARPERCOLLINS PUBLISHERS

Frontispiece courtesy of Elizabeth Olivier/UTsports.com

HarperCollins books may be purchased for educational, business, or
sales promotional use. For information please write: Special Markets
Department, HarperCollins Publishers, 10 East 53rd Street, New York,
NY 10022.

FIRST EDITION

Designed by Mia Risberg

Library of Congress Cataloging-in-Publication Data has been applied for.

ISBN 978-0-06-171926-4

09 10 11 12 13   OV/RRD   10 9 8 7 6 5 4 3 2 1

For Lara and Fox,
my two favorite people in the world

It is not the critic who counts; not the man who points out how the strong man stumbles, or where the doer of deeds could have done them better. The credit belongs to the man who is actually in the arena, whose face is marred by dust and sweat and blood; who strives valiantly; who errs, who comes short again and again, because there is no effort without error and shortcoming; but who does actually strive to do the deeds; who knows great enthusiasms, the great devotions; who spends himself in a worthy cause; who at the best knows in the end the triumph of high achievement, and who at the worst, if he fails, at least fails while daring greatly, so that his place shall never be with those cold and timid souls who neither know victory nor defeat.

THEODORE ROOSEVELT

This quote is inscribed on a plaque
outside Coach Phillip Fulmer's home
in Maryville, Tennessee

CONTENTS

ON
ROCKY
TOP

THE GRANDDADDY OF THEM ALL

IN 15 MINUTES IT WILL BE football time in Tennessee. Even though the Volunteers are 2,176 miles from Knoxville's Neyland Stadium in the visitors' locker room of Los Angeles's Rose Bowl. In a quarter of an hour 87 of the players currently gathered in front of an easel with General Robert Neyland's 7 Maxims of Football etched onto it will pour out of the long corridor beneath the stadium and enter the fading light of a California September afternoon. But now, in these final moments before the 2008 football season commences, the teammates congregate in a semicircle of folding chairs while student managers circle the room yelling out, "Gatorade, Pedialyte, water, drink up!" The student managers, undergrads at the University of Tennessee who work 30 to 40 hours a week with the football team, are wearing orange shirts and holding brightly colored bottles of liquids aloft in their hands. The Tennessee Volunteer players are clad in their road uniform of orange pants and white jerseys, orange numbers on their backs catching the locker-room lights when they move. They sit with heads bowed, their large padded shoulders and enormous bulky legs appearing to swallow the flimsy chairs. The players wait, bathed in the soft overhead lights of the visitors' locker room, for their coach to arrive. Other than the calls of the training staff, the Rose Bowl locker room is completely silent.

Coach Phillip Fulmer is in the corridor outside the locker room, huddling with his assistant coaches. Fulmer is a Tennessee legend, in his 16th full season as the Vols' head coach. With his ponderous lower lip that extends just a bit past his smaller upper lip, the full-stomached heft of an aging offensive lineman, a slightly sunburned face, a graying and balding head that is generally covered by an orange Tennessee cap, and a unique ability to use the word *heck* as subject, verb, and exclamation, Fulmer is a Southern football coach direct from Hollywood central casting.

Having won the Vols' second consensus national championship in 1998, breaking a 47-year-long championship drought, Fulmer recently signed a contract extension in the 2008 offseason that pays him nearly $3 million a year. Since that 1998 championship season, Fulmer's teams have not won an SEC title, losing three times in the SEC championship game in 2001, 2004, and 2007. This recent championship failure hangs around the stolid former UT offensive lineman's neck, an albatross of past expectations unfulfilled. Still, Fulmer has a street named after him outside Neyland Stadium, Phillip Fulmer Way, and he's just 27 wins from passing General Robert Neyland, who led the team for 21 years, to become the all-time winningest coach in UT football history.

Fulmer is wedded to the University of Tennessee in a way that few coaches have ever been connected to their schools. He's spent 34 of the past 40 years of his life at Tennessee. From 1968 to 1971 Fulmer played as an offensive guard on the football team, arriving as a 6' 1" 198-pound linebacker who believed he might become a dentist one day. He won an SEC title as a player in 1969, and was 30-5 during his three-year career (freshmen were not eligible then). Upon graduation, he worked his way up in the coaching ranks, with 5 years spent at Wichita State and 1 year at Vanderbilt. In 1980 he became an assistant coach at Tennessee under Head Coach Johnny Majors, and 12 years later, in 1992, he was named the 20th head coach in University of Tennessee history. Since that time he has amassed a career record of 147-45 (.766), which, on a percentage basis, makes him the winningest coach in college football with 10 or more years under his belt.

But Fulmer's connection to the university is not just individual. All four of Fulmer's children, his son, Phillip Jr. (39), and three daughters, Courtney (25), Brittany (23), and Allison (21), currently a senior, attended the school. In 2007 Fulmer and his wife of 26 years, Vicky, donated $1 million to the university, half to the athletic program and half to academics. He's the most recognizable man in the entire state of Tennessee . . . and there isn't a close second.

He's also the dean of Southeastern Conference coaches, and in his 16 seasons as UT head coach, he has seen the SEC evolve from a spirited regional pastime into one of the most profitable enterprises in American sports. In 1992, when Tennessee hired Fulmer, three other rival coaches in the SEC had played for and graduated from the schools they coached: Georgia's Ray Goff, a former quarterback; Ole Miss's Billy Brewer, a former quarterback; and Florida's Steve Spurrier, a former quarterback as well. What's more, five additional SEC coaches played for or coached under Alabama's Bear Bryant: Jackie Sherrill at Mississippi State, Danny Ford at Arkansas, Gene Stallings at Alabama, Pat Dye at Auburn, and Curley Hallman at LSU. In 1992 the only school in the SEC with a coach born outside the Southeast was Vanderbilt. SEC football was still a regional game, a sport played and coached by men of the South. Lots of men of the South. Since 1992, Fulmer has outlasted 46 head coaches at the 11 other SEC schools.

Now, as 2008 commences, Fulmer is the last of the regionalists— the only coach in the SEC to be born in the state where he coaches or to graduate from the school he coaches. Less than a month ago the SEC inked the most lucrative television contract in the history of collegiate conference sports—ESPN and CBS agreed to pay a whopping $325 million a year to televise league athletic events. With this money has come a newfound national prominence for the SEC. In fact, this very game, UT's season opener against UCLA in the *Monday Night Football* slot on ESPN, is a made-for-television contest. ESPN was able to get both universities to change their already-announced schedules to fit the telecast. Tennessee bumped back their opener against the University of Alabama-Birmingham (UAB) to September 13 and UCLA rescheduled their opener with Fresno State. Now both teams have the television stage entirely to themselves—the final game of the opening weekend of college football. This is no surprise; television owns college football. As UT athletic director Mike Hamilton said back in early April when the change was announced, "The opportunity to play unopposed on national television against such a quality opponent as UCLA was something we couldn't pass up." Hamilton couldn't pass it up because 85 percent of UT's athletes come from outside the state of Tennessee. And potential recruits are first exposed to the UT program through television events such as this one.

As Labor Day 2008 arrives, Fulmer's Vols are ranked #18 in the preseason polls, and are coming off a 10-4 season that included a narrow 21–14 SEC championship game loss to eventual 2007 national champion LSU. After last year's season Tennessee lost their offensive coordinator, David Cutcliffe, who left to become the head coach at Duke. As his replacement Fulmer has selected Dave Clawson, a 41-year-old former defensive back from Williams College who has spent the past four seasons as head coach of the University of Richmond Spiders, a lower-division college. Clawson, a thin man with a boyish face and closely cropped dark hair, is highly esteemed in the coaching profession, so highly esteemed that he's been hired with an understanding that if all goes well he will be Fulmer's successor at Tennessee. This fact is not yet public knowledge, but Clawson moved his wife and young family, a daughter, age 9, and a son, age 7, to Knoxville in June with the hope and expectation that this will be the final stop of his coaching career. His plan is to win lots of games, win some SEC championships, and score a lot of points. UCLA will be the first test of what Vol fans are already calling "the Clawfense."

Today Clawson helms an offense that returns nine starters. The biggest question is at quarterback, where the highly touted redshirt junior Jonathan Crompton will take over for the departed Erik Ainge, drafted by the New York Jets. The quarterback position is especially precarious given that 10 days before the start of the football season Crompton severely sprained his right ankle. It's bad enough that he has been wearing a walking boot in between practices.

At this very moment, surrounding the team that Fulmer and many college football aficionados believe will contend for an SEC championship, on three different locker-room walls rest three red digital clocks counting down the minutes and seconds until kickoff. Strength coach Johnny Long is standing in front of the team insisting that each of the players still standing in the locker room take one of the folding chairs in front of him. "Everybody sit down now. Rest your legs," says the dark-haired, goateed native of Louisiana. Only a few players remain on their feet. Defensive tackle Dan Williams is one of them. "I don't want to sit down," Williams says. "Well, I want you down, off your feet," says Long, his words clipped, dancing with the intensity one would expect from a man who is constantly drinking 16-ounce cans of Full Throttle energy drink. Williams, a 6' 3", 305-pound junior defensive tackle from Memphis, Tennessee, defers to Long, a diminutive 5' 6" package of dynamicism and curse words. He sits.

Arian Foster, UT's senior running back, who is just 685 yards from becoming the all-time leading rusher in Volunteer history, sits nearby, leaning over with his head between his knees. The 6' 1", 230-pound Foster went to high school in San Diego, and the Rose Bowl stands will be filled with family members and friends who have come to see him play. His father is a Los Angeles native and will bring Foster's grandmother, who still lives in L.A., to the game for her first time to see Arian play in college. Foster, a light-skinned black man with a thin beard, is flexing and unflexing his hands. In the process the tattoos on his arms ripple. Foster has 10 tattoos, snaking around his right and left arms. Soon after he graduated from high school in San Diego, Foster designed what was to be his first tattoo, a pyramid discovered in Mexico melded with a pyramid discovered in Africa. The pyramids represented the duality of his heritage: Foster's African American father and his Hispanic mother. But when he arrived at the tattoo parlor with his mother, Bernadette, in tow, the tattoo artist refused to ink the design because Foster was not yet 18. Although he's since gotten 10 other tattoos, he has yet to add this design, but is reserving his back for the mural.

Usually Foster wears the number 27, but today he dons the number 30, in honor of David Holbert, a UT fullback who suffered a devastating knee injury in the preseason. He considers Holbert to be more than a friend, more like a brother. Foster is a bundle of contradictions: outspoken but quiet, a violent runner who is majoring in philosophy and writes poetry in his spare time. When asked in July what game he was most looking forward to this season, the eccentric Foster replied, "All of them . . . I hope."

He looks at me now and nods. I feel strangely uncomfortable. I'm in the inner sanctum of UT football, a fan drowning in access. I can barely breathe. I close my eyes for an instant. My heart is pounding and my mouth is dry. I have been a Tennessee fan since birth. I'm named after my grandfather, a former Vol who played for General Neyland. I'm in awe of my proximity to this season, to my team.

When I open my eyes and take a deep breath, Fulmer is suddenly there, standing beside me. "Good to see you, Clay," he says. Fulmer's wearing an orange polo shirt and khaki pants and is intensely calm, much calmer than I am. "I saw you in here with us yesterday at the walkthrough. Didn't see you from the front and thought you'd snuck in. I pointed you out and told them to get you out of here." I laugh nervously. "You getting some good stuff?" Fulmer asks.

Words fail me. I sputter an answer that makes no sense. Fulmer looks me in the eyes, appraises me, finds me lacking in some degree, I'm sure.

Today is Coach Fulmer's 58th birthday. I know this because my dad advised me earlier in the week, "You might want to mention it to him, wish him a happy birthday." I'd nodded when my dad suggested it, silently thinking it highly implausible that sometime between Saturday and the Monday-night kickoff in front of a national television audience I was going to have an opportunity to speak with Coach Fulmer and mention his birthday. But suddenly that moment is here.

Fulmer reaches out his hand and we shake. He's moving now toward General Neyland's Maxims hanging on a dry-erase board in front of the team. It's time to address his team and commence the season.

"Happy birthday, Coach," I say, a few seconds belatedly. Fulmer looks at me slightly askance. Nods. I halfway expect to be pulled from the Rose Bowl locker room. Instead he continues walking, slowly, across the room to face his players. The trainers have stopped insisting that the players drink, and the room is completely silent.

Then Fulmer speaks and breaks the silence.

"Let me see the captains," he says.

The five senior captains—offensive tackle Ramon Foster, wide receiver Lucas Taylor, defensive end Robert Ayers, deep snapper Morgan Cox, and linebacker Ellix Wilson—spring forward out of their chairs. Fulmer steps to the side of the room and converses with the captains in such a whisper that their words are lost to the rest of us. Suddenly I realize that Tennessee's defensive coordinator since 1995, John Chavis, is standing beside me. Like Fulmer, Chavis has long-standing ties to Tennessee, having arrived as a walk-on defensive lineman and played football for the Vols in the late 1970s. Now Chavis is tapping his play chart idly on his leg. His mustache is tightly clipped and his dark black hair is as tightly combed as is humanly possible. It occurs to me that the grim-faced and dour Chavis might not have smiled since 1998.

When the red digital clocks show that there are only 13 minutes remaining until kickoff, Fulmer returns with the captains to the team and begins his speech.

"Get on one knee and grab the hand of the person next to you," he says. Everyone in the room drops, accustomed to the routine. It takes me a moment to lower myself onto my left knee and I don't take the hand of Chavis, crouching on the floor alongside me. I debate reaching for it, but by then we're already in the midst of the Lord's Prayer, and I decide it would be too awkward. The entire team is intoning the words as one.

"Our father, who art in heaven, hallowed be thy name . . ."

I haven't said the Lord's Prayer since my elementary school days in Nashville's Baptist day care, but the rhythm of the words returns to me and soon my voice joins in the chorus. As soon as the prayer is over, the players return to their seats and the managers and coaches stand.

"Well, we've worked and we've prepared and we've waited to get this special opportunity on Monday night with the entire nation watching. It doesn't get any better in college football than this," Fulmer begins. "Playing in what they call the granddaddy of them all, Rose Bowl Stadium, nice place to be, not nearly as good as home. There's a lot of people out there dressed in orange up in the stands, lot of people dressed in blue up in the stands, not a darn one of them have anything to do with what happens on the field.

"That gets back to the eleven on the field at that particular time getting their job done with a physicalness, with a speed of the game, with a finishing-everything-that-you-start attitude. When we walk out of this locker room there's no more talk, we have talked and talked and talked and talked."

Fulmer paces now, slowly, regally. His eyes are trained on his players, scanning his team from one side to the other. The players are tense, moving their arms on their thighs, tightening and untightening the gloves on their palms, twitching their neck muscles, breathing in through their noses and out through their mouths.

"Okay, we've practiced hard and we've worked hard and we've got that offense down to what we want it to be. We've got a whole hell of a lot to prove from the defensive standpoint where we need to be back to where John Chavis's defenses are.

"Offensively get our pads down and make those tough yards. It's a whole lot easier to call plays when it's second and six, anything normal, third and two, anything normal. Be sharp in our motion and alignments, smart and look efficient like we have in the past couple of scrimmages."

Fulmer claps his hands, bites his lower lip, holds it for an instant, then laughs softly to himself.

"It's not a scrimmage; this is the real deal with the world watching. An opportunity sitting here in front of you to show the 2008 Volunteer football team on national television. It doesn't get any better than that."

He pauses once more, turns in front of Arian Foster, who is now sitting on the blue carpeted floor of the locker room.

"I'm going to say it again: Regardless of what happens out there tonight, I'm proud of what you've done. To this point you've come together as a football team. We've got the pieces of the puzzle put back together to where we look like a football team, act like a football team. We are a disciplined group of guys that know how to go play the game. So play it like you're capable of playing."

Fulmer stands directly in front of General Neyland's 7 Maxims. He brings his large hands together in front of him, and the lenses on the reading glasses folded at the neck of his orange coach's polo—white power T sewn directly above his heart—catch the overhead lights of the locker room and flicker.

"We're going to say these game maxims and I'm going to tell you again: believe in your brothers all the way back to the twenties that have said these maxims. Understand what you stand for by putting on that orange shirt and that T on your helmet. It's something that's special. Maybe some of you freshmen don't really understand that yet, but by the time you get to be a junior and senior you will.

"Know what respect that commands from anybody that you line up against in this entire country. I had six or seven of their [other teams'] coaches come down there to shake my hand and talk about what we've done over the past sixteen years and how incredible it's been, the consistency that the Tennessee teams have had . . . in an admirable way, not in a negative way at all. Understand what you represent when you put your hand on the ground and you get ready to come off the ball on offense and you get ready to strike your butts on defense and what the Tennessee offense and the Tennessee defense has meant here for a long, long time."

Coach Fulmer gestures toward UT junior running back Montario Hardesty and says, "I am such an admirer of Montario Hardesty and what he's done for our punt team and our kickoff coverage team as an upperclassman. Taking on that role. To practice with the verve. And I know if he gets an opportunity he's going to go out and make a difference in the game tonight. You freshmen follow that lead.

"That's what you represent. With a T on your helmet you don't have to have an S on your chest. But you've got to respect what you stand for and where we've come from.

"You've done a hell of a job. Now let's go play our rears off tonight!"

The all-time winningest coach in UT history, the late General Robert Neyland, introduced his seven maxims of winning football in the 1920s, and since those days every University of Tennessee team has recited them prior to each game. My grandfather said them during his playing days in the 1930s. Now the players and coaches intone the maxims in a hushed and intense rush of words without pausing to take any breaths.

One: The team that makes the fewest mistakes will win.
Two: Play for and make the breaks and when one comes your way—SCORE.
Three: If at first the game—or the breaks—go against you, don't let up . . . put on more steam.
Four: Protect our kickers, our QB, our lead, and our ball game.
Five: Ball, oskie, cover, block, cut and slice, pursue and gang tackle . . . for this is the WINNING EDGE.
Six: Press the kicking game. Here is where the breaks are made.

The players chant the first six maxims at a fevered pace and then rise en masse, rushing toward the exit of the Rose Bowl locker room while screaming, "Seven: Carry the fight to our opponent and keep it there for sixty minutes!"

This last of General Neyland's Maxims is even more hurried than the previous six. It emerges as almost a single word. The players rush through the locker-room exit and pass beneath an orange sign in the shape of the state of Tennessee that reads: "I will give my all for Tennessee."

One by one the players leap and slap the sign with their palms. As the last of the players leave, a pair of defensive backs enact an elaborate alley-oop that ends in the touching of the T. Now the entire Tennessee Volunteer team is out of the locker room, with me amidst them, heading down the concrete ramparts in the direction of the field. The dull roar of the crowd filters down into our ears. The players' pace quickens, the clack of 87 pairs of cleats on concrete echoes, the season is nigh. My throat is so tight I can barely swallow. I'm as close as any football fan could ever be to his favorite team, and as kickoff nears I'm dizzy with excitement.

The team gathers in a large jumble of bodies leaping on the concrete beneath the stands, and now the players are screaming along with the rising roar of the Rose Bowl crowd. Above us UCLA fans are peering down beneath their seats and cursing the front lines of the Vol football players.

"They built this stadium with Tennessee steel," a player yells, pointing to the underside of the bleachers. It's true. The Rose Bowl's steel girders have been stamped with "Tennessee, USA." The team cheers in unison.

We pause at the field's entrance for a moment, suspended and packed together in a large bunch. I've been consumed by the football team and can barely see anything at all. Mere moments from an explosion, this is the calm before the orange-clad storm. Then, up above me, through the mass of the players' bobbing white helmets with orange T's, I catch the unfurling of a large Tennessee flag—orange with a bold white T—and then we're all moving inexorably and suddenly toward the field of the Rose Bowl.

Grass replaces concrete, and we run from the dimness of the locker-room tunnel to the sunlight-dappled field. After 9 months of exquisite slowness without football—winter's draining chill, spring's torrential rains, and summer's stifling heat across the state of Tennessee—the moment of actual arrival is sudden. Even though I know it's coming, the sprint onto the field is shocking, bracing in the way that jumping into an ice-covered lake is. Chills race along the length of my body. The 110th season of University of Tennessee football has begun.

CHAPTER 2

CALIFORNIA DREAMIN'

ON JANUARY 1, 1986, I WATCHED my first University of Tennessee football game on television by myself. I was 6 years old, and Tennessee was playing the University of Miami in the Sugar Bowl. My dad and several of his friends were at the game, sporting orange and singing UT's unofficial fight song, "Rocky Top," loudly in the New Orleans Superdome. I watched the game at home from an old yellow chair directly in front of the television. Occasionally my mom came to check on me. I don't remember standing or yelling or making a lot of noise or really ever moving from the chair at all. I just remember being overwhelmed by the game in front of me—and falling in love with the excitement of it all.

Tennessee was a huge underdog that game, but I was too young to understand what being an underdog meant or to know just how good Miami's Heisman Trophy–winning quarterback, Vinny Testaverde, or his top wide receiver, future NFL Hall-of-Famer Michael Irvin, were. I only knew that Miami was the enemy and that it was somehow important for me to watch this game and support my family's team.

As the seconds ticked down to kickoff, the University of Tennessee's

Pride of the Southland marching band, wearing fluorescent orange, formed the T and the UT players rushed out from the tunnel into the bright lights. For the first time in my life, I felt butterflies in my stomach.

Although Tennessee fell behind early, 7–0, it wasn't long before the world came undone in one long glorious medley of plays, one Big Orange touchdown after another. In the third quarter, my favorite player, Eric Swanson, number 27, a wide receiver with blond hair, caught a couple of passes leading to a touchdown that built Tennessee's lead to 21–7. I adored Swanson, not only because of his athleticism, but because I too had blond hair, which made us virtual brothers in my 6-year-old consciousness. When he caught a pass and fell to the ground, it was almost as if I, 560 miles away in my darkened Nashville den, had just caught the pass myself.

On the field Swanson lay wiggling his legs, his orange-striped white pants shivering with glee. For the next year my friends and I would pretend we were Eric Swanson, lying on the warm grass in the Tennessee sunshine, wiggling our legs in triumph as if we had just caught Sugar Bowl passes against Miami. Eric Swanson was my first athletic hero, and his celebration during the Miami game is still my favorite childhood sports memory.

When halftime arrived, UT's band took the field and the famous country singer/songwriter Lee Greenwood came out to sing "God Bless the USA," my dad's favorite song. When he hit the third stanza, standing at midfield, holding a microphone, and staring up into the stands, the 43-year-old Greenwood crooned about the "hills of Tennessee," prompting the predominantly Tennessee crowd to drown out his song with cheers. Later, when my dad came back from the game, he told me no less than a dozen times how loudly the stadium exploded with applause when Greenwood mentioned the hills of Tennessee.

"I just wish you could have heard it," he said.

After halftime came touchdowns four and five. When UT scored the fifth time, this fifth unbelievable and unanswered touchdown, to go up 35–7 on the not-so-mighty Hurricanes, my mom strolled into the den.

I was leaning forward with my hands clenched so tightly and my eyes fixated so intently on the television screen that she asked me if I was okay.

"Has UT won for sure?" I asked.

My mom looked at the television and saw the score. She was no sports fan, but she knew the rules.

"Your dad always says it's never over until the game actually ends."

Her answer satisfied me. I nodded my head, returned my attention to the TV screen, and kept up a ferocious rooting interest until the game's final play. When the referee blew the whistle, I jumped from the chair and did a small, private victory dance. I lay in bed that night for what seemed like hours. For the first time in my life, a sporting event kept me from sleeping.

The day after the game I spoke on the phone with my grandfather, Richard Fox, who played for General Neyland from 1931 to 1933. Given his heart troubles, my grandfather was under doctor's orders not to watch football games live, but when he'd finally gotten word that the Vols won, he'd stayed up long after midnight to savor the victory. "Sonny boy," he said, "it doesn't get much better than this."

That night my dad returned from New Orleans. He picked me up and twirled me around in the air. Then he taught me a new cheer, patting the couch in time to, "I say it's great . . . to be . . . a Tennessee Vol. I say it's great . . . to be . . . a Tennessee Vol." At the time this cheer seemed like the greatest invention in the history of mankind—even better than the General Lee car on *The Dukes of Hazzard*.

My mom, who evidently had caught wind of the fact that my dad was home when she heard the racket he, my sister, and I were making, sauntered into the living room.

"Well," she said, "how was the game?"

"It was the best night of my life," my dad said.

I think Dad might have slept alone that night.

The 1986 Sugar Bowl remains one of the sweetest victories in UT history. How much did this game matter to Tennessee fans? Said former

UT coach Johnny Majors, "Many years later a man came up to me and said that when he got depressed he would put on that game and immediately feel better. It was amazing the impact it had on the Tennessee people."

A FEW MONTHS SHY of 23 years after that Sugar Bowl game, on August 29, 2008, I drive to the Nashville International Airport to begin my season following the University of Tennessee Volunteers. I'm 29 years old, going on 6. I'm exceedingly optimistic about this year's season. Of course, I'm always a tremendous optimist before the first game of every season. According to my parents, I get this from my grandfather and my dad, both incurable optimists. No matter how much Tennessee's opponent is favored, victory is always near.

This year I've convinced myself all omens are breaking in our favor. Whereas in years past the offseason has sometimes been tainted by arrests, malfeasance, and, occasionally, the molestation of a yearling or a fowl, thus far the UT football team has remained out of trouble. This clean slate must be due at least in part to the team self-instituting an 11 P.M. curfew. Coaches are fond of saying nothing good ever happens after midnight. Which, to be fair, is entirely false. For instance, sex almost always happens after midnight in college. But this year UT's team has bent to the coaching cliché and stayed out of trouble.

As a fan I'm hopeful that this off-field discipline will translate into positive results on the field—discipline and the ability to make the winning play in tight ballgames. My spirits are buoyant as my 11:30 A.M. flight to Los Angeles nears.

I'm embarking on a sort of real-life fan fantasy camp this fall—following my favorite team with unlimited access for the season, with the intention of writing a book about my beloved Vols. In June I met with University of Tennessee officials and laid out a series of ridiculous requests for my "research." "I'd like to run through the T for the Alabama game, spend a week with the coaches, travel with the football team to an away game, watch several games from the sideline, be in the locker room for pre- and postgame speeches, do the Vol Walk, and ride in the big rig that transports the UT helmets and pads to an away game." I'd written all these requests down on a Holiday Inn notepad the night before our meeting, scarcely believing UT would comply with any of them. As long as I was going to be spending 5 months up close and personal with my favorite team, I figured, why not dream big?

Amazingly, Tennessee officials nodded their heads at each request. Inside the Stokely Athletic Center on Tennessee's campus, in a brightly lit conference room with Tennessee posters hanging on the walls, I attempted to contain my excitement. By the time I left Tennessee's campus 1 hour and 23 minutes later, I was humming "Rocky Top" on a baking-hot Knoxville sidewalk. Football season was over 2 months away, and already I felt like I could run through a brick wall if Phil Fulmer asked me to.

Now, at the airport 3 days before the season is to begin, throngs of orange-clad Tennessee fans, Tennesseans dressing up for the benefit of other Tennesseans, are waiting to board our Southwest flight to Los Angeles. Meanwhile, there's a ton of other people at the airport, non-Southerners, Yankees, probably, who are warily looking around in every direction, afraid of what might ensue on this flight. One of the first things you learn as a Tennessee fan is that it's of the utmost importance that people know you are from Tennessee. That's why you wear orange not just on game days but on the days spent traveling for football. The orange badge of courage must be displayed at all times.

And if your outfit does not announce your hometown allegiance, you must do so verbally. As a child, on family vacations, my sister frequently harangued my dad for being too friendly with strangers and telling them where we were from. "You don't have to tell everyone we're from Tennessee," she would say. Once, on a ride to the top of the St. Louis Arch, we shared a compartment with vacationers from New York. After talking for a short while my dad drawled, "Where do y'all think we're from?"

"New York," said the New Yorkers.

My dad's face broke. "No," he said, not seeing that they were teasing him, "we're from Tennessee."

Being from a particular city or state in the South still means something, even in the 21st century, when mobility and lack of connection to any one place has become a hallmark of our times. Every time my dad introduces my wife to people from Tennessee he makes a big deal of explaining that she's from Michigan. "Dee-Troit," he says, turning the city into a multisyllable, exotic, and faraway land.

I remember packing for trips to UT road games as a kid. My dad always insisted that we pack orange to wear for every day we were gone. He took our dress code seriously, even though he didn't pack for himself. Instead my mom took it seriously on his behalf, though she was a bit of a leery fan, always suspicious of the illogical basis of fandom and its impact upon her daddy, husband, and son. "Why do you care," she would constantly ask, "what a bunch of dumb ole athletes do in a *game?*"

Nevertheless, she could not undo my dad's teaching that Volunteer fans are an orange-clad army. If a day passed without our garish orange outfits being immediately identifiable to hunters in three adjoining states, we'd failed our team and our state. As a result, decades later, despite the fact that I live in Tennessee, am leaving from Tennessee, and it's still 3 full days until kickoff at UCLA, I'm wearing my orange shirt as I board the plane.

But if you think merely wearing an orange shirt 3 days before a game is enough to establish your Tennessee bona fides, you're wrong. Nor can you merely discuss the game with your orange-wearing seatmates, or exchange the sports pages from several different Tennessee papers as you fly across the country, or get away with exchanging a nod and a subtle, "Go Vols," or "Go Big Orange," as a lady wearing orange passes you in the aisle. No, that's not enough at all. That's amateur fandom hour. There might even be some people, shudder, who believe that there are Alabama fans flying on this plane. Plainly, this cannot happen. Nope, we have to establish that this plane is rooting for the University of Tennessee. After all, FAA rules require that all planes filled with Southerners announce their football allegiance as they cross the Mississippi River. Scout's honor.

How do you establish who a plane is rooting for? You persuade the Southwest flight attendant to blast "Rocky Top" on the PA system of the plane. Well, of course you do.

Somewhere above Oklahoma, I'm halfway through *The Courting of Marcus Dupree* by Willie Morris when I realize that the plane has gone eerily silent. I look up to see a drunken UT fan, sporting an orange shirt and blue jeans, warbling in the aisle of the plane. I'd previously noted this fan as the middle-aged man pulling out his own smuggled miniature whiskey bottles during the first beverage service. Then the fan had asked me, "How you think the UCLA puss will match up?" Now he stands just outside the captain's cabin with his orange-clad arm draped around a nervous flight attendant. "Y'all ready for some 'Rocky Top'?" he drawls.

Across the aisle from me a man in a Georgia hat angrily switches one leg over the top of the other. "Of all the goddamn cross-country flights," he mumbles. Then, over the Southwest public address system (the last use of which instructed us that there would be some turbulence over Arkansas) comes the first strident chords of "Rocky Top"—"I wish that I was on ole Rocky Top." The airplane begins to sing along as one. A few fans stand. One woman manages to unfurl an orange-and-white pom-pom and shake it in time to the music—on 30 seconds' notice.

Despite the absurdity of the situation, my throat clenches for an instant, then I grip my armrests tighter and begin to sing along as well, loving that my flight is all Vol.

We land in Los Angeles early, perhaps because the flight attendants and the pilots want to get rid of the orange-clad masses on the plane. Before the "fasten your seat belt" sign has gone off, a UT fan in an orange shirt and khaki pants undoes his seat belt and rushes down the aisle toward the back of the plane. He's balding, appears to be about 45 years old, and is moving in a tight crouch, as if standing up to his full height is more likely to draw attention than being a grown man running up the aisle of an airplane in a full crouch.

Behind him a blond flight attendant is calling for him to return to his seat. But the man either doesn't hear or, more likely, is choosing to ignore her. Having already turned on his BlackBerry, he has news to share: "Gerald Williams is eligible," he squeals. "Pass it along." Then he turns and sprints in a waddling crouch back to the front of the plane. Cheers rise up once more. Gerald Williams, a 6' 4", 240-pound linebacker, is a purportedly stellar defensive player who has been attempting to be admitted to the University of Tennessee since 2005. As the 2008 season neared, Tennessee's optimism that he'd be eligible this season has waned. Now he's eligible! Everyone on the plane exults. I feel another shot of adrenaline rush through my body. We've just landed on California soil and already we've received great news. Nothing, it would seem, can stop us now.

MERE MOMENTS AFTER MY fellow Vol fan declares Gerald Williams eligible for the Vols, a dark cloud appears. My full-size car at the Hertz rental station is "out of stock." As in, "We're sorry, Mr. Travis, your car isn't here." The woman behind the counter offers me a convertible instead.

"Is it a Chrysler Sebring?" I ask to make sure that I will not be forced to drive around L.A. for 4 days with my friend Kelly, who's flying out later in the day to join me, in the only car model I loathe.

The agent types on her computer for several seconds. "Oh, no, sir, it's not a Sebring."

"Okay, I'll take it."

"Great. You're in space nine-fifty-five."

Space 955 is all the way across a sun-bleached parking lot. The sky is a perfect blue, the Los Angeles smog almost undetectable. I take a deep breath and savor the scent of college football's eve. My pulse is racing, football fantasies darting through my head.

It's altogether possible that UT is going to win a national championship this year, the 10-year anniversary of the 1998 perfect 13-0 season. We'll beat UCLA and rush past UAB. Then, in the ultimate sign of redemptive justice, we'll spank Urban Meyer's Florida Gators and avenge the 59–20 beating I sat through last year in "the Swamp." Phil Fulmer will chest-bump me in the postgame locker room, maybe break out the elusive double high-five while the UT team serenades us with "Rocky Top" in the background. We'll make Urban Meyer cry, and Georgia's Mark Richt will understand, once and for all, that Jesus is all Vol. Nick Saban will leave Alabama after we vanquish him in Knoxville and he realizes that the Tide will never be able to compete with the Vols again. Steve Spurrier's South Carolina Gamecocks will meet the pimp hand of Vol football for the third consecutive season and he'll question why he ever returned to the SEC. Eventually, we'll run the table in the conference, go 8-0, arrive undefeated for the SEC championship game, which we'll win by 30 points over LSU, and every other fan base will be jealous of how dominant a season we've had.

Every image and thought rushing through my head is positive—I'm one of those ridiculous-looking people you see walking down the street with a full smile plastered on his face—until I reach the far fence and count down the cars: 953, an SUV; 954, a truck; 955 . . . a UCLA-blue Chrysler Sebring.

Oh, no . . . not the Sebring. In UCLA baby blue, of all colors.

My and my wife's history with the Sebring is a bit like the Israeli-Palestinian conflict, only with more enmity and discord. My wife bought a red Sebring in 2005. To her credit, she did this because I told her I liked the idea of having a convertible. But the piece of junk quickly became the bane of my existence. I soon learned that despite its small size, the vehicle has the same turning radius as the *Titanic*. It was impossible to pull into a parking space without executing 14 different steering wheel turns. Once I was aligned correctly, if I pulled up too close to the curb in front of me, my front bumper scraped over the offending parking curb and made a sound of metal being torn asunder. Presumably this was bad for the car. Park next to a curb, and I couldn't open the door without it becoming stuck. Park in front of our condo, and inevitably my wife would find me and say, "Clay, you parked too close to the sidewalk again, the car is stuck."

My distaste for the Sebring culminated in November of 2007 when my wife totaled the car while she was 6 months pregnant with our unborn son. As soon as I found out that both of them were fine, we cashed the insurance check and swore that we would never again come near a Sebring.

Now here the rental stands before me. Worst of all, the Sebring's in UCLA blue. I'm not typically superstitious, but my optimism has faded.

But I don't want to walk all the way back to the car rental place and stand in line again. I make a fateful decision that will echo down the annals of the UT 2008 season for all eternity: I get in the evil Sebring and drive away into the Los Angeles sunshine.

MY ONLY RESPONSIBILITIES FOR Friday afternoon are to check in at the hotel, pick up my friend Kelly, and make sure we set the wheels in motion for our trip to the Playboy Mansion.

Kelly believes we'll be able to visit the Playboy Mansion because his cousin married a former playmate, Miss May 1998, who supposedly has a permanent invite to the Playboy Mansion and can bring over visitors whenever she likes. "That's how it works," he's been telling me for the past month. "Once you're a playmate, you can go to the house whenever you want."

When pressed for the particulars as to how he knows this to be the case, Kelly is remarkably spare in his details. Namely, he provides none. Even still, as soon as I pull out of the Hertz lot, he calls me from the Nashville airport, where he's awaiting a later flight. "We'll be in the Playboy Mansion by tomorrow," he says.

Kelly raises the issue of what we need to wear to the mansion, debating whether we should bring our own swimsuits or whether Hef offers up extras to all his guests. He also instructs me that since he has a girlfriend, I should make sure that no playmates try to have sex with him. In sum, we have spent enough time to write this book twice talking about all the details surrounding our impending trip to the Playboy Mansion. All thanks to Miss May 1998.

I check into the Pasadena Sheraton and spend the afternoon reading *Athlon* and *Lindy's* preseason football magazines while idly watching news stories about John McCain's vice-presidential selection, Sarah Palin. For a long time I've been extremely selective about which preseason magazine I buy. Namely I select whichever magazine ranks UT highest. I do this because the other magazine, the one that ranks us lower, is clearly biased against my team. I consider it a sign of great emotional growth that I've purchased both magazines this fall.

In their 2008 preseason guide *Athlon* predicts UT to finish 17th overall but just 3rd in the rugged SEC East—behind Georgia and Florida. *Athlon* predicts UT will win eight games and lose to Auburn, and lists three games, UCLA, Florida, and Georgia, as toss-ups. *Lindy's* is less generous—pegging the Vols as the 24th-best team in the country. Angrily I slam the magazine to the ground. Clearly *Lindy's* is run by communists . . . or Florida Gator fans.

On the cover of *Lindy's* magazine is Tennessee's Arian Foster, the 22-year-old senior running back from San Diego, who has agreed to participate with me on this book. So far Arian and I have a great relationship. We've texted frequently and talked on the phone several times. We've met in person once—at the UT Alumni Picnic in July. On a hot July day, Arian arrived resplendent in a white suit, looking as big as a small hotel. I shook his hand, which is the size of some men's arms, and he brought me in for a more familiarizing chest bump. "All right, man," he said.

Awkwardly, we bumped chests.

We were in a media room at Nashville's Lipscomb University and we sat down on flimsy blue chairs that overlooked the basketball floor below. In front of us, through a large Plexiglas window, we watched as thousands of Tennessee fans milled about on the covered basketball floor awaiting the arrival of Coach Fulmer and the Vol players. Foster began to talk quietly, softly, not the voice I anticipated for such a violent runner.

He talked about his mother, Bernadette, and how frequently she posted on the Vol message boards. "She's a crazy fan now," he said. Earlier in the day Foster attended SEC Media Days in Birmingham, Alabama, where Phil Fulmer received a subpoena in a long-running lawsuit brought by disassociated Alabama boosters angry over Fulmer's role in Alabama's football probation. In the media room, Foster shook his head. "So many people paying attention to every word you say." He sighed, sympathetic to his coach. Then he leaned back in the chair, paused to run his right hand across his head, and stared down at the lines of Tennessee fans forming across the distant floor.

"Are they waiting for us?" he asked.

"Yes," I said, "you're going to be signing autographs for all of them."

Foster's eyes widened, and he adjusted the lapels on his white suit. "Is it hot in here?" he asked.

Just then a friend of Foster's arrived—a short black man with braces. Arian exploded off the chair and talked to the short guy with braces for the next half hour. Occasionally he glanced back over his shoulder and nodded at me. Idly, I checked my text messages (I had none), checked my voice mail (again, none), and decided to send text messages to friends for no reason. Arian came back and sat down beside me. "We gotta go sign autographs now," he said. Then Arian and I extended the same awkward chest bump again.

"Good meeting," Foster said.

Soon after Arian left, I met Phil Fulmer to discuss the book I'd be writing. I told him I'd like to follow him around for a week before a game to see if I could keep up. Fulmer nodded and looked me up and down.

"You're a young man, you should be able to keep up," Fulmer said.

Then he too was gone.

From a distance I watched him address a cheering throng of Tennessee fans. He closed with these stirring words, "Now let's go win a championship!"

AT 9 P.M. KELLY arrives from Nashville. Moments after he's placed his bag in the trunk of the Chrysler Sebring at the Los Angeles airport, he drops a bombshell. "Bad news," he says, "my cousin and the playmate are getting a divorce."

"You couldn't have found that out beforehand?"

Kelly, born in Michigan, stares dejectedly out into the California night. "Why do so many people have on orange?" he asks.

ON SUNDAY MORNING, AFTER two days of riding around Hollywood in the cheapest convertible in L.A., I drive to the Pasadena Westin Hotel, where I'm meeting the University of Tennessee team for a tour of Hollywood. I spend half an hour ahead of time contemplating whether it's appropriate to wear shorts on the tour. I lay out my shorts and khakis on the bed, weighing my options while wearing Tennessee Vol boxers.

Kelly glances over at me. "You look really nervous," he says. And I am. It's not every day you go on a Hollywood tour with your football team. "I'm going to wear the pants," I declare with great solemnity 10 minutes later, "because you can't go wrong with pants."

Kelly nods. "Solid analysis," he says.

I arrive at the hotel a few minutes before 11 A.M. and meet Bruce Warwick, the assistant athletic director in charge of football operations. A few of the team members are already materializing in the lobby, and I can see that wearing long pants has me overdressed. Most of the players are in their UT-issue Adidas workout gear.

Jonathan Crompton, UT's unproven redshirt junior starting quarterback from North Carolina, is leaning against the wall in front of me. The 6' 4", 225-pound Crompton is wearing headphones over his shaved head and is in control, more than any other single player, of whether the 2008 Volunteer season will be a success or failure. I study him, attempting to glean via his mannerisms and body language whether he's ready to play tomorrow, whether he's prepared to lead my team to an SEC championship this year.

Crompton, 21, with heavy-lidded, sullen eyes and a slightly crooked nose, arrived in Knoxville as a heralded four-star recruit in the late summer of 2005. The top college football recruiting site in the country, Rivals.com, ranked him the #4 pro-style quarterback in the country. A native of Asheville, North Carolina, just across the Smoky Mountains from Tennessee, Crompton started two games as a redshirt freshman in 2006—SEC losses to LSU and Arkansas. But he played well for a young quarterback, well enough that many Vol fans clamored for him to be given a shot last season when Erik Ainge was playing with a broken pinkie. Several seniors on that 2007 team, tight ends Brad Cottam and Chris Brown among them, have told me that Crompton will be special this season.

Crompton told his father at the age of 2 that he was going to play in the NFL. By third grade Crompton started at quarterback for the Erwin Warriors. Since that time he has only played quarterback. Crompton's dad, David, is a car salesman and his mom, Janet, is a social worker. He has one sister, 2 years older, named Brooke, of whom he said, "She's one of my best friends." Crompton's parents are equally close to him—they've never missed one of his college football games.

While other kids played at the pool during summers, Crompton practiced his two sporting loves, baseball and football. "My dad would take me out to the field and I'd field grounders for a couple of hours and then we'd move out to the outfield and I'd work on my drops [from center]," he recalled. A shortstop in baseball with a rocket for an arm, Crompton eschewed pitching. "The pitching motion and the quarterback motion are different," he explains. Asked how hard he can throw a football, Crompton shrugs. "People ask me that all the time," he says, "I don't know."

As he trained in the heat of the Asheville summers, Crompton's mantra was "Every day you ain't getting better, you're getting worse.

I really believe that." By eighth grade, Crompton knew he would be a college quarterback. So did the college coaches. After a spirited recruiting battle during his junior year of high school, Crompton selected the Vols over North Carolina, Clemson, Georgia, and LSU. Not content with merely making his own decision, Crompton worked the phones hard to persuade other top recruits to join him in Knoxville. Among his targets was the top-rated center in the country, Josh McNeil, a 6' 4", 270-pounder from Collins, Mississippi. "He'd call me all the time," McNeil said, "saying, 'Tennessee, it's all Vols, you with me?' He tried to get everybody to come join that class, receivers, running backs, defensive backs, he was always on the phone." The two young men arrived on campus in 2005 as freshmen roommates believing they were destined to be stars. Within months both were forced to take redshirt seasons due to torn labrums in their shoulders. Both also needed surgery, and neither played his freshman year. "We'd sit around in our dorm room and be like, 'This sucks,' " says McNeil.

Three years later Crompton is surrounded by older fans in the lobby of the Pasadena Westin, acolytes soaking up his single-sentence comments as if he were the Oracle of Delphi. "Last year they kept us all cooped up at Cal and thought we played tight. This year they want us to see stuff. Keep us relaxed." The fans, all with white hair, nod and stare contemplatively at this 21-year-old who carries the Volunteers' season on his strong right arm.

Crompton lifts his large headphones, places them over both of his ears, and begins walking—his large legs are like tree trunks—toward the team buses. What most fans don't know is that Crompton's right ankle has been killing him since 2 weeks ago, when he severely sprained it during practice. Since the injury, for 3 days each week until 11:30 at night, Crompton has received treatment on the ankle. After the treatment, before leaving for his apartment, he's put on a boot. But when he walks to class on campus, the subject of inquiring stares from classmates and staff, he does so without the boot. "I don't want people to know about it," he says.

He's been doing his best to keep the injury a secret, but his ankle is far from healthy. "In my mind, I'm never hurt," says Crompton. "But some nights after practice I can't even walk." Now, in the hotel lobby, Crompton concentrates on walking toward the buses without a limp.

There are four buses, and I'm to be on Bus 3. I board and sit alone, feeling out of place, half expecting one of the players or coaches to challenge my presence. UT tight end coach Greg Adkins, a former offensive lineman at Marshall, comes on and sits in the seat behind me. Adkins is a very tall man with a receding hairline and a mustache with a slight hint of red in it. He's on the phone with his wife talking about the upcoming tour of Hollywood. UT strength coach Johnny Long sits across from me, drinking a Full Throttle energy drink. Assorted special teams players file onto the bus. They look so young. Most of them I don't recognize in their UT-issue Adidas outfits, but a few players such as UT's field goal kicker, Daniel Lincoln, a comparatively short player with dark brown hair, stand out because the television cameras have focused on them on the sideline.

No one sits next to me, which makes sense because the bus is not completely full, but I sneak a glance around and see that most people have seatmates. I feel a bit sad, as if I've been the last person picked in kickball. Or not picked at all. Nevertheless, in a few moments four policemen on motorcycles peal out and begin stopping traffic for the buses. Our trip to Hollywood has begun.

As the bus executes a complicated turn on an empty Pasadena street, an elderly woman steps to the front of the bus and taps on a microphone. "I'm Janice," she says, "your tour guide."

Janice has dark brown hair with fringes of white, a strong nose, and pursed lips bearing a more than ample coating of auburn lipstick. Each comment she utters sounds a bit like a question, as if she isn't quite sure she's saying the right thing to the Tennessee football team. She's wearing an orange scarf and informs us that she'll be rooting for the Vols tomorrow. "You know, I don't have much orange, I had to look around for a long time for this scarf." She waits for a response, which doesn't come.

Eventually, we cross over the Colorado Street Bridge. To our right, in the distance, is the Rose Bowl. The players on the left side of the bus rush to the right, and the entire squad comes alive, snapping photos from the moving bus and jabbering excitedly about the upcoming game. Janice catches the enthusiasm. "There's the Rose Bowl," she says in a dull monotone, "so tomorrow that's going to be very exciting."

The rose on the outside of the stadium is visible for about 30 seconds, and then it's gone. We merge onto the 105 freeway, and as if on cue, Nirvana's "Smells like Teen Spirit" suddenly begins blaring through Janice's microphone. "Oh, dear," she says. "I like this better," says UT strength coach Johnny Long gruffly.

Eventually Janice regains control of her microphone. However, her attempt to connect with a young audience is not going so well. We pass St. Joseph's Hospital. "That's where John Ritter went when they misdiagnosed him. You all know John Ritter, right?" Crickets. Janice sticks with her planned punch line. "So if you get sick, don't go to St. Joseph's." For some reason this brings down the bus with laughter. Janice flushes red. "I shouldn't say that," she says, dabbing her forehead with the orange scarf.

Buoyed by the team's response to her hospital ridicule, Janice moves on to a joke about the Paris Hilton sex tape as we reach Hollywood. More laughter. Janice is killing. We pass the Hollywood sign and she tells us that originally, in 1923, the sign spelled out "Hollywoodland" because it was designed to advertise a subdivision. "They thought about taking it down, but people loved it. So in 1940, it became Hollywood. In case you were wondering, each letter in the Hollywood sign is fifty feet tall and made of steel."

The buses stop in front of Grauman's Chinese Theatre, which was known as Mann's Chinese Theatre from 1973 to 2001, and the entire Volunteer football team unloads onto the sidewalk. Arian Foster sees me amidst the crowd. "Man, I grew up in San Diego, but I've never been to Hollywood before," he says. Then Foster disappears into a swirl of football players and tourists.

"These guys are huge," a thin blond woman with a Midwestern accent says to her companion. Around us life-size characters from Hollywood films past and present parade on the sidewalk: Spider-Man, Captain Jack, the Tin Man from *The Wizard of Oz,* Wonder Woman. Some of these figures are more believable than others. "The Tin Man is smoking," says one Vol coach, "so I'm sort of thinking, nah, it kills the authenticity."

Coach Fulmer, wearing an orange track suit and tennis shoes, is standing on the concrete looking at the star handprints on the sidewalk. He has a daughter on either side of him, Brittany, 23, on his left and Allison, 21, on his right. Both are wearing jeans, and the resemblance among the three, particularly in the eyes, is striking. The daughters could be picked out as Fulmer's by anyone. Since they were young, Fulmer's daughters have accompanied him to midfield for the postgame handshake with the opposing coach, a tangible connection of Fulmer's family to football. Today, in the warm California sunshine, father and daughters are staring down at Johnny Depp's handprints. "Girls, is there anyone you want to see?" he asks, sounding just like any 57-year-old father on vacation. But this rare moment of anonymity doesn't last; a gentleman hawking DVDs has recognized him. "Get you a bootlegged movie, Coach?" he asks, holding up the latest *Batman.* Fulmer demurs. "No, thank you," he says.

Coach Fulmer and Hollywood are an incongruous pairing, a former offensive lineman who for the past 16 years has made a living eschewing the glitz and glamour of witty sound bites and the land of artificial spectacles. Hollywood, California, is a long way from Fulmer's rural hometown of Winchester, Tennessee.

Winchester, founded in 1809 by an act of the Tennessee legislature, is on the south-central edge of Tennessee, just 21 miles from the Alabama state line, and even by the year 2000 boasted only 7,328 inhabitants and a per capita income of just $16,533. Named for James Winchester, the first speaker of the Tennessee House of Representatives, the town's primary claim to fame until Phil Fulmer became head coach of Tennessee was being the birthplace of singer and television personality Dinah Shore.

By the time Fulmer was born on September 1, 1950, the Tennessee football program was at the height of General Robert Neyland's tenure. Indeed, the first few months of Fulmer's life would be among the greatest in Tennessee football history: The Vols lost just once, when Fulmer was 23 days old, to Mississippi State. The 11-1 SEC championship Volunteer team would outscore opponents 335–64 on the season. And 1950 was only the beginning; 1 year later, when Fulmer was just learning to walk, General Neyland won the first consensus national title in UT football history.

Fulmer's father, James C. Fulmer, a night watchman with an eighth-grade education, worked a second job hauling off boxes for the Hat Corporation. He died in 1989 never having made more than $20,000 a year. Born and raised in Winchester, James Fulmer served in France during World War II, where he was wounded in St. Lo, France. "I'm going someday," Phil Fulmer says.

Fulmer's mother, Nan, was a stay-at-home mom who, at 82, still lives in Winchester. According to Fulmer, the family's home was "modest but small, just a good Christian family. I was fortunate."

Winchester nurtured the young Fulmer, who excelled at baseball, football, and basketball. He played all three sports at Franklin County High School until after his sophomore year. "We got integrated and I went from the sixth man to about the eleventh man, I think," says a laughing Fulmer. "After that I was done with basketball." Instead he focused on football and baseball, playing both ways on the football team, tight end on offense and linebacker on defense, and as catcher on the baseball team.

Mike Morgan, a classmate of Fulmer's for 12 years, says that Fulmer developed a reputation as a tough and physical player in all sports. The summer after his junior year of high school, while playing on an American Legion baseball team, Fulmer dropped a ball from his catcher's mitt after an opposing player ran into him at home plate. "The ball rolled away from him, the guy scored, and the coach just got all over him. Screaming and yelling about how he needed to block the plate better. Phillip just looked at him and took it, didn't say anything. Later that game there was a ground ball to left field and a different guy tried to score from second. Phillip got up and ran forward up the third base line until he was almost halfway to third. He caught the throw there and instead of tagging the guy coming around third, he put up both forearms and caught the guy right in the chest, sent him flying into the air. The guy was laying there on his back and Phillip leaned over and touched him with the baseball for the out. He turned around and looked at the coach and just grinned. Nobody tried to score by running into him ever again."

Fulmer's varsity football career began slowly. "We got a new coach and my sophomore year we didn't win a game," he says. "All of us were just young guys, but we learned a lot and we got better and better." Fulmer played tight end—"I caught a lot of balls," he says—and linebacker. By 1967, his senior year, Fulmer was a standout on a Franklin County High School football team that over the next 3 years would send 27 players to play in college, including 9 to SEC schools.

Fulmer attended a few college football games growing up. "It's funny, we'd go up to Nashville and watch Tennessee State play in the afternoons and then go watch Vanderbilt play at night." Watching these games, a young Fulmer would think, "Gosh, if I could just get a chance to go to Austin Peay or Middle Tennessee State or somewhere."

As it turned out, Fulmer's college decision came down to Alabama and the legendary Coach Bear Bryant, 198 miles away from Winchester in Tuscaloosa, or Tennessee and Doug Dickey, 172 miles away in the big city of Knoxville. The Bear didn't visit Fulmer in Winchester. "Back then they signed about forty-five guys," Fulmer says. "They probably sent him to visit with the better players." Instead he was recruited by a 28-year-old Alabama assistant who he'd eventually coach against in the SEC, Pat Dye. "He's still a friend of mine." Fulmer did visit Alabama for a football game. "I remember I was down on the field and this big ole hand was put on my shoulder and kind of squeezed me and this deep voice. It was Coach Bryant, but I was so into watching them [Alabama] warm up that for a second I didn't even acknowledge him. But then I saw that it was Coach Bryant and I almost peed my pants."

His awe at the sight of Bear Bryant notwithstanding, Fulmer eventually accepted a scholarship to the University of Tennessee from head coach Doug Dickey, the man who would later hire Fulmer as head coach there. As a reward for his football scholarship, his dad presented Fulmer with a gift, a 1965 souped-up black GTO. "It was a hot little car. It didn't take long for me to get rid of it, because of the cost of the gas, and get a Volkswagen."

In 1968, Fulmer arrived at Tennessee as a 198-pound linebacker intent on becoming a dentist. "I wanted to be a dentist because the wealthiest guy I knew in Winchester was a dentist," he says. But his dream of becoming a dentist lasted for just two academic quarters. "I'd never made a D in my life, and I made a D in chemistry. I took it over again, because we were on the quarter system, and I made another D. Same professor, same class, same seat." Right then and there, Phillip Fulmer, D.D.S., died.

Early in that first semester, Fulmer also switched positions on the football field, becoming a guard on the offensive line. He recalls those first days of football as some of the most exciting times of his life. "My first flight was when we went to Notre Dame to play the freshman game. It was quite the sight. It was cooler there and I remember we had a walk-through on the day of the freshman game. The varsity was practicing. You saw the gold helmets and the blue shirts and the gold pants, and you were just thrilled to be a part of college football."

Not yet a starter, Fulmer split time at guard as a sophomore and junior before becoming a senior starter and co-captain on the 10-2 Liberty Bowl Champion 1971 Tennessee Volunteers. In three seasons Fulmer's teams went 30-5 and captured an SEC championship. Upon graduation, Fulmer worked for Vol coach Bill Battle while taking graduate courses. He was unsure what the future held. "I think probably, looking back on it now, I sort of had it in my mind to be a coach, but I was still thinking about law school, the business world, I didn't know."

The more time he spent around the Tennessee football program, the more he became convinced that coaching was his love. In 1974 Fulmer received his first coaching offer, a position at Wichita State University. The job paid $6,000. "I remember thinking, I'm getting paid to coach football!" Fulmer shared a house with four other young coaches. "It's a wonder my professional life ever survived," he deadpans.

Thirty-four years later, Fulmer is in his 16th season as head coach of Tennessee and mobbed by many delighted UT fans—sporting orange, of course—outside Hollywood's Grauman's Chinese Theatre. Fans gravitate to him like orange moths drawn to the football flame, requesting autographs, asking for pictures, shaking his hand, and wishing him luck. Time after time Fulmer stops what he's doing and indulges the many requests from UT fans. He turns down no one, and at no point does the smile on his face seem artificial or forced. Occasionally he glances back to his daughters, Brittany and Allison, to make sure they aren't frustrated with the wait. But the girls aren't; they're used to the interruptions, and they realize this is an important day. After all, there are only 26 hours until the 2008 season kickoff, when a superstitious Fulmer will ensure that two things he always takes onto the field with him, a lucky buckeye given to him a long time ago and a locket given to him by his wife of 26 years, Vicky, are both inside the pocket of his khaki pants. "I don't have any lucky underwear or anything like that," he says.

Several of the players, including Jonathan Crompton, have gathered on the sidewalk alongside a mediocre Michael Jackson impersonator. M.J. is moonwalking and holding his right hand up, palm facing out, in the direction of the players. As M.J. poses with a young child for a photo, Crompton calls out, "Keep away from those boys." The Jackson impersonator bristles and storms in the direction of the players. The team scatters, but Crompton stands his ground. Face-to-face with UT's quarterback, M.J. brushes his own shoulders off and then spins on his heel and walks away.

I breathe easier. For a moment I thought I was going to have to break up a fight between UT's starting quarterback and a Michael Jackson

CALIFORNIA DREAMIN' | 35

impersonator on the day before the season began. Up close, I notice that M.J.'s white makeup is beaded with sweat. I ask him what's the matter. "I cannot work with people like that," he says—gesturing toward the doorway that Jonathan Crompton has just entered.

In the atrium at the shopping center next door is a large water fountain, and UT's kicker, Daniel Lincoln, a sophomore from Ocala, Florida, who is listed at 6' 0", 204 (although he's probably closer to 5' 10", 175), takes off his shirt and runs through the streams of leaping water. I can't help wondering whether it's a good or bad sign that he's this relaxed before the game. Then I feel bad for even thinking about the game and trying to extrapolate anything from a college kid's cheerful behavior. I turn away, walk a few more steps, and then catch myself thinking again: Wait, is it a good or bad sign?

I head back to the bus because I don't want to be left behind, or, worse, be noted as absent from the team bus and have all the players and coaches sitting around waiting for a bearded writer they don't know to return. As I'm standing on the street, a goateed and sunburned man driving a convertible (not a Sebring, I notice) and wearing an orange shirt comes to a screeching halt as he spots several team members on the sidewalk and yells, "Go Vols!" Then he almost rear-ends the car in front of him. His female companion slaps his arm. "It's the Vols, honey!" he exclaims, defending himself.

Gathered back on the bus, we return to the interstate. The bus is silent now; our tour guide, Janice, has given up enlightening us with further Hollywood stories. Instead the players and coaches gaze out the windows at the desert hills in the distance. On the opposite side of the bus the city of Los Angeles rises into the smog, which is so dense the skyline looks like a mirage.

We're to be back at the hotel for only a short while. At 5 P.M., the bus brigade will leave once again, this time for the team walkthrough at the Rose Bowl.

TWO HOURS LATER THE players, wearing white Tennessee shirts and orange pants, congregate in the hotel lobby and load the buses. When we arrive at the Rose Bowl, employees swing open the gates to allow the buses to drive down into the stadium. About a hundred UT fans are already standing at the entrance a day in advance of the game, cheering and waving as we drive past them into the bowels of the stadium. The team steps off the buses and walks down the concrete rampart into the visiting locker room. On the day before the game, the players' jerseys, pads, and cleats are already laid out for them in the individual lockers.

The Rose Bowl is one of the most famous stadiums in the country. Since opening in 1922, it's hosted five Super Bowls, Olympic events in 1932 and 1984, the World Cup in 1994, and 84 Rose Bowl games since the first on January 1, 1923. UCLA plays its home football games here, and tomorrow, the 91,136-seat stadium that *Sports Illustrated* called the finest college stadium in America will be alive with the start of a new season.

Todd Blackledge, a former Penn State quarterback, Mike Patrick, a longtime announcer for ESPN who seems to be perpetually sleeping or stoned when the camera finds him in the booth, and Holly Rowe, a portly blond sideline reporter, will be calling the game for ESPN; all of them are standing on the sideline today chatting with Tennessee officials. The end zone is freshly painted, BRUINS on the side nearest our locker room and UCLA on the other. I walk out onto the field in my flip-flops, kick them off, and feel the Rose Bowl grass under my feet. It's as soft as you'd expect it to be, like a pillow.

The players arrive on the field, wearing their white shirts, orange shorts, and Tennessee helmets. They split into their different positions and perform their respective drills, the defensive backs practicing leaping catches with other defensive backs flashing in front of them at the last moment to try to block their view of the ball. Laughter rings out from the field; the team appears buoyant, relaxed.

Meanwhile, Coach Fulmer runs the offense through their sequence of plays. New offensive coordinator Dave Clawson stands alongside new quarterback Jonathan Crompton. "You ready?" Clawson asks. "Yep," Crompton says.

Tennessee strength coach Johnny Long walks up to me. "Today is relaxed," he says. "Tomorrow will be different. No offense, but tomorrow I won't even talk to you."

At the end of the walkthrough, after little more than 45 minutes on the field, as the sun is beginning to sink down behind the hills that climb into the clear blue sky above the Rose Bowl, Coach Fulmer gathers his players. "Tomorrow," he says, "is for real."

AT 2:50 ON SEPTEMBER 1, 2008, the UT team buses depart the Pasadena Westin for their season opener at the Rose Bowl. This is the first time the players have left the hotel all day. Earlier they met for a mandatory team breakfast from 9 to 10 A.M. in the hotel's Fountain I and II meeting rooms. At 10 A.M. came a team meeting with Coach Fulmer. Following that, the special teams met in a hotel conference room at 10:15 A.M. and the offense and defense meetings came at 10:30 A.M. in Fountain III and IV rooms. The team then returned to their rooms until 1 P.M., when they filed back downstairs for the pregame meal.

About a mile from the Rose Bowl we come upon our first UCLA fans, who upon spotting the UT buses point their thumbs down or pop their UCLA shirts aggressively into the air. The UT crowd is not impressed. "They're amateurs compared to the LSU and Florida fans," says a member of UT media relations. Several players begin to count how many fans flip off the bus. "Hey, we got our first," exclaims a player. "I got two," says another. "I got three," reports yet another. I look outside the window in time to spot this fan, a large man in a tight UCLA Bruins shirt, extending his middle finger skyward while he holds a newspaper in the other hand, an expression of benevolent derision— somewhere between a sneer and a smile—gripping his face. Then we're through the gate and into the Rose Bowl. "That's the fewest birds I've ever seen before a game," says the same UT media relations member, sounding vaguely disappointed.

The players and coaches unload the buses and walk to the center of the field, where they meet for a team prayer. They drop to their knees, arms thrown across one another's shoulders, and pray together. Already several UCLA players are stretching on the field.

At 3:20 P.M. UT quarterback Jonathan Crompton emerges from the locker room and begins to throw. Crompton is about to start the third game of his football career. This is his 4th year at Tennessee. During his redshirt freshman season, Crompton needed shoulder surgery and wore a sling for months. Three years later he throws tight spirals into the California sunshine. Other than occasionally biting his lower lip between passes, Crompton shows no nerves. At long last his moment is upon us.

Above Crompton, towing a banner behind it, a small plane flutters in the bright blue sky. The banner's advertising a new season of *Beverly Hills 90210*. Fourteen years before, in 1994, when the old *90210* was in its heyday, another team of Volunteers took the field for their season opener in the Rose Bowl. That year's team was led by a 5th-year senior starting quarterback, Jerry Colquitt. On the first series of the game, Colquitt tore his ACL. Soon after, a freshman named Peyton Manning took the field and began to rewrite the UT record books. The Vols would go on to lose that game, but in the process, a new era of UT football dominance was born. During 4 years of football, Manning would go 39-6 as a starter.

At 4:07 P.M. the Tennessee band arrives in the stands and plays the first "Rocky Top" of the season. My pulse quickens. Many fans incorrectly believe that "Rocky Top" is UT's official fight song—it isn't. That honor belongs to a radically different song entitled "Down the Field," which no one actually knows. "Rocky Top," written in Gatlinburg, Tennessee, in 1967 by a married couple named Felice and Boudleaux Bryant, wasn't actually played by UT's band until 1972. Now the song is inextricably linked to Tennessee, and even teetotalers overlook the lyrics of the song—about moonshining and murder. As the band plays, bright gold instruments glistening as they catch the afternoon sunlight, early-arriving UT fans shake their pom-poms in time to the music. Just now former hockey star Wayne Gretzky and former UCLA and Los

Angeles Laker star Kareem Abdul-Jabbar pass on the sideline with large sideline visitor passes draped around their necks. Both men look up at the band, but neither accompanies Vol fans in singing along to the chorus.

Rocky Top, you'll always be
Home sweet home to me
Good ole Rocky Top,
Rocky Top, Tennessee

UCLA's first-year coach, the 47-year-old golden-haired Rick Neuheisel, walks out onto his home field. Neuheisel played quarterback at UCLA, starting as a senior in the 1984 Rose Bowl, and later was the head coach at Colorado and then Washington. In 2003, the University of Washington fired Neuheisel, alleging that his participation in a high-stakes NCAA basketball tournament pool violated NCAA rules prohibiting gambling. After a protracted lawsuit related to his firing, the NCAA and Washington paid out a $4.5 million settlement to Neuheisel.

A little over 3 months ago, I stood across from Neuheisel at a charity golf event in Birmingham, Alabama, and asked him about a credit I'd seen at the end of the movie *Point Break*. Neuheisel was credited for the scene when Keanu Reeves and Patrick Swayze played football on the beach.

Neuheisel lit up. "No one else has ever asked me about that before," he said excitedly.

Indeed he had coached the movie stars for the scene. "It was crazy. Swayze would take breaks and do yoga and smoke in between the takes. He kept coming up to me and saying, 'Well, why can't we do it like this?' And I kept saying, 'No, no, no, we can't do it like that.'" Evidently dealing with Swayze was the easy part of his challenge, because Keanu Reeves was incapable of throwing a pass. "Keanu threw like a girl. He was a hockey guy, good athlete, but couldn't throw for the life of him. I worked and I worked with him. His footwork was perfect, but as soon as he threw the ball it was horrible. So eventually I told the director, you're going to have to dub somebody else's throw in here for this pass. I can get the footwork down but not the pass."

Upon this revelation, in a moment of unfortunate and unbridled excitement, I proved unable to control the peanuts I was snacking on. As I expressed amazement at Neuheisel's anecdote, peanut shrapnel escaped my mouth and sailed across the small distance between us, landing on his black turtleneck. I was horrified and frozen immobile in front of him during a brief, stunned silence. I'd just spit on the opposing coach for UT's opener. Then, without even mentioning the stray peanut detritus on his chest, Neuheisel reached down and flicked it off his shirt with an index finger. Our conversation was over.

My companion at the time, one of Alabama's finest radio show hosts, Ian Fitzsimmons, leaned over to me and said, "Dude, did you just spit on Rick Neuheisel?"

Yep.

Now, 3 months later, we're on opposing sidelines. I have no peanuts. I contemplate walking across the field and greeting him, but instead I return to the locker room to witness Fulmer's moving pregame speech and to say the Lord's Prayer with the team. Shortly thereafter, I burst through the tunnel with the Tennessee football players.

AS WE RUSH OUT onto the field and toward the sideline, everyone in the stadium is standing and screaming. Throngs of blue-and-gold-clad UCLA fans and, away in the distance, an entire end zone full of orange are here to watch the final game of college football's opening weekend.

An ESPN television camera that's anchored on a tow line above the field circles the UCLA kickoff team as they sprint onto the field. UCLA's players spread out across the width of the field, golden helmets catching the bright sunshine. Shortly thereafter the Volunteer kick return team rushes out onto the field to receive the kick. Tennessee sophomore defensive back and kick returner Dennis Rogan nervously checks and rechecks the tightness of his gloves, the "UCLA" goal line behind him bathed in light.

The UCLA kicker drops his arm and runs forward, the entire stadium takes a collective breath, and the kicker's foot meets the ball, which spirals high into the California sky and comes to rest in the arms of Tennessee's Rogan, who fields the kick cleanly and returns it 29 yards. Jonathan Crompton trots out onto the field and takes his first snap from under center as Tennessee's starting quarterback.

The sideline is a beehive of activity. Yellow-jacketed security guards and ESPN cameramen are everywhere, as is the odd sideline celebrity such as former professional wrestler Diamond Dallas Page, who does his famous Diamond sign as he poses for a photograph. Amidst the bedlam, Crompton hits a pass to Arian Foster that gains 9 yards. The sideline exults, but only for a moment. On Tennessee's third play from scrimmage, third and a short 1, a jittery Crompton steps back from under center without the football. As I'm craning my neck to see who recovered the football, security is checking for sideline passes. I don't have one. Tennessee emerges from the pile holding the football. But we're forced to punt. The yellow-jacketed security guard reaches me. Before he can say anything, I climb from the field up into the stands.

I join my friend Kelly in the UT section of the stadium, where I'm surrounded by my orange-clad brethren. Although I am not pleased with how the game is going (UCLA scores first on a blocked punt return for a touchdown), I immediately feel more comfortable in the stands than I had on the field. This is where fans are supposed to watch games, with a level of remove between them and the players on the sideline. It's easier this way, easier to be upset with Jonathan Crompton when he can't hit the broad side of a building with his passes, easier to stomach that Tennessee can have a jail break on special teams and allow a punt block for a touchdown. I don't have to see the fevered brows of the players or the coaches, or hear their muttered expletives; they're just anonymous people toiling in a football game I care way too much about.

On one of the final plays of the first half, with the score tied at 7 and the first few stars appearing in California's dusk sky, UT's Nevin McKenzie, a 6' 2", 215-pound linebacker from San Antonio, Texas, makes the Vols' fourth interception of the first half and returns it 61 yards for a touchdown. My Vols have their first lead of the season, 14–7. As McKenzie strides toward my end of the field, I'm jumping as one with the rest of the Vol fans in the end zone. We've traveled thousands of miles for this exact moment, for this exact play. The exultant roar in my section leaves my ears ringing through the halftime break.

Early in the second half UT threatens to put the game beyond reach. Arian Foster takes a handoff on first and goal from the 6. He's directly in front of me, moving right with the ball in the direction of our end zone when, inexplicably, he fumbles. Both teams scramble for the loose football, which UCLA recovers. My stomach sinks. The UCLA student section to my left, which had been quiet for over an hour, suddenly springs to life. With just one play the UCLA stadium is reenergized.

UCLA kicks a field goal to cut our lead to 14–10. I find myself looking at the clock, willing the time to run out. To our left the UCLA student section is one indiscriminate mob of sound.

To ward off anxiety, I try to distract myself by watching the UCLA cheerleaders. They're unbelievably gorgeous, the finest collection of cheerleading talent I've seen in some years. But right now they're the enemy, albeit an attractive and alluring enemy, the singing sirens of this Vol Odysseus. Before I know it, these vixens are tossing each other in the air with reckless abandon as UCLA drives the length of the field and scores a touchdown to go up 17–14.

As the stadium explodes in celebration, I'm seized by a flood of panicked thoughts: How are we losing this game? The 11 games to come, the epic disaster that can become of this season, the fact that I'm writing a book about it and might only sell 10 copies . . . to my parents. My team is losing to a team they're favored to beat by 8 points, to a team on their third-string quarterback who threw four interceptions in the first half, to a team no one thought we could lose to. I groan, a low and mournful wail that leaves me sinking to my iron seat.

The Tennessee offense takes the field and Crompton throws incomplete passes on first and second down. A tubby Tennessee fan behind me says, "It's going to be a long year if that's the best we've got at quarterback." Then comes the best play of the second half for Tennessee: Jonathan Crompton is sacked on third and long but in the process his face mask is grabbed. A personal foul and an automatic first down!

God is a Vol.

I leap from my seat. Perhaps the season is not lost after all. We move farther down the field, convert a fourth and 1, and then, unbelievably, miraculously, Montario Hardesty, the 6', 210-pound junior from New Bern, North Carolina, whom Coach Fulmer singled out for praise in his pregame speech, scores from 20 yards out on a toss sweep to give the Vols a 21–17 lead. There is only a minute and a half remaining in the game. I lose it, dive into the arms of other UT fans surrounding me, scream the words to "Rocky Top" as loudly as I can, and give Kelly a tremendous bear hug. We've stared defeat in the face and emerged victorious, come all the way across the country to California and begun our season 1-0. The season can still be a bright and shining city on the orange hill of seasons past. We are still Tennessee!

Starting away from us in the distance of the Rose Bowl field, the UCLA offense marches with alarming alacrity to just beneath our seats—directly in front of the UT fans, in front of the same end zone where Arian Foster fumbled what seems like so many years ago now. With 44 seconds remaining, UCLA has a first down at the 11-yard line. With 31 seconds left, they're facing a third and 2 at the 3-yard line. Then it happens: a UCLA touchdown pass right in front of the UT section, with 27 seconds left on the clock. A piercing dart from UCLA's third-string quarterback, Kevin Craft, directly to my heart. The score is 24–21 UCLA, and the Rose Bowl is a riotous mosh pit of blue-and-gold celebration. I can't manage to make any sound at all. I open my mouth but nothing comes out. Around me some UT fans are filing out of the stadium to begin the long trek back to Tennessee.

But fate has not exerted her final toll yet. UCLA kicks short. UT takes possession not far from midfield, at their own 43. Crompton completes a couple of clutch passes and suddenly, amazingly, has enough time left on the clock for a final play—a 47-yard field goal attempt to send the game into overtime. UT's Daniel Lincoln, my fellow Bus 3 passenger, who spent the previous day running bare-chested through the fountains in a Hollywood shopping center, lines up the kick. I slide down the now-empty bleacher row in the end zone for a better angle on the kick. Several Vol fans join me.

The kick is up and immediately we can see it's going to be straight and true. Now we just need the distance to be there. And it is. Joyous, rapturous celebration breaks out in the UT cheering section. Our team, our beloved Volunteers, are not done fighting yet. In the ensuing merriment I end up on six different rows, hug a variety of strangers, scream as loudly as I can. Victory, almost given up for good, is still out there, waiting to be taken from the cruel football fates.

There's a perfect symmetry to the evenness of this game and my own life as a football fan. Twenty-three years ago, in 1985, I attended my first UT football game—a home game that ended in a 26–26 tie between UCLA and Tennessee. At that game UCLA completed a late touchdown pass to tie the game. They scored directly in front of me. Even though I was only 6, the concept of a game ending in a tie troubled me because a stalemate seemed more complicated than a win or a loss, unfathomable, even. I was frustrated at the incompleteness of the outcome. "A tie is better than a loss," my dad said. Now, at long last, Tennessee finds itself in overtime against UCLA.

On the first overtime possession, UT's defense stands stout and forces a 42-yard field goal attempt. UCLA bangs it through.

Now in the end zone distant from us, Tennessee begins the possession that will either win, tie, or lose the game. Tennessee fails to gain a first down, and Daniel Lincoln strides onto the field to attempt a 34-yard field goal to send us into a second overtime.

Attempting an overtime field goal for a potential tie is the worst form of football torture. As I'm standing awaiting the kick it occurs to me that whoever came up with the term *sudden death* was a genius. Sure, through overuse and ubiquity the phrase has lost its power, but clear your mind of all previous connotations and think of the two words standing alone: sudden death. They're bone-chilling in their finality. One moment your team is alive and fighting and the next moment, you're finished.

It's dark in my end zone bleachers. There's a Jumbotron behind us. I turn to check the time outs; neither team has any left. There isn't going to be any last-second pause before the play. The ball is snapped. My heart is beating so hard that I understand why my grandfather's doctor told him all those years ago that he wasn't allowed to watch games live.

Lincoln takes his deliberate steps in the direction of the ball. His foot meets the ball and I bite my lip so hard I taste blood.

It's wide left.

Immediately the UCLA players flood the field in euphoric celebration. My stomach falls to my feet. We've lost. Twenty-three years later, I discover that my dad was right—a tie isn't so bad after all. Colorful fireworks explode over the stadium. I want to puke. I sink down to the hard metal of the bleachers and bury my head in my hands. When I look up, I turn to Kelly and say four words: "We are so fucked."

CHAPTER 3

RUNNING THE WRONG ROUTE

I CAN'T SLEEP THE NIGHT AFTER the game. The name of my first book about my 2006 road trip through the Southeastern Conference was called *Dixieland Delight*; I called the journey the "Dixieland Delight Tour," DDT for short. My friend Kelly describes the upcoming season as DDT part two, "Drunk, Dejected Travis."

Eventually I get out of bed, pack my bag, put on my orange UT shirt (after all, I'm traveling today and need to make sure people know where I'm from), and go downstairs to the cursed Chrysler Sebring convertible. I get on the interstate and make a discreet phone call to my wife, discreet because using cell phones while driving in California is against the law. My phone is sitting on my lap when she answers at her high school guidance office back in Tennessee.

"My team stinks," I say by way of greeting.

"No, no, no, Fox and I aren't putting up with this all fall," she says, laying on the guilt with a reference to our 7-month-old son.

"My team stinks and I don't want to do anything," I continue.

"How old are you?"

"Twenty-nine."

"That was a rhetorical question."

I drive in silence. The California sunshine is steaming up the interior of my stupid convertible. Eventually she speaks. "You have a son now. You can't be a baby every time your team loses a game. It's just one game."

"I don't want to write this stupid book," I persist.

"Clay"—my wife's voice is rising now—"we are not putting up with this! You're going to be on the road all fall and we're not going to wait until Thursday for you to be in a good mood again. You can't throw yourself a pity party. Everything is not stupid."

The conversation goes on like this until I get to the Burbank Airport, where I hang up and return the rental car, take a deep breath, and start to think maybe things will be okay after all. Even though my team has lost their opening game, they can't play this badly every week, right? Sooner or later the proverbial light will flash on inside Jonathan Crompton and our defense will be able to cover short slant passes in the fourth quarter. I force myself to think positive thoughts as I enter the airport.

I'm feeling better right up until the moment when I scan the departing flights and don't see my direct flight to Nashville on the board. I feel sick to my stomach all over again. I look down at my boarding pass only to see . . . yep, my flight leaves from Ontario, California, instead of Burbank—the opposite direction from Pasadena, east instead of west.

Oh . . . no.

Until you've attempted to reclaim a rental car after returning it to the wrong airport, you can't imagine what a disaster it is. Surfing in the desert is easier. Hertz has already swept away my UCLA-blue Chrysler Sebring and sent it off to some other unlucky fool. After many telephone conversations I learn that instead of taking a direct flight back to Nashville from another airport, I'll spend all day at the Burbank Airport and be rerouted through Las Vegas. This is the coup de grace on the season opener.

The first circle of fan hell, I soon discover, is the Burbank Airport.

The only thing worse than having to spend an entire day in the airport is having to spend an entire day in the Burbank Airport where every television in your immediate vicinity constantly replays highlights of your team's loss to UCLA. I want to break something, anything. Instead I sit and stew. Anger continues to boil inside me. How could my team let me down like this? How could they single me out in the very year I'm writing a book about them? I'm the victim here and there's nothing anyone can say to convince me otherwise. My sense of grievance is perfectly logical, I tell myself, every bit as logical as caring so damn much about a bunch of players and coaches I don't know in the first place.

In the midst of a near mental collapse, I get a telephone call from my friend Tardio, a Kentucky football fan who is, consequently, used to losing football games. "Am I going to see you on CNN getting arrested for going off on a stewardess?"

"Maybe," I say.

"You should have won. Honestly, I don't know how you managed to lose. It's not that bad."

"Yes, it is."

"Did you get to go to the Playboy Mansion?"

"No."

Tardio is silent for a few moments. "At least you're not Jonathan Crompton," he says.

After hanging up I sit and stare at the flat-screen televisions in the sports bar replaying UCLA's win. Here, in a town where no one really cares about college football, the loss is particularly grating. I'm in an enemy airport, my team has just lost, and UCLA fans don't even really care that they've won. They're already over their victory. It's one thing to lose to another fan base that cares as much as you do, but the worst thing of all is to lose to an apathetic fan base.

But here's the deal: I'm not a fan because it makes me feel better. I'm a fan because I can't imagine not being a fan. Times have been better for Tennessee fans, much better. In an effort to block out the constantly repeating lowlights of last night's loss, I pull out a notepad and write down the 10 best moments of my Tennessee football life, games that have made me proud to be a Vol fan:

1. Tennessee 20, Florida 17 (1998)

In an overtime game at Neyland Stadium, Tennessee beat Florida for the first time after five consecutive losses. Tennessee announcer John Ward's memorable overtime call, "And the kick this time is . . . no sirreeeee! No sireeeee! Final score Tennessee twenty, Florida seventeen . . . Pandemonium reigns!" still gives me chills every time I hear it. In fact, I later had Ward's call recorded and would listen to it on cold winter mornings during my college years up north when I didn't want to get out of a warm bed.

2. Tennessee 41, Alabama 17 (1995)

Another redemption game. Tennessee hadn't beaten Alabama since 1985, though we did tie them in 1993. Peyton Manning was a sophomore and the first play of the game was an 80-yard touchdown pass to Joey Kent. From here the Vols rolled against Alabama, winning 9 of the next 10 games in the series. But I can't tell you how sweet this win was; I went through the day-to-day routine of high school smiling for a week.

3. Tennessee 23, Florida State 16 (1998)

In the immediate aftermath of this national championship victory, Tennessee's first outright title since 1951, Coach Fulmer said he felt the presence of his father, who had died at 69 years of age 9 years earlier: "Everything stopped, stood still, in slow motion, and I felt his presence." When I saw Coach Fulmer raise the trophy on television, I couldn't help agreeing with him on how surreal the entire night truly was. You felt like every Vol fan who had ever lived was aware of what was happening. I can't explain it exactly, but it's how I felt. And I've never felt like that at the end of any other game.

4. Tennessee 34, Florida 32 (2001)

By 2001, winning on the road in Gainesville had become as challenging for UT as finding Florida undergrads without fat arms. We just flat-out couldn't do it. And we'd been hearing about this failure for at least a decade. Then, in that year's away game, rescheduled because of 9/11, we went in as 17-point underdogs and won. This victory produced one of the greatest feelings of satisfaction of my life. Of course, my joy would be destroyed by abject despair the next week in the SEC championship game when UT lost to LSU. But the 6 days between the two were pure bliss.

5. Tennessee 35, Miami 7 (1986)

The first Vol game I ever watched on television, more than any other, made me a Tennessee fan for life. I probably would have become a Tennessee fan anyway, but this game injected my blood with orange. Adults often compare their subsequent relationships with the unbridled joy of their first time falling in love. For me that's exactly what this game is.

6. Tennessee 28, Arkansas 24 (1998)

The most miraculous play of my life as a Vol fan was Arkansas quarterback Clint Stoerner's fumble late in the fourth quarter of this game, which gave Tennessee an opportunity for a miraculous victory. This play inspired Arkansas fan—and author of the amazing book *The Courting of Marcus Dupree*—Willie Morris to write to President Bill Clinton: "Now if we could just take that Razorback fumble back with 1:49 left. I was yelling for the Hogs and it damn near killed me." Rumor has it that this game led diehard Arkansas fan Bill Clinton to seek solace from an intern, Monica Lewinsky.

7. Tennessee 35, Notre Dame 34 (1991)

My dad and I watched this game from our den, where at the age of 12 I saw my characteristically upbeat dad sink into the depths of despair. Tennessee fell behind 31–7 and my dad pronounced the Vols dead. As the first half came to a close, Notre Dame attempted a field goal. Tennessee blocked the kick and returned it 85 yards for a touchdown. That brought the score to 31–14 at the half. Then came a potent dusting of Volunteer second-half magic. Tennessee dominated the second half and took a 35–34 lead with 5 minutes to play in the game. Not to be outdone, Notre Dame drove the length of the field and set up for a 27-yard field goal attempt to win the game, only Tennessee's Jeremy Lincoln partially blocked the field goal with his rear end and the Vols escaped with the win. "I thank my mom for giving me a big butt," Lincoln said later. "When I go home she says, 'You've got a big butt.' I tell her, 'I can't help it. You gave it to me.' I put it to good use this time." After the game, Notre Dame's coach Lou Holtz said, "I've been in this game a long time. That was as difficult a loss as I've been associated with, ever. Ever."

8. Tennessee 21, Auburn 14 (1989)

I was a 10-year-old Vol fan attending this rainy game against fourth-ranked Auburn. Early in the game Tennessee got two safeties and a field goal to go up 7–0. I remember the elderly Vol fan in front of me turning around and screaming, "By God, we got seven the hard way." This was the year of the immortal Reggie Cobb and Chuck Webb tailback combination, memorably nicknamed the CobbWebb. Late in the first half Reggie Cobb broke a 79-yard touchdown run, prompting Neyland Stadium to erupt in the highest volume of cheering I'd heard up to that point. Cobb and Webb would run for 354 yards combined in the game. Alas, the glory did not last for long; the next week was Cobb's final as a Vol—he was kicked off the team for failing a drug test.

9. Tennessee 20, Ohio State 14 (1995)

We were facing off against the great Heisman Trophy–winning Eddie George Buckeye team that we'd heard all about for the entire season. Ohio State lost the final game of the season to Michigan and then arrived in Orlando's Citrus Bowl as heavy favorites over my 10-1 Vols. With under a minute to go in the first half, UT tailback Jay Graham broke a 69-yard touchdown run to tie the game at 7. From there the Vols held on to finish the season with an 11-1 record.

10. Tennessee 30, Florida 28 (2004)

On the final play of the game Tennessee's kicker, James Wilhoit, drilled a 50-yard field goal, which erased his earlier missed extra point that threatened to hand Florida a 28–27 victory. The game also featured a late penalty against Florida receiver Dallas Baker, and a resulting clock error that made the win possible. I considered this an evening of the score for the Jabar Gaffney touchdown "catch" in 2000, where officials ruled the game-winning play a completion although Gaffney seemed to have control of the ball milliseconds at best. Wilhoit's winning kick sent the largest crowd in Volunteer history, at 109,061, into a frenzied ecstasy.

CHAPTER 4

THE RECLAMATION PROJECT COMMENCES

TWO WEEKS LATER THE LOSS IN California has not faded. In fact, all the buzz on message boards, talk radio, and other places where Vol fans congregate for news has been about firing Coach Fulmer. Worst of all, the UCLA loss was followed immediately with a bye week, so there has been no immediate game, no second chance, to erase the sting of defeat or quell the "fire Fulmer" talk. It's taken me the better part of 10 days to get over the UCLA loss, longer than normal.

UT's 45-year-old athletic director, Mike Hamilton, is similarly worried. It was Hamilton who initially received ESPN's offer to rearrange the schedule and play UCLA in the first game of the 2008 season. Being the head of the athletic department with a public e-mail address listed, Hamilton has been receiving angry fan e-mails in the wake of the defeat. He tries to respond to most e-mailers, at least those who manage not to curse. Amazingly, he began receiving some of these e-mails during the game itself—as he watched from his box high above the Rose Bowl field. In just one night, Tennessee has gone a long way toward reversing the goodwill garnered during the 2007 run to the SEC championship game.

The more he thinks about the UCLA game, the more Hamilton is convinced that the Vols shouldn't have lost. "My immediate thought was we let one get away that we should have won, but I've always been told by coaches that teams improve the most between their first and second game," says Hamilton who has a receding gray hairline, a nose like an arrow, and small, round eyes. He's mindful that Tennessee traveled across the country with a new quarterback and a new offensive coordinator, and he's hopeful that the squad will show rapid improvement.

Hamilton arrived at the University of Tennessee in 1992—the same year that Phil Fulmer was named head coach of the football team. He was born in Brevard, North Carolina, on August 3, 1963. Neither of Hamilton's parents graduated from college. His father, James Hamilton, worked 44 years for Olin Corporation, a producer of paper products. His mother, Winky, worked as an office manager for a doctor. Hamilton grew up in a middle-class household playing baseball, basketball, and football, but was an average athlete. He stopped playing sports in the 10th grade after a knee injury and grew up rooting for several nearby universities: Duke, Wake Forest, and North Carolina State. Prior to arriving at college, Hamilton had been to only a handful of collegiate athletic events in his life.

In 1981 he enrolled at Clemson University, 48 miles south of his home. Arriving as a chemical engineering major, Hamilton switched to accounting within 6 weeks. During his college years he became a big Clemson Tigers fan, ultimately helping to coordinate the release of 365,000 balloons at the 1984 Clemson-Maryland football game. This is still the Guinness World Record for most balloons ever released at the same time. Pulling off organizational stunts like this put him in the good graces of the Clemson athletic department.

Upon graduating with a degree in accounting, Hamilton moved to Tampa and worked as a banker for a year. Then a job opened in the fund-raising arm of the Clemson athletic department and Hamilton returned to accept the job and complete his MBA. When he finished his MBA, he turned down a job at another bank and instead accepted a position in Wake Forest's athletic department. After 4 years at Wake, Hamilton answered an ad he saw in the *NCAA News* newspaper in 1992, a small classified listing for a job at the University of Tennessee.

Hamilton mailed in his résumé, and in August 1992, at 29 years old, he started at Tennessee as an assistant athletic director for development. In late November of that same year, Phil Fulmer replaced Johnny Majors as head coach at Tennessee. For the next 11 years Hamilton worked his way up the athletic department ladder until 2003, when he replaced Phil Fulmer's former head coach, a retiring Doug Dickey, to become the seventh men's athletic director in Tennessee history. (Tennessee also employs a women's athletic director for women's sports.) Now Hamilton lives with his wife and two children in Knoxville.

Hamilton will be the ultimate judge of Phil Fulmer and the 2008 football season, and right now he still believes that Tennessee has a chance to have a very good season, due in no small part to the opinion of his coach. "For years Coach Fulmer has been telling me that 2008 will be the year. That's what he tells me . . . 2008," says Hamilton.

Despite the UCLA loss, Coach Fulmer is not worried about his job security at Tennessee. He signed a new contract extension in the off-season, played the eventual national champion LSU Tigers to the final minutes in last year's SEC championship game, and he's currently renovating his house in Maryville, Tennessee, so that he can better host recruits on campus visits. Since his return to Knoxville to take an assistant coaching job in 1980, Fulmer has firmly ensconced himself at Tennessee.

Indeed, Fulmer's rise at Tennessee seems so inevitable now that it's remarkable to believe it almost didn't happen. In the spring of 1992 Fulmer was the offensive coordinator at Tennessee. He interviewed for the head coaching position at East Carolina University. "It was my first head coaching interview. We met in Dallas and it went great. Really great. I had my staff together and was ready to go," says Fulmer. Instead East Carolina settled on Steve Logan to be their next coach. Logan would eventually go 69-58 in 11 years as ECU's head coach, and as the 2008 season dawned was offensive coordinator at Boston College.

In early 1992 Fulmer was named interim coach as Johnny Majors recovered from open-heart surgery. Fulmer led the Vols to a 3-0 start, including a huge 31–14 upset victory over #4 Florida and Steve Spurrier and a come-from-behind win on the road over Ray Goff and Georgia. At 2-0 in the conference during the first season of SEC divisional play, Fulmer and the Vols already had two victories over the two best teams in the SEC East; a trip to Birmingham, Alabama, for the inaugural SEC championship seemed likely. As Fulmer's star ascended in Knoxville, Majors rushed back to coach his team, winning his first two games over Cincinnati and LSU. The 5-0 Vols surged to #4 in the country.

Then disaster struck. Tennessee lost a home game 25–24 to Arkansas, a team they were heavily favored over. Next came a 17–10 home loss to Alabama, Majors's seventh consecutive loss to the Crimson Tide. Anger among the Tennessee fan base grew as the Vols plummeted down the rankings. But the season was not yet a wash; all Majors and the heavily favored Vols needed to do was beat South Carolina, Kentucky, and Vanderbilt for Tennessee to win the SEC East.

Instead, the Vols lost their third consecutive SEC game, 24–23, failing to convert a 2-point conversion in the final minutes against the Gamecocks. It was the death knell for Majors. In just 28 days his undefeated 5-0 Vols fell to 23rd in the nation and out of contention in the SEC East. Fans believed that Majors was too tough on the Vol players, and that they tightened up in big games. Phil Fulmer's 3-0 start stood in marked contrast to Majors's three consecutive SEC losses.

As if that weren't enough, the Arkansas Razorbacks were also pursuing Phil Fulmer to be their next coach. "Frank Broyles [Arkansas's athletic director] wanted me," Fulmer says. "It was an exciting time; I was getting ready to probably take a job at Arkansas as the head coach." Arkansas's interest in Fulmer and Majors's implosion and difficult relationships with Tennessee officials forced athletic director Doug Dickey's hand. Just one day after the final game of the regular season, on November 29, 1992, he named Phil Fulmer head coach of the Tennessee Volunteers. Fulmer promptly rewarded the faith shown by his former football coach, winning his first game as head coach, the Hall of Fame

Bowl over Boston College, on January 1, 1993. Since that day, he has won 143 more games.

Despite his impressive record, Fulmer is a bit wary of Mike Hamilton. "With Coach Dickey it was more informal," Fulmer says. "He knew what it was like to be in athletics. He was a player and coach. Mike wasn't. He's from the business side of things, it's more corporate with him. More about the money."

After 34 years spent at Tennessee as both a player and coach, Fulmer feels secure that he can turn around the 2008 season. Privately, Fulmer acknowledges that opening on the road at UCLA was a mistake: "We made the decision to do that and I thought Jonathan would handle it, but I wouldn't do it again. It was a good chance to be on national television, great focus for our program from a recruiting standpoint, but as it turned out I wish I hadn't done it. The last ten minutes our defense fell apart." Fulmer pauses, returns to coach-speak: "But hindsight is always twenty-twenty."

At 0-1, Fulmer has to reclaim the season and redirect the Volunteer ship into safer, victorious waters. He's done it before and believes he can do it again, and despite all the radio and message board chatter calling for his head, Fulmer doesn't listen to sports talk radio or read the message boards. He'd rather listen to any music on the radio than sports talk radio, except rap. "I don't do rap," he says. Despite the disappointing opening loss, he feels like he's far removed from the precarious nature of his coaching status when he returned to Tennessee as an assistant in 1980. Back then, Fulmer told his wife, "Don't buy drapes."

ON SEPTEMBER 12 MY friend Junaid arrives at my Nashville home to accompany me to Knoxville for the home opener against the University of Alabama-Birmingham. We've got an important date to keep. I've scheduled dinner with UT running back Arian Foster's mother, Bernadette, that evening.

"I can't believe we're going to dinner with our starting running back's mother," says Junaid.

"That's nothing," I say. "She almost rode up to Knoxville with us."

Junaid rolls his eyes. He's my best Vol friend, a 2001 UT graduate and a fellow 2004 graduate of Vanderbilt Law School. We spend hours during the football season discussing strategy and analyzing matchups. He's 29, tall and thin, ran a 5.3 40 this past winter, and has recently entered into a serious relationship with an Alabama grad. "At least they're not that good right now, either," he says.

Junaid is the deputy legal counsel for Tennessee governor Phil Bredesen. To put that into perspective, there is only one chief counsel and one deputy. So Junaid is one of two attorneys the governor turns to when he needs legal advice, including at executions, where Junaid mans the phone in the event the governor or the courts decide at the last minute to stay an execution. Because of this job, I've nicknamed him "Lights Out," and each time his phone rings I worry about what crisis is upon the state.

Knoxville, our destination on today's drive, is the third-largest city in the state of Tennessee. Founded on the banks of the Tennessee River in 1786, Knoxville was Tennessee's capital for the first 23 years of statehood, and the city was named after the nation's first secretary of war, Henry Knox.

Surrounded on all sides by steep hills, deep ridges, and picturesque valleys, Knoxville lies just 20 miles from the dramatic blue sunrises of the Great Smoky Mountains. It was here, in 1794, that the University of Tennessee was founded, originally called Blount (pronounced "Blunt") College. In 1826 the university moved to its present location, a 40-acre tract named Barbara Hill in honor of the then-governor's daughter. During the Civil War the campus was nearly destroyed by shelling, the buildings were used as hospitals, and students left to join both Union and Confederate armies. Fifteen years later, in 1879, the school officially became known as the University of Tennessee. Women were admitted in 1893 and the first black students enrolled in 1952, though not in the undergraduate population until 1961. Compared to other Southern universities, Tennessee did not experience great racial turmoil.

The city of Knoxville, inextricably connected to the University of Tennessee, however, experienced its own turmoil at the dawn of the civil rights movement. Once known as the "Underwear Capital of the World" because 20 textile and clothing mills operated in the city, Knoxville entered rough times as this industry collapsed in the late 1950s and families moved to the suburbs. It took several decades for the city to recover. Thanks to attractions like the 1982 World's Fair, which brought the Sunsphere, a golden orb in a downtown park, to the Knoxville skyline, people returned to the city. After the World's Fair, the Sunsphere fell into a couple of decades of malaise, culminating in 2003 when European starling bird droppings threatened to ruin the 24-carat gold dust exterior. At the last moment, the city procured a device that emits a sound that makes the birds uncomfortable and keeps them away. Doubtless many of the artists who have called Knoxville home, such as James Agee, Cormac McCarthy, Quentin Tarantino, and especially *Jackass*'s Johnny Knoxville, were pleased by the Sunsphere's rescue.

In the early 1890s the university began to compete in a new sport: football. And it's football for which the city of Knoxville and the University of Tennessee are now best known. Football is the metaphorical front porch of the University of Tennessee, the place where residents of the state and future students first encounter the school. During the late 1990s the university purchased advertisements across the country highlighting this connection:

THE UNIVERSITY OF TENNESSEE

2 NOBEL LAUREATES

7 RHODES SCHOLARS

6 PULITZER PRIZES

10 ASTRONAUTS

WE ALSO PLAY A LITTLE FOOTBALL

The campaign proved so popular that Vol fans clamored for T-shirts.

KNOXVILLE LIES 184 MILES east of Nashville on I-40, a road I've been traveling for most of my life. According to the always reliable Clay Travis baby book—a blue book embossed with orange lettering that says "Our Little Boy" and features a blue teddy bear with an oversize head sitting beside building blocks—I first made the trip to a UT football game at the age of 2 years, 6 months, and 4 days.

My family stayed for 3 nights at the Hyatt Regency hotel in downtown Knoxville (my dad has helpfully recorded the cost as $50 a night). We were there because Tennessee was playing Georgia Tech. I didn't go to that game; my dad considered me still too young. Instead I spent that Saturday with my mom at the Knoxville Zoo.

According to my dad's recollection, I enjoyed riding the elevators up and down in the hotel and watching the UT pep band as it marched into the hotel and played "Rocky Top" prior to the game on Saturday. I remember none of this, but my dad recorded the score of the UT–Georgia Tech game in my baby book, just in case I later wondered. The Vols won 10–7.

And that's not the only time he recorded a score in my baby book. The first night my parents spent away from me was November 11, 1979, when they traveled to Knoxville to watch UT play Notre Dame. I was 6 months and 5 days old. My grandfather, former UT player Richard K. Fox, and my grandmother, Ruth Fox, traveled up from Chattanooga to babysit me. Doubtless my grandfather watched the game and held me up in front of the television while telling me all about the team I would grow to love. According to Mom's notes in the baby book, "When we came back, Clay cried when he saw me."

Probably because she didn't take me to the damn game.

At the bottom of this write-up about the first night a mother spent away from her firstborn child, my dad added the notation, "UT 40 Notre Dame 18!"

And that's not all. At the age of 1 year and 1 month, in May 1980, my mom dutifully recorded my first words in my baby book: "UT, oh, no, there, hot, and ball." Shortly thereafter, that same month, came my first sentence: "Where the ball go?" My first two-syllable word was *water*. The second was *money*. The third? *Touchdown*. Football domi-

nated my consciousness even before I was conscious of having a consciousness; I was a baby with a looming football obsession even before
I knew what football was.

ON THIS FRIDAY, ALMOST 3 decades later, Junaid and I are on our way,
yet again, to Knoxville, but we're facing a challenge actually getting
there—namely, there is hardly any gas in the state of Tennessee as a
result of Hurricane Ike, which made landfall yesterday. The gas drought
is particularly alarming, given that we're traveling east on I-40 and
about to run out of it. As we're searching for a gas station, we learn
from the radio that the governors of Kentucky and Arkansas have de-
clared states of emergency over the absence of gas. Idly, I wonder what
the requirements are for the state of Tennessee to declare a gas emergency. Before I can finish wondering aloud, Junaid has rattled off the
Tennessee statute and informed me of the last time the state of Tennessee brought its might to bear on unsuspecting merchants who tried to
gouge consumers. "They charged Memphis hotels with violating the
state of emergency statute after Katrina," he says.

"Are we declaring a state of emergency?"

"Governor decided not to," says Junaid. "We had meetings about it."

"Could we get the governor's plane to go to a game?"

Junaid deadpans, "UT football games aren't official state business."

As we're driving, radio hosts George Plaster, Willy Daunic, and
Darren McFarland on Nashville's 104.5 sports radio station are fielding
calls from irate UT fans discussing whether Jonathan Crompton is the
worst quarterback in UT history. He's started three games in his career,
one this season. "I'm telling y'all, he's the worst they's ever been," drawls
a caller. Plaster, a Nashville sports radio fixture for over 2 decades is
apoplectic. "Now hold on just a minute," he says, "you're saying this
after *one* game?" As the debate rages on Tennessee airwaves, my phone
rings. It's Bernadette Foster. "Arian Foster's mom is calling me," I say.
"We're going to be late for dinner."

In our quest to find gas at interstate exit after interstate exit, we're not just late for dinner. We miss it entirely. So now we're scheduled to meet Bernadette at the Vol team hotel, the Crowne Plaza in downtown Knoxville. The UT players spend the Friday night before home games at the hotel so the coaches can ensure that the players stay out of trouble, eat well, and attend team meetings, and so the curfew can be more easily enforced.

Bernadette Foster, wearing an orange top, is sitting on a couch in the hotel lobby when we finally arrive. I've told her to watch for a bearded guy walking beside a black guy, figuring this will narrow us down. She spots me and Junaid immediately, but I'm not sure it's her. Arian Foster's mom is petite, light-skinned, and looks far too young to have a 22-year-old son.

"Clay," she says, reaching out her hands, "good to finally meet you."

Bernadette has brought her first grandson, her daughter's son, Cerron, to visit Arian, but by the time we arrive Arian has returned to his room as part of the 10:30 P.M. team curfew. Arian's father, Carl Foster, is also in the lobby. For the past several months, Bernadette and I have been e-mailing. Initially we met through the UT message boards, where Bernadette is a regular poster under the name Foster-mom. Arian is now a 5th-year senior running back and she's been posting on a variety of Vol message boards about his career, the team, and her own opinions for 5 years. "They all know me on there now," she says.

Part of the reason they all know her is because Bernadette has never hidden behind a false screen name. In fact, her online life has led to some flare-ups: "Once Trooper Taylor [a former beloved UT assistant coach] pulled me aside and really reamed me out—he could do that to me because he's like family—for posting something that shouldn't have been posted on the boards. He was upset because I mentioned that Tennessee was thinking about using a two-back set [two running backs lined up behind the quarterback] during the 2007 season. I didn't think it was a big deal, but he did. After that sometimes I bit my tongue so hard it bled when I read things that I knew weren't true, but was worried about posting. Another time Coach Fulmer pulled me aside and said, 'I hear you're on the message boards.' I was so embarrassed."

Bernadette admits that her online activity has exposed her to nasty criticisms of Arian, racial slurs on opposing teams' message boards, and outright attacks on her from some she's feuded with herself. "I used to take everything so personal," she says. "Now I've realized it's just a place for fans to vent."

Even still, Bernadette believes many posters don't know what an influence their messages have. "The players know what's said, the coaches know what's said, and some of the other players' family members are on there too," she says. "They're just doing it anonymously." All of this, the Internet message board culture, the fans' obsession with the day-to-day activities of the players, the erosion of personal space, came as a surprise to Bernadette when her son arrived at Tennessee. "I had no idea how much people cared. It really gets to them, their lives. I never expected it, not here, not anywhere."

Arian's arrival at Tennessee is, in itself, no small miracle. Initially discovered in San Diego, California, by former Tennessee offensive coordinator Randy Sanders when Sanders went to recruit a high school teammate of Foster's, Arian didn't even play on offense for 2 years. "A high school coach told me, 'Arian's not running back material,'" says Bernadette. It took Arian returning kickoffs for touchdowns to convince the coaches to give him a chance on offense.

Arian's high school career began in Albuquerque, New Mexico, where Bernadette still lives—she's employed by her alma mater, the University of New Mexico, as an administrative assistant with the African American history department. She met Arian's father, Carl, at the university during freshman orientation. Carl was a wide receiver on the New Mexico football team who arrived there from Compton, California. The two were married for 22 years and are now divorced. They have three children, and Arian is their youngest. The divorce was tough on the family and on Arian in particular. "He acted out," says Bernadette, "and I knew I had to send him to live with his father." It was while living with Carl that Arian came into his own as a San Diego high school athlete and was spotted by Sanders.

Now in her 5th year of traveling to Tennessee to watch games, Bernadette has made the transition from mother to fan. "I love it," she says. "They give the alums [former football players] the right to buy season tickets, and the other day I was telling Arian I want him to buy the tickets for me so I can keep coming. Even when Arian leaves I'm not going to stop being a fan."

On a recent trip to the Knoxville Kroger's, Bernadette and Arian were shopping for Arian's apartment when Bernadette spotted a cluster of Vol merchandise gathered in the center of the aisle: fold-up chairs, Tennessee plates and silverware, balloons, all evidence that if you stamp an orange T on any product in the Knoxville area it will sell better than it would without it. "I ran over there to shop and Arian was shocked," says Bernadette. "He turned to look at me and said, 'Now you're one of them, a fan.' Then he just shook his head and grinned. But I can't lie, I'm a fan now."

With this fandom has come a better realization of why fans react the way they do—often irrationally and with extreme emotions—on message boards. Bernadette says she realizes that the posters are divorcing themselves from the individuals behind the performance. "These kids aren't people to them anymore; they're just players." Plus, now that Arian's in his 5th season, she's seen it all before on the message boards and has developed a thick skin to protect her from the criticisms of her son. "Nothing new happens anymore. After the first fumble it was hard, but now, it's all the same things."

The "first fumble" was the first costly fumble of Arian Foster's Tennessee career. As he went in for a touchdown against South Carolina in his redshirt freshman season, Foster fumbled. South Carolina recovered the ball in the end zone and the Vols ended up losing the game 16–15 on a last-second field goal. Had Foster not fumbled and scored instead, Tennessee would have likely won the game. Indignation exploded across the Volunteer message boards, as everyone blamed Foster for the loss. Bernadette Foster took it very hard. "It was so difficult to read what everyone said about my son."

The criticism didn't let up the next year, Arian's sophomore season, when he fought through injuries for most of the year. He returned healthy for the Outback Bowl against Penn State. In that game, with the score tied at 10 and with Tennessee driving for a late fourth-quarter score, Foster fumbled once more and Penn State returned the fumble 88 yards for a touchdown. Those points were the difference in the game. Once more the message boards exploded in outrage.

Still more. Last season Tennessee fought back from a 28–6 deficit at Florida to cut the lead to 28–20. The Vols had just taken possession when, on the first play of the series, Arian lost control of the football on a handoff and it bounced into the arms of a Florida player who returned it for a touchdown. Ballgame. Later that same season, against South Carolina, Arian Foster fumbled in a close game as he cut into the open field. This time the ball bounded past several South Carolina players and ended up in the arms of a hustling UT lineman. The Vols went on to win in overtime. Many hoped this would be the fumble that erased the Foster curse. But it was not to be.

In the third quarter of the UCLA game almost two weeks ago, Foster fumbled at the UCLA 6-yard line. Many Vol fans trace the ultimate defeat to this single play, arguing that this was when the tide of the game turned. By this point, however, Bernadette has learned to deal with the criticism that athletes, and their parents, must bear. "That stuff doesn't faze me anymore," she says. "I've seen it all. I've been joking that I should have given Arian the middle name 'but,' because fans always say, 'Arian's going to get the record but . . .'"

While she can joke about the fans' response, the criticisms do, at times, bother her 22-year-old son. While we're talking, Arian's nephew keeps busy by throwing a small airplane down the stairs of the hotel, running circles around us while giggling uncontrollably. Bernadette tells me that her grandson, soon to turn 4, is very good at baseball. She told Arian the same thing earlier that night. "Good," Arian said, "don't let him play football."

This kind of negativity alarms Arian's father, a towering, dark-skinned man of 50 who doesn't appear to have a single ounce of body fat and looks like he could play pro football today. (Later Junaid will say, "That man could kill both of us so many different ways it's scary.") Arian's father has a deep voice that's occasionally punctuated by a sharp laugh. "I tell Arian what I've always told him before every game he's ever played: 'Have fun,' because if you're not having fun, what's the point?"

Arian's father, Carl, attended the UCLA game along with 74 friends and family members. He returned to Nashville on a flight full of UT fans. "No one knew who I was," he says, "but they were ripping Arian for that fumble. Saying he was worthless, that he had no shot in the NFL. If they only knew."

The fact that Arian is even playing in this, his redshirt senior season, is a bit of a surprise. He almost left for the NFL last season, after his 4th year in Knoxville. When asked how close he came to leaving, Bernadette Foster holds her index finger and thumb so closely together I can't see the space between them. "So close," she says. "The toughest day for him was watching the draft. When he saw Mayo go so high [UT linebacker Jerod Mayo was drafted 10th overall by the Patriots], he got really upset because he thought he could have helped himself like Mayo did. I told him not to put himself through that, that his day would come."

I ask Bernadette what the difference is between watching her son's games today and watching her ex-husband play at New Mexico over 26 years ago. She laughs and then looks over at Carl. "Watching his games was fun," she says. "Watching Arian's is stressful, way more stressful."

I comment that sitting beside her for a game must be an experience. Carl Foster laughs. "Better you than me," he says. "I can't sit beside her, she's crazy." Bernadette nods. "I lost a flip-flop at last year's game because I was jumping around so much. It fell all the way down underneath the bleachers. No one could get it until after the game was over.

Arian came by and gave me a hug and I said, 'Great game, could you go get my flip-flop for me?' "

But these are the good memories. Worse is seeing a player's mother react when her son is injured. Bernadette's voice lowers and her expression darkens. "In 2005 Jason Allen [a UT defensive back] got injured on the field and his mom was sitting near me. She jumped right over the fence and ran down onto the field. No one could stop her. She moved that fast. I don't think I would have done that, but I don't blame her, either. People forget that these are our kids."

ON THE WAY BACK to our hotel, I can't escape Bernadette Foster's final words. Inside Neyland Stadium are 106,000 fans. Most of them, like me, have never had any real connection to any player on that field. That's what fandom is like for almost all of us—we root for anonymous men in our team's helmets to beat anonymous men who aren't wearing our team's helmets. Once there's any form of personal connection to the players on the field, the illusion of the game begins to vanish.

I realize that's why I felt more comfortable climbing into the Rose Bowl stands to watch the UCLA game than I did on the sideline. For better or worse, fans experience their teams with a filter, a remove, some distancing mechanism. That can be television, the radio, or a view from the seats. Most fans don't know the people on the field: We don't hear their voices and we rarely see their faces. For 3 or 4 hours a week these strangers put on pads and cleats and play a game. We watch and root for them to succeed. That's the fan bargain. But for Bernadette and many others, the players on the field aren't pawns on the football field; they're people, people who spend a very small portion of their lives playing a game.

Of course the reality is that being a football player isn't something these guys *are*, it's merely something they *do*. These 12 regular-season games take up a very small percentage of Tennessee's football players' time during the course of their year. How small? The average college football team competes for around 40 hours in a year. Forty hours, the average workweek. Yet we, as fans who only see these games, believe that in those 40 hours we're provided a unique entrée into the soul of the players. We concoct our own cast of characters: the hard worker who doesn't have great natural talent, the malcontent who is blessed with talent but no work ethic, the quitter, the genius, the dumb guy. You name it and we've typecast all these guys into specific roles, roles that will, at times, stick with players for the remainder of their lives, long after their time on a football field has passed.

Now, as we're driving back to our hotel well after midnight, just 11 hours until UT will kick off their home opener against UAB, I'm trying to come to grips with the absurdity of my fandom. For many fans the sting of losing a football game lingers much longer than it does for many players. Get too close to the players, and your own fandom suddenly seems ridiculous.

Junaid is thinking the same thing. "You know," he says, "it's a lot easier to be a fan if you're detached from the players. Like after the 1997 game against Florida I went down on a student bus. We lost and damn it all if we didn't get a flat tire on the bus and have to sit in Gainesville all night long. Meanwhile we got telephone calls on the bus about the UT team already being back in Knoxville. They just hopped on a plane after the game and were out at parties living it up on Saturday night. Here we were miserable in a Gainesville parking lot. I remember thinking, 'How is it that this loss is making me feel worse than it is them?' "

Junaid shakes his head. Back at the hotel we set the alarm for early the next morning. We've got to be up early because I'm doing the Vol Walk with the team.

NEYLAND-THOMPSON SPORTS COMPLEX, WHICH hosts the UT indoor practice football field, the coaches' offices, and the UT football museum, is swarming at 9 A.M. on September 13. Young recruits are walking in and out of the indoor football field, and I stand off to the side near the wax statues of Peyton Manning and Tee Martin inside the UT football museum.

Both men's wax statues are eerie and make the players look much older than they actually are. The lettermen's jackets give them a dated look—as if they are heroes from the 1950s. Both are smiling, but their smiles are forced, which makes sense because their mouths have been molded into a smile with wax. An involuntary chill runs down my spine. In a matter of minutes Peyton Manning and Tee Martin have gone from being my heroes to the stuff of nightmares.

I've got some time to kill before the Vol Walk leaves at 9:30, so I work my way through the museum. I pause in front of a large photograph of Neyland Stadium and read about its history. Construction began on the stadium (then called Shields-Watkins Field) in 1919. Colonel W. S. Shields, who was president of Knoxville's bank, provided the initial bequest for funding. By 1921 the first stands on the west side of the stadium were finished. The stadium seated just 3,000 people, but Tennessee football had a home on the banks of the Tennessee River.

The next year, in 1922, Tennessee began to play in orange jerseys. The orange color was chosen in honor of an orange daisy that grew on the hill, near the center of Tennessee's campus. UT orange is now officially designated as spot color PMS 151 and is licensed by the university. Want to paint your house official UT orange? Home Depot sells the exact color. Go ahead and paint your bedroom while your wife's away for the weekend. She'll love the color. Promise.

In 1926 33-year-old Robert Neyland, then a captain in charge of the campus ROTC, took over coaching duties at Tennessee. The chairman of athletics made Captain Neyland's responsibility clear: "Even the score with Vanderbilt."

Neyland graduated from West Point in 1916 and during his collegiate years was a star football player, baseball player, and national collegiate champion in boxing. Neyland did better than evening the score with Vanderbilt. In 1939 the dark-haired, thin-lipped, taciturn coach helmed the last team in major college football to complete a season without being scored upon.

Neyland, a native of Texas, would twice be recalled to the military during his 21-year coaching tenure at Tennessee. First, in 1935, he was recalled to Panama, and then during World War II Neyland served in the Asian theater as a general in charge of supply lines across the Himalayas. At the end of World War II Neyland returned to coach at Tennessee—promptly winning an SEC championship in his first year back. All of this success made Tennessee football a statewide passion. And with that passion came a need for more seats.

Stadium expansion ensued in 1926 and 1929. By the time my grandfather, Richard K. Fox, was playing in 1933, the stadium seated 17,860. After that came expansions in 1938, 1939, and 1948. In 1951, when Tennessee won their first consensus national title (they shared national titles under Neyland in 1938, 1940, and 1950), the stadium seated 46,390. Neyland retired in 1952 with a career record of 173-31-12, but the popularity of Tennessee football did not wane.

In 1962 the stadium was renamed in honor of General Neyland, who had died in March of the previous year. Still-further expansion of Neyland Stadium occurred in 1962, 1966, 1968, 1976, and 1980. By the time I watched my first game at Neyland Stadium in 1985, the stadium seated 91,249. Official capacity is now 102,037, although work continues on the stadium—club-level seats were completed in 2008. The largest crowd to ever see a game in Neyland Stadium was on September 18, 2004, when 109,061 people attended the UT-Florida game—a 30–28 Vol victory.

During these 109 complete seasons, Tennessee has won 771 games— good for the ninth-most wins in college football history. The Vols have also played in more bowl games than all but two programs, Alabama and Texas.

As I continue my tour of the museum I come upon a quote from Peggy Neyland, the general's widow. In the 1960s Tennessee's Charles Brakebill, a vice president for development, was raising money for the school and, when he called her, pronounced her name "Nay-land," infuriating her. She stood up and tapped her knee. "It's Knee-land," she admonished him, "like my knee."

Mispronouncing Neyland Stadium is a common error even for Vol fans. Truth be told, I'm ashamed to admit that I pronounced it "Nay-land" up until this exact moment. What have I been doing with my life that I can't even pronounce my own team's home stadium correctly?

Incanting "Knee-land, Knee-land, Knee-land" repeatedly in my head in an effort to correct my decades-long mispronunciation, I head upstairs and take my place with the football team for the Vol Walk. The Vol Walk—a tradition that began in 1989—is the players' procession, which leaves from the side door of the Neyland-Thompson complex approximately 2 hours and 30 minutes before kickoff of UT games. UT PR director Tiffany Carpenter shuttles me outside, where I stand alongside the UT managers and the Vol players' black Adidas bags. Each of the bags has a name tag on it, and they're strewn so haphazardly on the ground that I almost trip and fall several times as I attempt to find a place to stand where I won't be in anyone's way.

At 9:45 the doors open and the players march outside and gather in the morning sunlight. Wearing suits and ties, they mill around and try to locate their bags.

Someone calls out, "Seniors and captains up front," and the players align themselves thusly. Then we collectively take a right turn on Johnny Majors Boulevard, named for the head coach and former Vol player who preceded Coach Fulmer, and the first Vol Walk of 2008 has begun.

The first thing we pass on the Vol Walk is the UT Wall of Honor outside the Neyland-Thompson Sports Complex. The UT Wall of Honor bears the names of all Vol lettermen since the 1920s, including Johnny Majors, Herman Hickman, Walt Slater, Phillip Fulmer, Reggie White, and Peyton Manning. Several players run their fingers gently along the grooves of the names engraved on the granite. Earlier Arian Foster told me that the all-time rushing record wasn't as important to him as being remembered as a Tennessee player. "That's what it's about, belonging to something bigger than you." Now he traces his fingers along the wall. Tennessee's junior center Josh McNeil does the same. The image is awe-inspiring yet elegantly simple, a tangible connection among generations of Vols.

From Neyland-Thompson's Wall of Honor we take a left onto Lake Loudoun Boulevard and pass the first real collection of Vol fans. They greet the team, call out the players and coaches by name, extend their hands out in the narrow walkway for players and coaches to clasp, a tactile football connection.

Vol fans shout out coaching advice to defensive backs coach Larry Slade. Lots of advice. Since the UCLA comeback Vol fans have expressed outrage over how conservative the defense's game plan was in the fourth quarter, when UT allowed UCLA quarterback Kevin Craft to complete one short pass after another. Many fans blame this soft coverage for our defeat. Now they want to make sure, 2 hours before the kickoff of the second game of the football season, that Coach Slade has made the right decision on coverage for the UAB game. The unsolicited comments rain down upon him.

"Hey, Coach, let's play them closer this week, all right?" implores one fan wearing orange camouflage suspenders to hold up his orange camouflage pants.

"We gonna play some of that man this week, Coach Slade?" asks another fan holding a beer can covered in an orange coozie.

"Don't waste Berry and Morley now, Coach," says still another orange-clad football savant.

"Let's press 'em now, Coach."

Coach Slade, a thin black man born in North Carolina in 1951 who has been coaching defensive backs at Tennessee since 1999, responds to all of these fans—and today there will be dozens offering advice—with the same basic comment: "Hey, thank you, how 'bout we go out and have us some fun and win a football game?"

Stephen Darville, a senior defensive end from Rome, Georgia, who is built like a keg, low and squat, turns to me and says, "Make sure you get down how much advice our fans give our coaches on the walk. Like the coaches haven't even thought about their ideas." Darville is among the most popular of the Vol players on the walk because he's sporting an orange-and-white seersucker suit, which the fans love. "It's from Chattanooga," he says of the suit. He walks a few steps and then turns back to me. "Special-made," he says, popping the lapels and grinning.

Just across the street from the athletic dorm at Gibbs Hall, we make a right onto Volunteer Boulevard. Here Vicky Fulmer, Coach Fulmer's long-legged, auburn-haired wife for the past 26 years, gives each of the coaches and players a hug. She's standing with two of her daughters, including Courtney, who is holding Fulmer's first grandson, Joseph Phillip, born less than 2 months ago. When Vicky Fulmer gets to me, she pauses, stares at me, waits for a glimmer of recognition to alight in her eyes, and then, when it never comes, reaches out and lightly taps me on the shoulder with a smile.

"Go Vols," she says. The words sound soft amidst the cheering bedlam.

Before I have completely passed she has wrapped Coach Larry Slade in a full embrace.

On we walk, farther down the hill in the direction of Neyland Stadium. We turn right on Peyton Manning Pass, and the closer we get to the stadium the deeper the collection of Vol fans grows. There is no organized cheer, just the general roar of fans' joyful exclamation in close proximity to their heroes. But as the crowd has grown more substantial, the reach of fan hands has become all-encompassing. Young and old, boys and girls, white and black, all have come to serenade their Vols on to victory. Now, closer to the stadium, the pathway has narrowed. We're all moving single file, a narrow infantry of Vol troops advancing on our destination—the massive stadium looming above us. It's a bit claustrophobic now with the single-file line and all the hands and cheering and the depth of the fans on either side of us; I feel as if I've been swallowed by a huge orange snake and am slowly making my way through the belly of the beast.

Still the hands of the fans come, patting you on the back, slapping your shoulders, gripping your hands tightly in their own, or just running their fingertips along your own palm, a light dusting of Volunteer spirit.

Occasionally the players step out of line to greet a family member or friend, creating bottlenecks now in the Vol Walk. Often these bottlenecks form near groups of attractive girls in sundresses. Sure, there is a game to be played, but the players are college-aged men, and if the pregame walk permits a detour by a coterie of amply cleavaged coeds, well, the coaches won't notice.

Except when they do. "Don't be getting no numbers now," calls Coach Slade to one of his players, who has slowed to talk with a girl. There's another slow-up near a midget wearing a full orange dress suit. Each player is exchanging fives with him. "Little dude is working his orange," says safety Demetrice Morley.

The team turns onto Phillip Fulmer Way, makes a final frenzied lap, and finishes up in front of Gate 21 of Neyland Stadium. I breathe easier now, noticing for the first time that I'd been involuntarily holding my breath in the tight orange enclosure.

A player passes by, walking side by side once more with a teammate. "I saw you make out with two different girls," the player says. Then he slaps his teammate on the back. "You ready to play, dawg!" he exclaims.

From what I understand, the first Vol Walk of the season was a relatively mild one because of the early hour of the kickoff. Tennessee strength coach Johnny Long grabs me by the arm and says excitedly, "Next week, Clay, next week against Florida! That's the one!"

The team enters the stadium through a newly bricked, arched entranceway. In descending order, four phrases are inscribed on the four different arches above us: NEYLAND STADIUM VOL WALK, SEC CHAMPIONSHIPS (with the 13 years that the Vols have won championships since the SEC formed in 1933), NATIONAL CHAMPIONSHIPS (6 years are listed), and HALL OF FAMERS. The players pass the brand-new Lettermen's Lounge on the right as they walk out onto the fresh grass of Neyland Stadium.

The stadium is empty as the players gather at the midfield T for their prayer. The sun has not yet risen above the stadium walls, but already it's warm inside. By the end of the prayer some of the players have stripped down to wifebeaters or T-shirts. As I leave the stadium, I walk through the checkerboard end zone and, just for fun, knock off the pylon with my foot. The pylon springs off easily. For a moment I look up into the stands and pretend I've just scored. When I bend over to reattach the pylon a grasshopper hops beside my foot and stops, looks up at me quizzically. I decide there's no better place on earth to be a grasshopper.

Outside the stadium Junaid greets me. "Did I see you slapping hands with Vol fans?" he asks.

THE SEASON-OPENING VOL CROWD is announced at 99,000, but actual attendance is much smaller. Scads of upper-deck seats remain empty as kickoff nears, and many lower-deck seats as well; the hot sun glints off their aluminum bases, a tangible reflection of fans' absence. As if that weren't enough, it's an antsy crowd, still angry, buzzing with imprecations over the UCLA loss, and still nervous about what this season will bring.

Generally Tennessee games at home in September are played in the evening, unless television dictates otherwise. For the second time this season, television has dictated otherwise. In order for the largest possible crowd to watch on television, UT has changed the starting time of this game as well. Jefferson-Pilot/Lincoln Financial/Raycom, the conglomerate that broadcasts SEC games, is enacting their final bit of revenge on me for despising them: it's an early kickoff.

Athletic director Mike Hamilton breaks with tradition to maximize the television audience because Tennessee football provides the lion's share of the revenue that supports the school's athletics. For the 2008–2009 year the UT athletic department anticipates revenue of $87.5 million. Of this money 85 percent is generated by football. Men's basketball at Tennessee makes a small profit and women's basketball breaks even.

Every other collegiate sport loses money. So, effectively, football is the engine that powers the Tennessee athletic program.

Football is so successful at Tennessee that the athletic department as a whole makes money. Unlike all but 10 other athletic departments in the country, the University of Tennessee is fully self-sustaining and profitable. In fact, the athletic program at UT actually provides scholarship money *back* to the university. In 2007 the athletic program gave $1.375 million to the University of Tennessee for academic scholarships. That money funded scholarships for 2,400 non-athletes. Virtually all of this athletic largesse is reliant upon Tennessee football revenues remaining strong. This means that Hamilton and crew have to ensure that their ticket-buying public is happy. Happiness starts with winning. And if you're not winning, or not winning enough, uneasy lies the headset on the coaching crown. Right now Coach Phil Fulmer, one game into the season after an SEC East title, is embattled.

Fortunately for Fulmer his starting quarterback, Jonathan Crompton, looks better in today's game, but the Vol offense still appears out of sorts. In the first half, Crompton completes two touchdown passes to wide receiver Gerald Jones. Jones, generously listed at 6', 185 pounds, is a 19-year-old sophomore from Oklahoma. He's the Vols' most explosive offensive playmaker, and, like many of the Vol players, he comes from a single-parent home. The move to Tennessee has been difficult for Jones, because he left behind a child; he's been a father since he was 16, making his mother a grandmother at 29.

At halftime today, UT is honoring its former gridiron heroes. Lined up outside the locker room, ready to take the field, are the Vol players I grew up watching in matching orange shirts and khaki pants: fleet running back Tony Thompson; Peyton Manning's playmaking wide receiver, Joey Kent; the clutch kicker on the 1998 national championship team, Jeff Hall; quarterback Tee Martin; and Fiesta Bowl co-MVP Peerless Price. The players are organized by the decade they played in.

In the 1980s section, one player says to another, "Hey, Jim, aren't you supposed to be in the 1960s?" Everybody cracks up. As I walk up the hall in the direction of the 2000s, I hear the same joke repeated over and over again, at a dozen different players' expense.

I chat briefly with UT fullback Will Bartholomew, a blond-haired Nashville native whose grandfather also played for the Vols in the 1930s and who graduated from high school the same year I did. Now he's a former player, but a part of Bartholomew is still a fan as well.

"Pretty cool, huh?" he asks, excited to be back in the tunnel.

I agree. As I stare down at the long line of hundreds of Vol players whom I've rooted for in the past, I realize how few of them I can really recognize. Without their helmets, their jerseys, and their youth, many of them could be just normal fans themselves. If I passed the majority of them on the street, I'd never know that they played football at the University of Tennessee. For the vast majority of the players, those who didn't go on to NFL careers, the final time they ran through the T on game day was one of the last times they'd be recognized as Volunteer football players. It's no coincidence that the University of Tennessee provided them with name tags.

Over the PA system, the former Vols are introduced at halftime to raucous applause. Instead of being individually announced by name, or even by year, they're clumped together en masse by decade. Some players raise their hands and wave to the crowd; others merely step forward into the bright sunshine as the announcer recounts each decade's win/loss record. Finally, the announcer bellows how many SEC titles each group of players won in its decade. The decades are amazingly similar in their relative success levels; since the 1930s every decade's win/loss percentage has been between .680 and .697.

As the end of halftime nears, I return to my seat and, in the process, assist a man named Walter Slater to his own seat. Slater is the oldest Vol football alum in attendance. Sporting a head of white hair and some fashionable sunglasses, he's 88 years old and played under General Neyland before and after World War II. He played for UT before the war, left to serve as a B-24 navigator in World War II, was shot down over Sweden—where due to the neutrality of the country he was forced to remain for a year before he was paroled—and returned to play once more for General Neyland in 1946. He's just under 6' and lean, with a mouth that's perpetually inclined to smile. His face is wrinkled, but the flesh is still tight on his cheekbones; he looks younger than his 88 years.

"I don't know how many more times I'll be able to make it to games here, I have trouble with the steps now," he says. His voice is strong, fierce enough to rise above the sound of the crowd surrounding us.

As I'm talking to Slater, Jonathan Crompton throws his second interception of the game and boos rain down upon him. Slater winces. This is the first time in my life as a Vol fan that I have ever heard the UT team booed in Neyland Stadium. And it's certainly the first time the team has been booed in the second half of a game they are winning.

Slater regales me with stories about his years as a player for General Neyland. "He was only a major when I started," says Slater. "I came down for a tryout at the stadium. In those days everybody had to try out in front of the coaches before you got a scholarship. Six of us came and only four of us got offers. Should have given us all offers. There were some damn fine players in that group."

On the field UAB kicks a field goal after the Crompton interception. Fulmer seems more animated than he has in years, moving rapidly up and down the sideline, exhorting the team by waving his arms in rapid circles, at all times encouraging them to pick up the pace. The team responds, primarily though a methodical rushing effort. UT commits to Arian Foster and begins to pound the UAB defensive line. Foster rushes just 12 times but gains 100 yards on those carries. This offensive-line dominance fires up Fulmer, the old offensive lineman. "Feel goddamn proud of yourselves," he says, rushing over to the sideline and yelling to his offensive linemen in front of us. "That's what Tennessee football is supposed to look like. Taking their will away."

As the Vols slowly gain control of the football game, Slater continues to talk. He arrived at UT after being all-state in hockey, baseball, and football in Rhode Island. He wanted to go to Brown to play football, but his family was poor and his academics were subpar. "I remember going down to the Brown field and pressing my face up against the fence and thinking, 'Boy if I could ever get to put on a jersey and play with them, that would be the best thing.' But I couldn't because I never took a book home in high school. I didn't know. I was just a poor boy from the tenements then."

When he accepted his offer to play for Neyland at Tennessee, Slater says, "I'd never heard of Tennessee, but all I wanted to do was play football." And play football Slater did: He had several big scores, a punt return for a touchdown against North Carolina and another against Kentucky that was the only score in the game. Against Alabama in 1946 he ran out the clock in the end zone with 15 seconds left to preserve a victory.

In those days Slater and other players played a quarter at a time. And they played both offense and defense. Neyland's strategy was to sub out the entire team at the end of the quarters no matter the situation. Once against Alabama the quarter ended with the offense on the 4-yard line. Slater was not happy about being pulled from the game. "I passed Neyland on the sideline and I said, 'Thanks a lot for that.' He heard me and made me run."

Another time Slater landed himself in Neyland's doghouse by returning late for summer practice. He'd been working as a lifeguard in Rhode Island. Neyland had him run laps around the stadium in the hot summer sun, but Slater outsmarted his coach by hiding behind the bleachers where Neyland couldn't see him. "I'd hide behind there and drink some cold water. Then I'd make a lap and do the same thing over and over again.

"Boy, that would really tick me off sometimes. He had his rules and he stuck to them. Neyland, he was very aloof, he didn't love you, put his arms around you. Nothing like that. Once he got into a fight with a player. Neyland had been a boxing instructor and he knocked the guy down in the dirt. Socked him good. There's no way he could handle these players today. Not without fighting them."

As part of the football team at Tennessee, Slater lived in the dorms at Shield-Watkins Stadium and was required to help groom the field. An old man named Hoskins was in charge of the field and he kept a notebook with all the players' names inside, marking a cross beside the players' names when they showed up to help him groom the field. When he was a freshman, Slater got a tip from an upperclassman: Put the cross in yourself and you never had to work on the field. "From then on, I never worked another day on the field. But I didn't tell anyone else because I was sure no one else would groom the field."

Being a player in those days at UT did come with some perks, though. Beer was 10 cents a bottle back then, but most of the guys didn't have a lot of money. "They gave us five dollars a month for laundry, but we got to keep that because they did the laundry for us. Sometimes we'd go out and none of us would have a dime. So we'd sit around and pretty soon a fan would come over and buy us a round or two of drinks."

During the season the teams traveled to games by train on Pullman cars. In 1946 the team, SEC champions with a record of 9-1, traveled on a train to Biloxi, Mississippi, to prepare for the Orange Bowl. While there, Slater and several of his teammates went out late one night, well past the curfew. When they returned, they found Neyland, back from World War II and a general now, sitting in a rocking chair on the porch of their hotel. "We all thought we were done for." Slater walked up the stairs and said, "General?" kind of softly. Nothing happened. "So we all filed in really quiet. Turned out the general was really drunk and passed out on the porch. He never found out about us." The Vols went on to lose that Orange Bowl 8–0 to Rice.

After his career at Tennessee, Slater headed to the NFL, where he was drafted in the 3rd round, the 36th pick overall by the Pittsburgh Steelers. He led the NFL in punt returns his first year. For this he was paid $5,500. Buoyed by the results after his first season, Slater went to management and said, "Look here, you need to give me a raise. I want five hundred dollars more or I'm leaving. They told me to leave."

So Slater did leave. He took jobs coaching football and eventually moved to suburban Tampa, Florida, where he lives to this day. He's tried to make at least one game in Neyland Stadium every year for the past several decades.

Sixty-two years after his final game at Tennessee, in the stadium that now bears Walter Slater's former coach's name, UT is successfully running the ball on every play with third-string tailback Lennon Creer, a sophomore from Texas. Nevertheless, this game has done little to mollify the fears brought on by the UCLA loss, and the indifferent crowd is beginning to quietly file out of Neyland Stadium.

When asked what he thinks of the criticism falling on Coach Fulmer's shoulders, Slater says, "I don't know. I like a coach to get madder on the sideline. But football has changed so much since then. I couldn't keep up. There's lots of guessing going on." He's silent for a few moments and then he confesses, "I've kind of always liked Spurrier myself."

On this day the Vol offense behind Jonathan Crompton has rolled up big numbers—282 yards passing and 266 running the football. After 2 weeks of stewing over the UCLA loss there's reason to be at least a bit optimistic about Florida coming to Neyland.

Then, as the final minutes tick off the clock at UT's 2008 home opener, one of the last living men to play under General Neyland stands and makes his way back up the concrete steps of Neyland Stadium. I watch him go until he disappears into the shadows of the tunnel.

IN THE RECENTLY REDESIGNED Vol locker room, a hoarse Fulmer addresses the team. "This was a damn fine win," he says. "Now we can all start thinkin' about what we been thinkin' about anyway."

Fulmer calls first-year running backs coach Stan Drayton and first-year offensive coordinator Dave Clawson into the center of the locker room and congratulates them on the team's offensive performance.

"Next week is going to be a big boy's ballgame," he says.

The players cheer and, as per UT tradition, celebrate their victory by singing. The song they sing is the same after every victory; only the state mentioned in the last line changes depending on where the opponent is from. This leads to the stirring closing line today, "We don't give a damn about the whole state of Alabama . . . the whole state of Alabama . . . We're from Tennessee!"

The players sing enthusiastically and their voices echo around the new locker room. At the end of the song Phil Fulmer stands before his team once more.

"Stay out of trouble now," he tells the team. "Now that you're winning games you're going to have people who want to hang around you. Be careful."

Ah, yes, the eternal struggle of fighting off groupies after wins over bad Conference USA teams. But quickly this snarky thought vanishes from my consciousness and I'm left once again with a jolt of excited nerves.

It's Florida week once more. A win in this game and all the torment from the UCLA loss will be erased. But even in the wake of a 35–3 win, the haunting specter of the UCLA loss lingers, especially since the same UCLA team that defeated Tennessee lost 59–0 on the road at Brigham Young University in their second game of the season.

That afternoon, as we drive back across the sun-drenched Tennessee landscape with the air conditioner blowing freezing cold air into our faces, I ask Junaid what he thinks our chances are of beating Florida. Without skipping a beat he responds, "No better than one in ten."

CHAPTER 5

GATORS VS. CRIMSON TIDE: A LOATHSOME DUEL

TENNESSEE FANS ARE EVENLY SPLIT ON whether they hate Florida or Alabama more. Like many things in life, this is partially a function of age.

From 1986 to 1995, Tennessee did not beat Alabama. Included during this period was one tie game, 1993's 17–17 tussle in Birmingham that still makes Tennessee fans want to bomb Mobile (as soon as Tee Martin's family has been safely relocated). During this streak of epic defeats Tennessee could do no right and Alabama could do no wrong. Game-winning field goals were blocked, inexplicable goal-line fumbles snatched away victory. Tennessee fans sat around and speculated about how untalented a collection of players could put on crimson jerseys and still beat the Volunteers. (Most fans suggested that a good high school team could manage the feat.)

After another bitingly close 17–13 defeat at home in 1994—in which true freshman Peyton Manning missed a wide-open receiver on fourth and goal—*Sports Illustrated* had the audacity to call UT-Alabama "the South's most overhyped rivalry." I remember reading the article in my dentist's office as a sophomore in high school. I was so angry I swallowed the fluoride treatment. At that point I was 15 years old and could not recall Tennessee ever beating Alabama. From the ages of 7 to 15, the formative years of one's fandom, my team lost to our biggest rival again and again and again and again. There are probably all sorts of psychological issues that can be traced to this exact history, but I'd prefer to pretend those didn't exist. And so would my parents. So, moving along . . .

But then came the blessed year of 1995. I got my driver's license, gained the freedom to go wherever I wanted in Nashville in an ugly red 1985 Volvo station wagon, and Tennessee traveled to Birmingham and executed a joyous 41–14 beatdown of Alabama. This set off a winning streak that spanned from 1996 to 2001. All but one of these games was a double-digit victory. As I came of age, at long last my team owned the series.

Alabama broke the string of losses briefly in 2002, but then lost again in 2003 and 2004. Since that time the teams have traded victories in 2005, 2006, and 2007. So the defeats of my youth became the victories of my adolescence and young adulthood. For better or worse, Phil Fulmer owned Alabama and the pain of my youthful losses began to somewhat subside.

And then came Florida.

Unlike Tennessee and Alabama, whose rivalry has been a blood feud since its inception in 1901, Tennessee and Florida weren't traditional rivals before the SEC was divided into divisions in 1992. In fact, prior to 1990, the teams had only played 19 times in their history, with Tennessee holding a decided 13-6 lead in the all-time series. Ten of these Vol victories, however, came before 1954. Occasionally a decade or more passed between meetings.

That all changed in 1990. Since then the teams have faced off 18 times in September of every season (with the lone exception being the rescheduled 2001 game played in December as a result of 9/11). Florida's won 12 of those games and Tennessee's won 6. As a result the all-time series is now virtually even—Tennessee leads 19-18.

The reversal in fortune and the rebalancing of the rivalry came courtesy of Stephen Orr Spurrier. Beginning in 1993, Spurrier ran off five consecutive victories over the Vols. Each game was more painful than the last, with Spurrier playing Lucy to the Vols' Charlie Brown. Just when it seemed possible that the Vols might finally win, Spurrier and the Gators yanked the ball away, running a post pattern for a fourth-down touchdown, for instance, and snagged another victory. Anxiety among the Vol faithful mounted.

At long last, just as my Vols had finally overcome one blood-feud rival in Alabama, a new adversary emerged. Worse, Florida was an early September game, often the first SEC game of the season. At least Alabama had waited until late October to break my spirit. Now the Gators ruined my team's season before autumn even arrived. The temperature would be over 80 degrees, leaves would be bright green, the air conditioner would be running, and already my team would be done for.

Like many UT fans, I came to hate Florida with a boundless passion and unquenchable fury. Once I dreamed that the Florida team plane crashed in a damp and fetid swamp and there were no survivors. In a bit of dreamed irony, the bodies of the players were consumed by alligators. The team was traveling in full football uniforms (naturally), so the alligators had to bite through shoulder pads and helmets, crunching bit by bit my mortal enemies. I woke up smiling.

After years of frustration and torment, finally my Vols broke through, beating Florida in 1998 en route to a national championship and then winning again in 2001. After that 2001 victory Spurrier left for the NFL and Ron Zook replaced him. My Vols won two of the next three. At long last I was psychologically sound and emotionally mature. I married, became a practicing attorney, and convinced myself that college football was only a part of my life and not the sum total of my existence.

But then came Urban Meyer's arrival in 2005. Since that time the Gators have rolled up three wins in a row, including a crushing 59–20 victory in Gainesville in 2007 that included a late touchdown with less than 2 minutes remaining. Yep, a new coach was running up the score on my Vols. We weren't just being outclassed by our newest rival, we were being embarrassed. All of these losses conspired to make the Gators my most hated rival. But that's just me. Some Vol fans, like my 63-year-old father, still hate Alabama more than Florida.

"I will never hate anyone more than I hate Alabama. I lived through eleven losses in a row," he growls, sounding a bit like a veteran of the Battle of the Bulge.

For the first time I tell him about my dream about the Florida football team. He's silent for a long time. Finally he speaks. "That's pretty weird, Clay," he says.

CHAPTER 6

URBAN MEYER: MIDGET WRESTLER

FLORIDA WEEK DOESN'T EVER PASS QUICKLY in Tennessee. Monday of Florida week is an exquisite torture, a prolonged exercise in immaturity writ large. I send and receive taunting e-mails with Florida fans who are doctors, lawyers, and scientists in charge of important research projects. My friend Neville, a Florida grad, takes a break from working in the International Criminal Court in The Hague to call and talk trash from overseas about the game.

I'm filled with an irrational degree of optimism, primarily because I'm one of those fans who always believes his team has a good chance of winning as kickoff nears. In e-mail after e-mail all week, I insist that this is a "we're still Tennessee" game, by which I mean that our program has not deteriorated to the point where a rival can come into Knoxville and completely dominate us. Conveniently, I ignore the fact that Tennessee is 1-7 against top-10 teams in our last eight home games.

On Thursday, I hop on I-40 and head to Knoxville, where my first stop is Neyland Stadium. Outside the stadium I meet Andrew Haag, a Tennessee student manager from Hendersonville. Andrew has dark hair and bright blue eyes, an optimist's eyes. He's agreed to take me into the locker room two nights before the game so I can see what the student managers do to get ready for a big game.

"You think we're going to win?" I ask him.

"I'm feeling pretty good," he says.

The two of us walk down the Gate 21 ramp of Neyland Stadium where the Vol Walk ended last weekend and take a left at the new Vol Lettermen's Lounge. We walk a short way down a brick hallway and then turn left and enter the locker room. Inside 15 other managers turn to look at us.

"This is Clay, y'all," says Andrew, "he's writing a book about UT."

The brightly lit, newly renovated UT locker room has just opened as part of a $15 million rehab of Neyland Stadium. It's spacious and beautiful. Immediately upon entering six floor-to-ceiling columns confront you. The columns are wrapped with black-and-white photographs of UT games and greats from the past. Peyton Manning, Reggie White, and Jason Witten, among others, encircle the columns. The lockers are cherry brown, and each player's name and number are affixed above them. The jerseys are not in the lockers yet, but the pads are. In the very center of the locker room are the Tennessee helmets, white with the orange power T on the sides. Two huge dry-erase boards stand to the right and left of the locker-room exit; the one on the left is permanently covered with General Neyland's 7 Maxims.

The managers love the conveniences and luxuries of the new locker room, particularly when they compare it with the one it replaced. "The old one was like a Super 8 Motel," says Andrew, "it got the job done but you don't want to stay there that long."

It's 7:30 on Thursday evening and work stalls shortly after I arrive because dinner has arrived from Bayou Bay in Knoxville. Dinner, of course, is gator. Huge, heaping mounds of fried alligator. The 16 managers jump in line and await their turn to chow down. The managers' eating gator is a tradition for Florida-Tennessee week that goes back at least a decade. I stand in line with them and prepare to consume my rival. But not before I ask a stupid question.

"Do you always eat your rival before the game?"

Nobody speaks for a moment and then one of the managers dead-pans, "Georgia week is rough."

What with eating bulldog and all. Right.

The gator tastes like chicken mixed with a bitter garnish of defeat, and while we eat I learn that the 16 mangers are each assigned to a specific coach on the staff whom they're responsible for working along-side all season. Each manager works between 30 and 40 hours a week during the football season, and as a result many of them take a reduced course load in the fall. The top 8 most senior managers get tickets to the games, and the top 10 managers get a per diem when they go on road trips. NCAA rules allow per diem distributions for meal money even though all teams provide their own meals on the road. Effectively, the players get cash to spend as they see fit. The top two managers get full scholarships.

Currently the top manager is senior Chris Cutcliffe, the son of former Tennessee offensive coordinator David Cutcliffe, who left after the 2007 season to accept the head coaching position at Duke. Also on the managerial staff is Cutcliffe's adopted son, Marcus, another senior at Tennessee. Marcus is black and was adopted by Cutcliffe during his days as head coach at Ole Miss. Chris and Marcus met during sixth grade in Oxford and became fast friends. When he was in eighth grade Marcus's mother died of lung cancer. His mother's final request of Cut-cliffe's wife was that she ensure that Marcus receive a college education. The Cutcliffes did more than that. Now the two seniors, brothers by adoption, are inseparable.

Quickly I learn that black, white, or green, the number-one goal of all the managers is, as Marcus puts it, "Don't get yelled at." Some coaches are more likely to yell than others, and manager glory can be very fleeting. Marcus tells me a story about another student manager, Doug, who impressed Trooper Taylor once by making a catch on the sideline. "We were watching film and a pass went out of bounds and Doug made the catch and Trooper was like, 'Nice catch.' So after that Doug tried to catch everything." Eventually Doug dropped a catchable ball and Trooper treated him like a player. "Doug had to drop and do push-ups in front of everyone," says Marcus.

After dinner, the managers gather in a circle of seats around the helmets, which are piled in the center of the folding chairs. So superstitious are the Tennessee managers that after wins they keep the same seats that they had for the prior game—in this case the victory over UAB. And that's not all. Each week one manager wears the upcoming opposing team's helmet while he helps prepare the UT helmets. So long as UT wins that same manager keeps the helmet on for the following week, but if the team loses he selects another manager to work with the helmet on.

This week's helmet-wearer is student manager Cody Sunderland, who's wearing an orange Gators helmet. Sunderland's Gator helmet comes from a collection of opponent helmets that the managers pull out of the storage closet for game week. The Gator helmet is particularly despised.

"It's a rough week to have to wear the helmet," Andrew Haag acknowledges.

The managers pass the Tennessee helmets clockwise, performing different jobs based on seniority. There are three primary jobs, each different, that the managers must complete to get the helmets ready. Where they sit dictates their stature—the closer one is to a completed helmet, the more senior he or she is. Newbie managers scrub the helmets with rubbing alcohol to remove the vestiges of paint and scratches; managers who have been around for a while are stripers who must affix the orange stripe stickers along the crest of the helmet; the most senior managers, "T-ers," are responsible for putting on the sticker T's. Once a helmet makes the circuit, the head manager, this year Chris Cutcliffe, ensures that it looks perfect.

Stripped of their adornment on the Thursday before a big game, the helmets are just plain and white, naked of any connection to Tennessee history or tradition, blank canvases of football paraphernalia. Seeing the plain white helmets without the orange T's is jarring, like seeing

Darth Vader suddenly removed of his mask in *Return of the Jedi*. The power and majesty of the helmets are gone.

But as the helmets move around the manager circle, they slowly come to life. First the orange stickers are affixed to the crown of the helmet, then a hole is cut in the top of the helmet to allow the padding inside to be inflated on game day (this inflation helps to cushion the impact on collision), then, finally, the helmet reaches the T'ers. The T's come from large sheets of stickers covered with orange T's in the trademarked Volunteer Orange—spot color PMS 151.

UT's only female manager, Katrina, instructs me on the intricacies of properly affixing the orange T stickers to the helmet. "You can't put the T's straight on the sides," she says, "because then the helmets look wrong when they're worn. The helmets aren't worn straight. See, the helmets slide back on their heads so you have to angle the T to make sure it looks right when they wear them." She puts a T on and tilts the helmet back a bit so I can see the result.

The UT student managers are a lively bunch, making fun of one another as they work and playing, of all things, telephone. They band together during the season by playing as an intramural flag football team and competing in an annual Thanksgiving Day game on the indoor practice field against the athletic trainers, the Hemo Bowl. Chris Cutcliffe, who wants to be a head coach like his dad someday, coaches the managers, who have a sheet of football plays that they run. Last year the team coached by Chris was undefeated and won their league championship. This year things have not gone as smoothly. "We lost last week," says Cutcliffe, shaking his head.

When asked what his go-to play call is when he has to get a first down, Cutcliffe beams, happy to reveal the secret to his flag football juggernaut. "We bring a guy in motion and set an illegal pick with him, then throw to the other guy coming outside. It's been in the UT playbook for years."

"Has it ever been called as an illegal pick?"

Cutcliffe smiles again. "Never."

As a manager Chris Cutcliffe is assigned to the new offensive coordinator, Dave Clawson, the man who replaced his father when David Cutcliffe left for Duke. Asked how much difference he sees in the new offensive philosophy as opposed to when his dad coached, he says, "Not much, honestly. Offensive football is offensive football. You might change the order that the practice is run or what you call things, but the same basic stuff is still there."

As we talk, Cutcliffe is examining all the helmets. He finds one that doesn't meet his specifications. "Look at this one," he says, holding up a helmet that appears to look exactly the same as the others. Cutcliffe recognizes that I'm not seeing anything wrong with the helmet. "Look underneath the stripes."

Sure enough, underneath the orange stripes is a black mark on the crown of the helmet. "That's not going to work for a television game." He rips off the orange stripe and tosses the helmet back to the start of the line. "We need to get this black mark scrubbed," he says.

Attention to managerial detail descends from UT's equipment manager, Roger Frazier, known by everyone as Fraz (pronounced "phrase"). This is Fraz's 25th season as equipment manager at the University of Tennessee. He graduated from the university in 1984 as a sociology major and immediately took the job. "I was a manager then and the head equipment manager was ill and not able to do some things. I sort of stepped into his role and I've been here ever since."

Fraz is a large man with a dark mustache, a receding hairline, and a near-permanent smile stamped on his face. He walks slightly hunched over, his head pointed down a bit, as if he's always carrying a load of helmets on his shoulders. As he moves about the locker room, he's got a joke to share with everyone.

Fraz says that he always knows how a season's going. "Pressure filters down to us. We can feel it," he says. I ask him how this season is going. He lifts his eyes skyward. "There's pretty good pressure already."

When asked how things have changed during his 25 years as equipment manager, Fraz explains, "The wow factor has become even more important than it used to be. First, we got that indoor practice facility in 1989 and it was the best of its kind and now it's already been passed. Now we've got the new locker room and it's the best but it just keeps getting nicer and nicer for the recruits."

As part of his preparation for each week's game, Fraz has to know exactly how many jerseys, helmets, and the like the team needs. "For home games in conference, you can dress eighty, and fifteen [more] can dress but they can't participate." Consequently, the new UT locker room has 95 individual player lockers. But for out-of-conference games at home there are no such restrictions, which can make preparing a challenge. "In the 2004 game against Notre Dame we dressed the most we've ever dressed," Fraz says. "We dressed one hundred and twenty-seven players then." This number is enormous when compared with conference road games, for which only 70 players can dress.

As he prepares for the Florida game, I ask Fraz whether he considers the Gators to be the Vols' biggest rival. He grins. "I'm older than some of these guys," he gestures out at his managers, "but I still consider Alabama to be our biggest game."

Leading the managers in their final preparations, Chris Cutcliffe is patiently affixing SEC stickers in UT orange to the helmets. "The conference sends us these," he says, holding up a sheaf of SEC stickers. The conference also requires that the American flag be affixed to the helmets. "Every now and then the conference mandates new stickers. Like after Katrina we had a black sticker of the states that were impacted," Cutcliffe explains. In 2006 Tennessee also affixed stickers to the helmets for players badly injured in a game against Air Force: 92 for Justin Harrell and 29 for Inky Johnson.

The helmets are piling up in a stack, ready for the battle against Florida that will come in 2 days. Some of the managers begin to place the helmets in the proper lockers. After 3 hours of work, the managers are moving quickly now, ready to finish and head out into the late-September night. I say my good-byes then, step outside of the locker room, and walk down the brick tunnel toward the entrance of the field.

There isn't a soul in the stadium. The night is clear, moonlight spilling down onto the seats and the grass and the uprights. Tumult is coming, but for now, in the peaceful darkness of the evening, the stadium is so quiet that it seems impossible loud voices will ever rise from the seats surrounding us.

I walk out onto the field and look up into the south end zone seats where I used to sit as a kid, close my eyes, and for just an instant I'm still 6 years old and the game is as fresh as it ever was, as pure as the new-fallen snow that occasionally dusts the Tennessee hills. I don't yet hate any opposing team, and I don't yet understand why any fan would ever use the word *we* when referring to a football team. The band is marching and soon they'll split to form a T for the team to run through. My dad is grabbing me by the shoulder and pointing. I'm just about to become a fan for life.

But then I open my eyes.

It's Florida week and the mere thought of this game sets my heart racing. I want my team to win more than I want anything on earth right now—even though I know how irrational my desire is, how insignificant this game is in the grand scheme of life. All of us, we fans, always say that we realize there are things more important than sports. Yet, even still, why do we feel the need to make this claim if we don't, at times, doubt whether this is actually true?

Deep down in all of our hearts, we're all a bit ashamed, frightened even, by how much we care.

MY FRIENDS KELLY AND Tardio don't care who wins the Florida-Tennessee game. Both men say they're rooting for Tennessee because they're afraid that if Tennessee loses I might jump into the Tennessee River from the bridge near our hotel. But tonight, two nights before the game, all they want to do is drink. Our first stop is country music singer Pat Green's concert in the World's Fair Park in downtown Knoxville. Early on in the night, before Green begins his concert, Phil Fulmer takes the stage and, in a remarkable departure from his generally restrained demeanor, announces that we are going to kick Florida's butt. The crowd roars.

It's a cool night and the crowd packs together near the front of the stage as Pat Green plays. Behind us, a miniature football field features an orange-and-white checkerboard end zone. Tennessee fans consume beers and relish the anticipation of the Florida game. As we stand drinking beers and watching the concert, a vendor approaches and offers free T-shirts. Kelly and Tardio refuse them. I take three. My philosophy is that you never turn down a free T-shirt, no matter what.

"What am I going to do with a free T-shirt? We're lawyers, we don't need free T-shirts," Tardio says.

I explain that I never say no to a free T-shirt.

Tardio waves his hand in my direction. "You going to carry around three T-shirts all night at the bar?"

After the concert, three shirts in tow, we head to the bars. Throughout the town everyone wants to talk about the Florida game, including our cabdriver. He's wearing a Tennessee leather jacket and has long dark hair and a graying mustache. His seat is reclined so far that Tardio's knees are resting in the small of his back. I'm sitting up front with the T-shirts draped over my shoulder. I look vaguely like former Georgetown coach John Thompson.

Our cabdriver soon reveals that, like practically every person in the state of Tennessee, he is not a fan of Jonathan Crompton. When asked what he thinks will happen in the Florida game, he replies, "Awww, we're going to get beat. We don't got a quarterback worth shit."

We're driving down Cumberland Avenue in the direction of the Strip, a collection of bars and chain fast-food restaurants just off UT's campus, where red brick buildings climb high into the night sky. We cross James Agee Street where it meets Phillip Fulmer Way. If we turned left it would be a short drive to a quiet Neyland Stadium. It's a perfect night, cool but not cold, and the UT coeds are out in the streets in abundance.

"Shit," says our cabdriver, pointing to a girl in a short dress, "girls don't wear no clothes anymore. Y'all picked the right spot to go looking for pussy."

"You like to go out here?" Tardio asks. Of late Tardio has developed the ability to ask ridiculous questions without breaking a smile. I suspect this comes from all the depositions he conducts as a medical malpractice defense attorney.

"Shit, no, but with some of these skirts being so short, late at night, I like to watch these girls take pees in the street."

"You like to watch girls pee?" I ask.

"Shit, yeah. I'd take their picture if I had a camera with me."

Our gallant cabdriver stops next to the Half Barrel, a wood-paneled bar that fronts on Cumberland Avenue. In a gesture of munificence, I strip one of the three T-shirts off my shoulder and ask if our cabdriver wants one.

"Shit, yeah," he says, "always take a free T-shirt."

Inside the bar, Tardio is squeamish. "That girl peeing talk made me a little uncomfortable." We remedy his discomfort by drinking Scotty Hopson Shots—Kentucky Bourbon mixed with orange juice. Scotty Hopson is a top basketball recruit from Kentucky who signed with the Vols in the spring of 2008. The drink named in his honor is the invention of UT fraternity brothers Taylor and Chris from Sigma Phi Epsilon, and mixes the big orange with Kentucky bourbon.

"I'm not going to lie," Tardio says, "that did not go down smooth."

All talk in the bar is about the Florida game. Tennessee fans are not optimistic. A short student with blond hair slams the wooden bar in front of me. He's wearing a Tennessee polo and he can barely stand up.

"I never woulda believed it, but we're a damned basketball school. It's September and I'm ready for basketball season. Does that make me a bad person?" he slurs.

"It's still early in the season," I say, doing my best to rally a fellow Vol fan. "We can still turn things around."

He grabs my arm, stares at me intently. "Is it even fall yet?"

Technically, it's not. It's September 18. "No," I say.

He steps back from me again. "I quit on the Vols and it's still summer!" he wails. Loudly. Several people turn to look at him. He runs his hands through his blond curly hair and seems on the verge of rending his garments. He closes his eyes and leans over with both hands resting on the wooden bar in front of him. From nowhere, a girl with long brown hair materializes. She smiles crookedly at me.

"He's taking the season really hard," she says.

By now we've been joined by several third-year law students at the University of Tennessee, and we head to another bar, Cool Beans, whose televisions are all turned to Thursday night football. West Virginia is playing Colorado, and we post up at the bar.

Kelly and Tardio are in heaven because they can buy rounds of beers and shots for under $20. "I'm the old, rich uncle at the bar," Kelly says. "Yes!"

The rest of us talk about the upcoming game. Tennessee fans are restless, uncertain about the future of the program, and acting as if Florida is much more than the 7-point favorite they actually are.

"I don't think we can keep it close with them," says one law student. "Fulmer's done." His friends echo his opinion.

"It's time," he says, "for a change."

ESPN runs a preview of the UT-Florida game. The sound on the television is off, but two younger guys in jeans and polo shirts move closer to the television as Phil Fulmer's face comes on the screen. The two men say nothing; instead they simultaneously raise their right hands and slowly extend their middle fingers in the direction of the television screen.

No one in the bar reacts.

THE NEXT DAY I spend much of Friday morning watching ESPN, whose broadcasters are giving Tennessee zero respect. ESPN is scrolling Phil Fulmer's career record against Florida, 5-11, and, as if that weren't bad enough, they're spelling Fulmer with two l's, Fullmer. I note this error early in the morning. By the evening, when my friends and I leave the hotel for a night in Knoxville's Old City, the error remains on ESPN's scroll.

We leave from our hotel, the Marriott, which costs $400 a night now that a game weekend is here. The hotel lobby is swarming with Gator fans wearing their blue shirts, orange tops, and Gator 1 jerseys. In the room next door to us four Gator coeds check in just after midday. Tardio insists that we leave the curtains open on our windows so they can see us lounging in the room drinking beer.

"They might decide to stop by," he says.

They don't.

As our cabdriver is pulling away from the hotel, she comes to a screeching halt and picks up two old prostitutes, about 15 years past their prostitute heyday, large pendulous breasts swinging in front of them like rocks in a sock. One is blond, the other is brunette, and both are wearing dresses with plunging necklines.

They need to be dropped off at a rest stop on Interstate 81. Of course. As soon as the cab leaves I'm convinced we're going to get pulled over and my friends and I are going to be arrested for solicitation. I'm terrified I'll be spending the Florida game in a jail cell.

The prostitutes decline to explain how they got from the rest stop to the parking lot of our hotel. "It's a long story, honey," says the blonde. "This is just like that show in taxicabs where you confess," says the brunette. "What's it called?" The brunette laughs, snorts like a pig.

"*Taxicab Confessions?*" asks Kelly.

"No, I don't think that's it," she says.

Our female cabdriver calls back from up front, "Just you wait—once we get these boys dropped off we'll have a good time!"

Mercifully, my friends and I get dropped off in Old City without being arrested and head out to the bars. Knoxville's Old City is a row of old warehouses in the northeastern part of downtown. Train tracks still traverse the area, and at least one flour company is still in business. During its heyday, when downtown Knoxville was known as the

"Underwear Capital of the World," these tall brick buildings bustled with manufacturing activity. But when the manufacturing industry crumbled, the companies abandoned the buildings and the area fell into disrepute. In the past 15 years, developers have rehabilitated the neighborhood, and bars, clubs, and restaurants now flourish. Tonight, Old City, just over a mile from Tennessee's campus, is swarming with Vol and Gator fans.

The Gator men are easy to spot; they're short and have gelled hair. Also, they may or may not have sleeves on their shirts. The women are similarly easy to detect—they all have 7 or 8 extra pounds of fat on their arms. As we enter the first bar of the night, Barley's, "Sweet Caroline," the white national anthem, is playing, and a few Gator fans instigate nearby Vol fans by doing the Gator Chomp.

Barley's, a vast two-story bar with a large patio, is a restaurant during the day. By night it becomes a live music venue and popular watering hole. Tonight, the bar's so crowded it's impossible to get a drink. For 20 minutes we attempt to get a beer. Gator and Vol fans put down their animus and redirect it at the wait for drinks.

Tardio is apoplectic. "Every man who orders anything other than a beer and pays with anything other than cash should be castrated right now."

"Can you get me an orangetini?" Kelly calls.

"They do know there's a game tomorrow that a lot of people are going to?" asks a Gator fan standing near us. "All we wanna do tonight is drink." He taps his gelled hair to assure no stray hairs have emerged.

Much later, Kelly drops a beer bottle on the side porch of Barley's. The bottle has shattered before Kelly even realizes the bottle is no longer in his hand. Mercifully, neither Tardio nor I, both wearing flip-flops, lose a toe. Everyone on the porch boos Kelly as Tardio and I pretend not to be with him. He's standing all alone on the patio when he does what any man would do in the face of booing Volunteer fans: He commences the Gator Chomp.

I can't believe he survives.

After the bars close I run into a friend, a UT undergrad and law grad who is one among tens of thousands of Vol alums back in Knoxville for the Florida game. She's with her perturbed boyfriend, who keeps calling her "baby." As in, "Baby, we gotta get outta here," or "Baby, it's time for us to go." Only he sounds just like Elvis. It's uncanny. She rolls her eyes. After the 14th "baby" she grabs my arm. "He's from Mississippi," she says by way of explanation.

As we stand on the street awaiting a cab, she asks who I'm in town with and I gesture in the direction of the street.

"Two of my friends from law school," I say.

She looks into the mass of drunken revelers, both Gator and Vol fans, on the sidewalk and in the street, and then says, "Those guys eating from the pizza box about to get into the car with that old chick?"

"That's them," I say. "They're very good lawyers."

Kelly and Tardio have met a middle-aged woman who appears to have consumed approximately 28 piña coladas during the evening. Since we can't find a cab anywhere, they've convinced her to give us a ride home. She's with a bedraggled man wearing one of those tuxedo T-shirts and an unzipped fleece jacket. Tuxedo T-shirt sits up front, and after I say good-bye to my friend we all clamber into the back for one of the wildest rides of our life. For the next 15 minutes we drive on empty streets around downtown Knoxville while the woman gives us a running monologue on all her life's depressions.

"Clay's writing a book about Tennessee football," says Kelly, attempting to cut off our chauffeur.

"Fuck Tennessee football," says our driver as she brushes the long brown hair from in front of her eyes. "That's all anybody ever talks about here. Fucking Tennessee fucking football."

"So you're not buying the book?" Silence. Mission accomplished.

When our driver drops us off, Kelly tries to give her money for the ride. It's 4 in the morning on Saturday. We stumble into the silent Marriott lobby.

"Kelly," says Tardio, "that wasn't a cab."

It's game day in Knoxville.

WHEN I AWAKE THE next morning, my tongue is as dry as sandpaper. I feel as if I've been tackled 19 times by Reggie White on a field of broken glass. But it's almost football time in Tennessee, and I need to rally.

As we walk across the Tennessee campus near 11 in the morning, the tailgating scene is well under way. Tennessee fans deploy large orange tents, unfold long tables heaped with every food imaginable, and fire up their grills. Smoke rises into the morning sunlight and encircles bright orange Tennessee flags flapping in the morning breeze. Tennessee fans take their pregame preparation so seriously that tailgating isn't even limited to *land*. Down on the Tennessee River behind Neyland Stadium, the Vol Navy, a large collection of gleaming white boats, bobs gently in the current.

In 1962 former Vol broadcaster George Mooney began to park his boat on the river to avoid game day traffic. In the 46 years since Mooney's decision, the practice has exploded. Now over 200 vessels of varying size and color are docked for the game. Drunken fans, women in orange dresses and cowboy boots, men in jeans and orange polos warble from one boat to another, a land bridge of floating tailgaters.

"Rocky Top" blares from stereos at tailgates on land and water in a thousand different directions. Walt Whitman heard America singing; on a Saturday morning in Knoxville, I hear America tailgating. And at tailgate after tailgate, Vol fans are nervous. "I keep telling myself that we can win, but then I remember that Florida has Tim Tebow and Percy Harvin," says a dark-goateed Vol fan holding a bottle of Jack Daniel's in his right hand as he liberally mixes it with a dash of Coke held in a red plastic cup in his left hand. "We ain't got a prayer."

Before big games, I don't drink much. Some small part of me remains convinced that I might need to make a play call on third and 16. I care too much to be drunk. But this morning, Vol fans are drinking heavily, even more heavily than usual. Lori Stockton Mills, a blond-haired

2001 UT grad wearing orange shorts and an orange cardigan, lowers her orange eyeglasses skeptically. "You're not drinking anything? I think you're gonna need to drink," she says.

As kickoff nears, the alcohol flows. And it's not just Vol fans partaking to excess on a sunny Saturday morning. Gator fans are also keeping pace. Last week a high-ranking UT employee informed me that when Florida comes to town, Tennessee adds to the payroll. "We hire twice as many security guards for them as for any other team." She paused and then added, "We need them too."

By noon, three and a half hours before kickoff, I head to my friend Brad Lampley's tailgate in the shadows of Neyland Stadium. Lampley, a former Vol offensive lineman in the 1990s who is now a lawyer in Nashville, is wearing orange pants and a white dress shirt. The blond-haired Lampley pulls me aside. "Jackson did the funniest thing ever," he says.

Jackson, Lampley's son, recently turned 7 and one of his birthday presents was a big-boy room. Lampley took down all the cars and airplanes and baby toys that had been in the little boy's room and replaced them with a more mature football theme. Jackson's green bedspread replicated a football field, a large painting of Tennessee football rose above his bed, and SEC pennants lined the top of the walls. "It was perfect. We had the six SEC East teams lined up on two walls, and then the six SEC West teams lined up on the other two walls. Jackson walked into the room and his jaw dropped."

But there was a problem.

Jackson didn't like the location of the Florida Gators pennant. "Jackson pulled me aside and said, 'Dad, is it okay if I move the Gator pennant?' I said, 'No, Jackson, I know we hate them, but they're in the conference too.' And he looked right back at me and said, 'I want to put them above the bathroom door.' I said, 'Why would you want to do that?' And he said, and I've never been prouder of him, 'Because I want to make sure they're always next to my pooper.'"

Lampley beams, lifts his bourbon, and toasts me. "I got the ladder and moved it immediately."

Outside the stadium sits a large pile of *Knoxville News-Sentinel* newspapers that are free for the taking. The headline on the front page reads "Remember the Swamp," a reference to Florida's 59–20 triumph in last year's Gainesville game and a play on "Remember the Alamo," Texans' cry of freedom at the Battle of San Jacinto in 1836. The resulting triumph led to Texan independence. Likewise, what all Vol fans want is SEC East independence at the top of the standings.

My friends and I buy tickets outside the stadium for $100 each. Face value on the tickets is $70. Multiply that by the number of available seats, over 100,000, and you're talking about Tennessee netting, on a single day, over $7 million in ticket revenue alone.

Our seats are high in the upper deck of Neyland Stadium, section PP, row 27. As we climb high into the afternoon sky, the fans' clothing shifts from orange and white to orange and blue. My spirit sinks as I realize we've bought tickets in the visiting Florida section.

I've been to every SEC stadium and can say without a doubt that the worst possible seat to have anywhere is at your home stadium in the visiting team's section. It's horrid, far worse than sitting in a road stadium surrounded by opposing team fans. There you expect to be alone; you've gone on the road and geared up for the taunts, the subtle (or not so subtle) derogations of your heterosexuality, the danger of watching a game amid the enemy. But at home? It's the fan equivalent of watching the game in your own house while surrounded by fans of the opposing team. The view is familiar, the feeling of anticipation and excitement is similar, your immediate surroundings are the same, but your seat is so uncomfortable you might as well be perched atop a pile of sharpened razors.

On my way to the seat I have to brush past a passel of Gator fans doing the chomp. There are few things in life more mind-numbingly painful than being surrounded by fans doing the Gator Chomp. In fact, I can only think of a few: surgery without anesthesia, listening to JP/LF/Raycom call a game, STD testing swabs inside your peehole, and sawing your own leg off with a penknife while R. Kelly plays in the background.

Immediately to my right is a Florida fan in a blue Gator sleeveless T-shirt, who doesn't stop doing the Gator Chomp for the 30 minutes before the game starts. He's one of those fans who constantly tries to get other fans riled up, incessantly standing and pumping his fist in the direction of other Gator fans. I hate these people.

But the sleeveless T-shirt condemns this fan in my mind. Knoxville is 544 miles from Gainesville, Florida. From another Gator in my section, I learn that this guy is a student at UF, which means he didn't just wake up in the morning, realize he was in Knoxville and his favorite team was going to be in town, and then stumble over to Neyland Stadium in the sleeveless T-shirt. No, he made the conscious decision to *pack* the sleeveless T-shirt to wear to a game. In fact, he was in his dorm room over 500 miles away, throwing clothes into a duffel bag, a toothbrush, underwear, jeans, and he thought, "Can't forget to put that shirt inside." Because that's the shirt he's wearing to the game—the one without sleeves. This is indefensible.

TODAY'S GAME IS SEISMIC. Florida is ranked #4 in the country and undefeated. The Gators are 2-0, having dispatched Hawaii and Miami by a combined score of 79–10. Today's game is the SEC opener for both teams, and if the Vols hope to have a real shot at repeating as SEC East champs, they absolutely must win. But today's hatefest is even bigger than that—Phil Fulmer has to prove he can beat Urban Meyer.

Meyer is 44, 14 years younger than Fulmer. He's been Florida's coach for only three complete seasons and already he's won an SEC title and a national title. But Meyer and Fulmer are separated by more than just 14 years of age. Meyer is what the SEC has become, a coaching mercenary who has been successful at every stop on his college football journey.

Born in Ashtabula, Ohio, in 1964, Meyer is already head coach at his third university. After 13 years as an assistant coach, Meyer earned his first head coaching job at Bowling Green University in 2001. In just 2 years he ran up a record of 17-6, but before he could begin his third season at Bowling Green he was already off for his second head coaching gig. Meyer moved to Utah, a state he had no connection to, and took over the helm of the Utes program. While at the Mountain West school he went 22-2 in two seasons. In his second and final season, 2004, he led the Utes to a perfect 12-0 mark and a win in the Fiesta Bowl. It was Utah's first perfect season since 1930.

After just 4 years as a head coach, Urban Meyer was the most sought-after coach in college football. Heavily courted by both Notre Dame and Florida, Meyer accepted the head job at Florida even though being head coach of Notre Dame had been his lifelong dream. Meyer coolly analyzed the resources of the two schools and determined that Florida had the better program—the route most likely to lead to championships. In selecting Florida, Meyer followed his head and not his heart.

Despite having no connection to the state of Florida or the SEC, Meyer seized the reins of UF football in January 2005. Success quickly followed. By 2006 Meyer had led Florida to a national championship. Included in his national championship season was a 21–20 come-from-behind win at Neyland Stadium. In the final 20 minutes of that road game, Meyer rallied his Gators from a 17–7 second half deficit. If Fulmer had won that single game in 2006, he wouldn't just have beaten Florida, he would have won the SEC East, advanced to the SEC title game, and Urban Meyer would have neither an SEC nor national title. But Fulmer lost that home game and Florida is ascendant.

Now, in just his fourth season at Florida, Meyer is 34-8 overall. Three of those wins have come against Tennessee, including last year's 59–20 stomping in Gainesville. Many consider this year's undefeated Florida team to be Meyer's strongest.

His team is led by quarterback Tim Tebow, God's answer to the question, "What is 21st-century physical perfection on the football field?" Tebow is honest, forthright, and indestructible. Meyer is conniving and duplicitous. In 2004 Meyer recruited Tim Tebow to Gainesville. In the process Meyer spurned a previous quarterback commitment, Jevan Snead, who ended up at Ole Miss. Snead saw Meyer on television at one of Tebow's high school games and immediately asked Meyer what he was doing. Meyer told Snead he was recruiting Tebow as a linebacker.

Down on the Neyland Stadium field 4 years later, Tebow, now a Heisman Trophy–winning quarterback, is jumping and waving his arms. Meyer, a tall dark-haired man wearing a blue Gator polo and khaki pants, stands still on the sideline, coolly surveying the players running on the field before him. Phil Fulmer is clapping, always clapping, on the opposing sideline.

Even with Fulmer's failure against Meyer in the past three seasons, I'm optimistic, cautiously so, buoyed by an offensive game plan that UT center Josh McNeil calls the best he has ever seen. As Tennessee's Pride of the Southland band marches across the field and opens into the power T, the Vol team explodes out of the tunnel and onto the field. The Gator fans around me hiss, but every single person in the entire stadium, all 106,138 of us, stand and roar. It's time, yet again, for the 60-minute Tennessee-Florida hatefest.

Florida returns the opening kickoff to near midfield. On their first drive Meyer's Gators score a touchdown on a Tim Tebow third-and-goal jump pass. Less than 5 minutes into the game the score is 7–0 and I'm surrounded by Florida fans doing the Gator Chomp. Tardio leans over. "At least that girl has nice cleavage," he says, pointing at a Gator girl in the row in front of us.

On our first drive, we turn the ball over on a fumbled screen pass. Florida kicks a field goal. It's 10–0 Florida. We take possession, fail to do anything on offense, and punt directly to Florida punt returner Brandon James, the same 5' 7", 186-pound Brandon James who has already returned a punt for a touchdown against Tennessee in 2006 and 2007. (The punt return in 2006 was called back for a phantom block in the back.) In the moments before the football lands in his arms on this September afternoon, he's returned four punts for touchdowns in his career. Two of those touchdowns came against Tennessee. The other two were against Western Carolina and Hawaii.

In typical Tennessee fashion, we kick directly to him. James catches the ball, makes approximately 48 Tennessee defenders whiff on the tackle, and is gone for the touchdown. Suddenly Tennessee trails 17–0 and the first quarter is barely halfway over. Brandon James has now returned punts for touchdowns against Tennessee in three consecutive seasons. Has that ever happened before in the annals of modern football? The answer is no.

What's even more frustrating about this is that Brandon James has only returned punts for touchdowns in 14 percent of his 29 career games. Here's a roster of the teams who have given up these touchdowns: Tennessee, Western Carolina, Tennessee, Hawaii, Tennessee. Is anyone else seeing a pattern here? No? Let me break it down further. James's punt return touchdown percentage against the rest of the SEC in 15 games? Zero percent. In three games against Tennessee? One hundred percent.

As if that weren't enough, Western Carolina and Hawaii potentially could have been surprised by James's explosiveness or simply not had the athletes to match Florida's blocking or speed. UT, not so much. In fact, you can't even argue that Florida has some incredible punt return system. Prior to James, Florida had not had a punt return for a touchdown since the year 2000.

In the stands, I'm apoplectic, furious with Coach Fulmer and everyone on the sideline wearing orange. A winter, spring, and summer spent waiting to play your most hated rival on your home field and this is the result? Urban Meyer's Gators have now outscored my Vols 48–0 in the past 30 minutes of football. All around me Gator fans are chomping and I'm seething.

The frustration is not so much that Fulmer's teams have consistently failed in all facets of the game, but that he's consistently failed in the same ones over and over. Namely, special teams punt coverage. Year after year the Vols make the same mistakes. In last year's opener against Cal, the Vols kicked to wide receiver DeSean Jackson and allowed him to take a punt back for a touchdown. In this year's opener against UCLA it was a jailbreak blocked punt returned for a touchdown. And now, here, in the biggest game of the season, the game that will likely determine whether the Vols have a chance to win the SEC East, for the 3rd year in a row we've failed on punt coverage.

Tennessee responds to the latest special teams failure by taking possession of the football and executing a decent drive. We arrive on the doorstep of success, first and goal inside the Gator 10, when, once more, disaster strikes near the goal line: Jonathan Crompton runs into his fullback and fumbles the ball. The Gators recover.

You know how sometimes in horror movies the villain chases his victim without running? The victim runs at full speed, arms and legs windmilling pell-mell, and the killer doesn't move a step quicker than a determined walk but always seems to be on the victim's heels? That's how I feel about Urban Meyer right now. I feel like no matter what my Vols do or where we go, Urban Meyer is going to beat us there, traveling in a cool methodical walk. He won't even be sweating when he guts us. This analogy makes even more sense when you consider the obvious: Urban Meyer is pure evil.

I believe this. Firmly. And not just because he's my rival. I disliked Steve Spurrier, but I never felt he was evil. I'm not particularly fond of Georgia's Mark Richt or Alabama's Nick Saban, either, but I don't think they're evil. Urban Meyer? He's pure evil. There's just something about the way he walks, his absent chin, the steely flint gaze in his eyes. Put it this way: If Urban Meyer had to strangle five midgets with his bare hands to win one football game, I think he'd say without a moment's pause, "Show me the midgets." Then he'd strangle the midgets in Haiti (where strangling midgets is perfectly legal), smile for the camera, put the resulting tape up on YouTube, and text all his recruits the link of him feeding the dead bodies to alligators.

This might be a slight exaggeration. But I feel sort of like one of those imagined strangled midgets right about now.

I turn to Tardio. "I'm ready to go," I say.

"You can't leave," Tardio says, "you've never left a game early. Plus that girl is still here. I might talk to her."

"My team hasn't ever played this stupidly before," I say. "And you're not going to talk to that girl."

"You're writing a book on the season. What are you going to write about if you leave?"

"Leaving."

But I decide to stay. Moments later I get hit in the head by a Gator Chomp when Florida drives the length of the field and kicks a field goal. It's 20–0 Florida. Tennessee takes possession and Jonathan Crompton throws a horrible interception. Florida returns it to around the UT 20-yard line.

But wait, merciful heavens, the Gators have 12 men on the field! It's the best offensive play of UT's season, at least since Jonathan Crompton was tackled by his face mask against UCLA and we were the beneficiary of a 15-yard penalty. After this gift from God the Vols drive to inside the 2-yard line. On three consecutive plays we're stuffed. The clock is ticking down to halftime and we mismanage our time outs. I'm cursing in the stands. Rather than elect to kick a field goal, Fulmer rolls the dice and goes for a touchdown on fourth down. Our go-to offensive play appears to be this: quarterback sprints backward, offensive linemen choose not to block anyone, entire Gator defensive line pursues quarterback, quarterback throws ball to Gator defensive back.

Because that's what happens.

Full-throated boos rain down on the team as the half comes to a close. There's no uncertainty anymore: UT fans are booing the home team. We're losing 20–0 to Florida, but the worst thing about the first half is that we'd be losing to any team in the SEC. For the first time this season, I consider that I might just be watching an awful football team.

The first half has gone so badly that I don't want to move from my seat. This is another of my fan superstitions: when things are going badly, I don't like to move. While I sit and stare morosely down at the field, I convince myself that things can't possibly go worse in the second half. The band is on the field, but all I can do is sit and stare at the clock

ticking on the scoreboard, willing the second half to commence. For a
fleeting instant I allow myself to imagine what I'd feel like if we come
back to win 21–20. A rush of adrenaline buoys my spirits as I picture
the Gator fans around me, particularly Sleeveless T-shirt, trudging back
down the long ramps at Neyland Stadium. I imagine the sleeveless Gator
fan depressed and shivering in the evening coolness sweeping down off
Knoxville's surrounding majestic mountains.

I'm jolted from my daydream as the chorus around me, led by Sleeveless T-shirt, gains in volume. "If you ain't a Gator, you're gator bait,"
he screams. I hope Urban Meyer strangles him one day to impress a
recruit.

Sadly, the second half is more of the same. Florida scores to go up
27–0 midway through the third quarter, and shortly thereafter the UT
band shows up in my section to play "Rocky Top." No Vol fans are
singing and the Gator fans do the Gator Chomp in time to the music. I
get a text from Junaid.

"Not a lot of positives today," he writes.

"I'm not sure we will ever beat Florida again in my life," I respond.

In the fourth quarter Tennessee scores to bring a desultory cheer
from the crowd. The score is 27–6, and based on a convoluted set of
mathematical principles, Fulmer goes for 2. This way Tennessee only
has to score two more touchdowns, convert two more two-point conversions, and kick a field goal in the final quarter to *tie*.

Right.

But, of course, the 2-point conversion play fails as well. Later Florida tacks on a field goal to make the final score 30–6.

I've stayed for the entire game surrounded by Gator fans. Florida's
sections appear to be the only full ones remaining in Neyland Stadium.
On Monday I'll get an e-mail from a Vol fan suggesting that Phil Fulmer
be placed in charge of FEMA, since he was able to clear out a stadium
of over 100,000 fans in less than 2 hours.

As the players walk off the field, my friends and I leave the stadium
and begin the walk back to the Marriott. About five blocks from the

stadium, a couple jogs past me. They're both wearing yellow shorts and white T-shirts, happily smiling at each other in the September evening, oblivious to the massacre that has just transpired at Neyland Stadium.

After the joggers pass me, I turn and watch them. They veer off on a bridge over the Tennessee River and, I'm confident, don't even think about jumping off the side. They're happy and healthy and taking advantage of a beautiful day in late September. Football losses are entirely foreign to them. Fall Saturdays are for healthy fun, not obsessive wars with the fan's soul. I'm envious.

I get into my car at the Marriott and head west on I-40. On the outskirts of Knoxville, my wife calls. The game has been over for an hour. "So," my wife says, "what happened in the game?"

Lara has been out of the house all day rehearsing for her alumni performance with the Tennessee Titans cheerleaders for a home game against the Minnesota Vikings next week. As part of this preparation she took our son, Fox, to the Titans' indoor practice facility, where dozens of Titans cheerleaders oohed and aahed over him. At 7 months old, this may be his sexual peak.

"UT won," I say, just because I want to know how our conversation might have gone if they'd actually won.

"Really?" she exults. "Awesome!"

Then I tell her the dark truth.

"Well," she says, "Fox still loves you."

Shortly after midnight I arrive back in Nashville. My son is asleep in his crib, and my wife is also asleep in our bed. The entire house is dark and silent. I open the door to my son's nursery and stand looking down at him. He's sleeping deeply, chest rising and falling in the dark room, blissfully unaware of wins and losses.

Lara has him dressed in his UT pajamas. They're bright orange with a white T on the right side of his chest. Fox is on the road to UT fandom, and he's unaware of what sleepless fall nights await him. Although, to be fair, he's already felt the brunt of his dad's obsession. In late March, as he neared 2 months old, I'd attempted to feed him a bottle during the UT-American opening-round NCAA Tournament basketball game. Tennessee was a 2 seed and American was a 15 seed. Despite this seeding disparity, the Vols were in a tight game. Fox was crying, so I gave him his bottle. For 10 minutes he was silent, but then he began crying again. I couldn't figure out why he was upset until I realized that the new nipple on the bottle wasn't yet open. For 10 minutes, during the closest part of the second half, he'd been attempting to feed off a bottle that didn't yield him any nourishment. And I hadn't even noticed.

I stand there looking down at him tonight, thinking, "Do I really want my son to grow up a fan? Is it worth it for him to retrace the same old steps that his dad has already taken? Will he slam doors and stomp his feet and curse and make his mom scared for his future sanity? One day will my wife storm into my 10-year-old son's room and say, 'Fox Clay Travis, you are not going to grow up and be the kind of UT fan who beats his wife when the team loses!' just as my own mom said to me when I was 10?"

And if so, is being a fan really worth it? Especially when you're smart enough to know how irrational it is to feel so bad about your team, a collection of young men you don't even know, losing a game? Half the people in the world have never made a phone call, hundreds of millions are starving, billions can't read or write, yet, at this exact moment, I just might sign the papers for every Canadian simultaneously to be infected with chicken pox if only my team could have beaten Florida.

I stand looking down at Fox. He rolls over, sighs deeply in his sleep, flutters his eyelids. Once there must have been a time when I slept this well after the Vols lost to Florida or Alabama. But I'll be damned if I can remember it. I give him a kiss on his forehead, and he rolls away from me, blissfully unaware of anything but sleep.

I climb into bed next to my wife. She rolls over.

"Hey," she says, "I'm sorry your team lost."

My team losing is horrid. There is no escaping this. But in the wake of the lecture I received after the UCLA loss, I know the only way she might be willing to sleep with me right now is if I pretend not to pout.

"It's no big deal," I say, "we just aren't very good."

She gives me a peck on the lips. "You're doing a really good job taking this loss," she says. "Much better than after UCLA."

"I'm growing up," I say, kissing her back more passionately.

"It's late, Clay."

She rolls back over, away from me. And once more I'm alone with my defeat.

CHAPTER 7

MATT MAUCK AND THE MYSTERIOUS QUARTERBACK SNEAK

I'D BE LYING IF I TOLD you I didn't stay awake for a couple of hours that night staring at the ceiling fan in my bedroom, watching it slowly spin interminably around and around and around, thinking about all the plays that could have been made, and the plays that were made instead. Even though my Vols lost by 24, I still retrace each play, each turnover, each fumble, and each interception. Eventually the plays take over my mind and I'm fully awake.

When dawn finally breaks and sunlight begins filtering into my bedroom, I've barely slept at all. How defeated am I? I turn down a chance to watch the Tennessee Titans play the Minnesota Vikings, a mile and a half from my home. I can't bear to watch another football game this soon. I spend the day lying on the couch moping. I don't get dressed, I don't shower until after dark, I forget to eat. All I can think is, "Why does one game make me feel so bad?"

Eventually, by that evening, I find myself in the depths of a fan's depression. I've lumped this loss in with other horrific losses from my life as a Tennessee fan. And all of these losses have congealed inside me until I'm convinced I can taste the bitterness on my tongue, like moon-shine left in the bed of a pickup truck for a decade, the acid reflux of fan defeat. In my head I compile a list of Tennessee's most painful losses. Keep reading, if you dare:

1. LSU 31, Tennessee 20 (SEC Championship Game 2001)

My Vols were #2 in the country and coming off one of the greatest wins in school history, a 34–32 triumph at Flor-ida. Beat LSU for the second time this season and Tennessee would win the SEC title and travel to the Rose Bowl to play Miami for the national championship. Tennessee fans were feeling confident, to say the least. My dad even said, "I don't see any way it's possible that we lose this game."

Early on it looked like he was correct. The Vols stormed out to a 17–7 lead, knocking LSU's starting quarterback and starting running back from the game. And then they folded in the second half under a barrage of turnovers, poor tackling on the quarterback sneak (a play that seemed to astound the UT defense with its amazing complexity: take snap, run), and other assorted individual collapses that took years off my life.

As if this weren't enough, 5 days later my first-semester law school exams started. The only benefit of this loss was when midway through my torts final, I started to get sleepy, then thought back to the second half of the SEC champi-onship game, got fired up with indignation and anger, and powered through. (And by powered through I mean got a gentleman's B+.)

What makes this loss particularly difficult to swallow several years later is that this game represented two foot-ball programs passing in the night. LSU won the SEC title in 2001, destroyed Illinois in the Sugar Bowl, and then went on to win SEC and national titles in 2003 and 2007. Tennessee? We still haven't won another SEC title.

2. Alabama 9, Tennessee 6 (1990)

Tennessee, at 4-0-2, had risen to #3 in the country, the highest ranking for a Tennessee football team since 1969. The Vols were heavily favored to break Alabama's four-game winning streak. Not just an SEC championship but a national championship hung tremulously within our grasp. The longed-for rout didn't develop; instead both teams traded a pair of field goals and victory or defeat loomed on every snap as the fourth quarter waned with the teams tied 6–6. Tennessee lined up to attempt a 50-yard field goal, and Alabama blocked the field goal, recovered the football, and kicked their own 47-yard field goal to win 9–6. Afterward I cried and my grandfather remonstrated me for crying after a football game by asking, "Is Johnny Majors crying? Men don't cry about football games."

3. Alabama 17, Tennessee 17 (1993)

Sometimes ties count as losses. How so? When a tie game ends with the other team, whom you haven't beaten in 7 years, converting a 2-point conversion with all-everything offensive weapon David Palmer lined up under center. Alabama was defending national champions and Tennessee outplayed them on their home field, yet we still found a way to make a tie feel just as bad as a loss. To this day, if you utter the name David Palmer, I kick something. Hard.

4. Florida 35, Tennessee 29 (1996)

I've never looked forward to a single game more in my entire life, and instead I ended up barefoot in the street cursing Steve Spurrier. Before halftime.

The year 1996 was Peyton Manning's junior season and Vol fans believed this was our year to finally beat the Gators. The 1995 season had included a brutal 62–37 loss in Gainesville. It was the only game the 1995 Vols lost, and Manning and company squandered a 30–14 lead in that game. The 1996 game would provide redemption for the 48 consecutive points that a gleeful Steve Spurrier ran up in the Gainesville rain.

At least up until kickoff, that was the thought. Then Florida scored 35 straight points to begin the game, meaning my Vols had been outscored 83–0 in the past three quarters against the Gators. There are still places in Tennessee where if you mention this game, you'll be fed to ravenous grizzly bears. To the tune of "Rocky Top" of course.

5. LSU 21, Tennessee 14 (SEC Championship Game 2007)

With the Georgia Dome filled to the brim with Tennessee fans (I was one of about 60,000 Vol fans) and a 14–13 fourth-quarter lead, our senior quarterback, Erik Ainge, threw a third-down interception that LSU returned for a touchdown. I've called this interception the single most debilitating play in my life as a sports fan.

As if that weren't enough, Erik Ainge threw his second interception of the game on first down from the LSU 15 with just under 3 minutes left. LSU won another SEC championship and went on to win yet another national title. This loss was all the more painful because I'd been convinced that karma was going to reverse itself and that we'd beat LSU in an SEC championship game to make up for the loss in 2001.

6. Tennessee 26, Auburn 26 (1990)

Tennessee went on the road against a favored Auburn team and absolutely dominated for three quarters. As the fourth quarter began Tennessee scored to take a 26–9 lead. I was 11 years old and convinced that life could get no sweeter.

Then the world came undone. Auburn converted fourth downs, Tennessee dropped multiple easy interceptions. The collapse culminated when the Vols missed a field goal with 15 seconds left.

After this game my dad attempted to teach me a sporting life lesson by saying, "Clay, right now there is a boy the same age as you in Alabama who is really happy that his team tied Tennessee. Sometimes you'll be happy and sometimes he'll be happy, but you really aren't that different." Wrong. I still hate that boy.

7. Florida 27, Tennessee 23 (2000)

Despite dominating the game—Tennessee running back Travis Henry ran 37 times for 175 yards—Tennessee couldn't pull away from Florida. At least twice Henry broke into the open field, where not a man stood between him and the goal line, yet Henry managed to stumble. The result was field goal after field goal. Tennessee would eventually kick five.

With 14 seconds left and the Vols leading 23–20, Jabar Gaffney "caught" a touchdown pass that gave the Gators the victory. In his ensuing celebration, Gaffney gave the Vol crowd the throat-slash gesture. Later replay analysis confirmed that Gaffney had possession of the football for four one-hundredths of a second before dropping it. The referee who made the call, Bobby Moreau, received death threats from Vol fans. In fact, Moreau has never officiated another Tennessee game.

Almost a decade later, Phil Fulmer still winces when this game is mentioned. "He didn't catch that football, Clay," he says.

8. Notre Dame 34, Tennessee 29 (1990)

Notre Dame was #1 in the country, with Raghib "the Rocket" Ismail on their team, when they came into Knoxville on November 10, 1990. This was my first chance to ever see the #1 team in the country play, and I was giddy with excitement. I watched the game with another boy my own age, Jeremy Birdwell, one of the few Catholics in the small suburban town of Goodlettsville. He'd come to the game wearing a Notre Dame T-shirt under a coat. But he'd been afraid to take off his jacket inside Neyland Stadium for fear Tennessee fans would ridicule him.

It was a tight game, one that Tennessee led 23–20 early in the fourth quarter. But then momentum shifted. Notre Dame scored two quick touchdowns to go up 34–23. The second score, with just 3:33 remaining, was a Raghib Ismail 44-yard touchdown run. I remember crumbling to the ground in dismay. Many UT fans, including those surrounding me and Jeremy, left. I refused to leave early because my dad, sitting in another section, had taught me never to do this. For a short while it seemed that my dedication might be rewarded.

Tennessee went 68 yards in just 1:48 and scored a touchdown. The 2-point conversion failed, making the score 34–29. Then, miraculously, Carl Pickens recovered the onside kick and Tennessee advanced to the Notre Dame 20. Vol quarterback Andy Kelly, who'd passed for 399 yards in the game, was picked off throwing for Carl Pickens, who had 10 catches for 165 yards on the day, in the end zone. Notre Dame intercepted right in front of me and I can still see it like it was yesterday.

9. Memphis 21, Tennessee 17 (1996)

In Peyton Manning's junior season the Vols traveled to Memphis to play a downtrodden 2-6 Tigers team. Disaster struck. Memphis scored three touchdowns: a 76-yard interception return, a disputed 95-yard kickoff return (the returner should have been ruled down by contact when the arm holding the ball touched the ground), and a touchdown pass with 34 seconds left.

The entire state was stunned. In his postgame news

conference Coach Fulmer said, "This is the most disappointing game I have coached." Florida coach Steve Spurrier, never one to miss an opportunity to kick the Vols while they're down, pronounced Tennessee, a team that began the 1996 season with dreams of a national championship, "Knox County Champions."

10. *Alabama 28, Tennessee 20 (1988)*

Tennessee was 0-5 when the Alabama game rolled around in 1986. At age 7, I was there with my dad in Neyland Stadium to see it. Many of the UT fans wore bags over their heads, which infuriated my dad: "I just want to rip those bags off their heads," he growled. A local joke was making the rounds: "UT head coach Johnny Majors is buying up all the 7-Eleven convenience stores and renaming them 0-Elevens." Most Tennessee fans weren't laughing.

That October 15, Alabama rushed out to a 14–0 lead, but Tennessee fought back, slicing the lead to 14–9 by halftime. We would get no closer and Alabama pulled away before a late Tennessee score. By the time the Alabama game was over, Johnny Majors was over halfway to 0-11. But the Vols would rally, running off five consecutive wins to finish the season 5-6. The next season the Vols would rebound and win the first of two consecutive SEC championships.

CHAPTER 8

PEYTON MANNING, MEET JONATHAN CROMPTON

WHEN YOUR TEAM IS LOSING, IT'S impossible to escape. Everywhere you look—television, newspapers, in the mirror—you're reminded of defeat. When your team is losing and you're writing a book about the season, not only is it impossible to escape, but you have to relive all the memories by writing about them. Such is the case with me. I'm miserable. In the wake of the Florida game I've developed a horrible cough. The cough is debilitating, unlike any cough I've ever had before. I'll be walking along, a cough will come, and I'll double over in pain. My wife believes I am exaggerating the cough.

Fox is almost 7 months old and now he pretends to fake-cough when he hears Daddy coughing. After he fake-coughs he wiggles his feet and grins up at me. At moments like these, I wonder why I let my team make me feel as bad as I do. Especially when it's Auburn week—the one game all offseason that I wrote off as a loss. Tennessee has not beaten Auburn since that magical championship season of 1998. It feels like a century ago now. Winning two games in a row appears impossible, much less 13 in a row. What's more, has it really been a decade since the 1998 season? How has time passed so quickly? Shouldn't we all still be concerned about Y2K and Bill Clinton's dalliances with interns? As I make my way down to Auburn in late September, I can't stop thinking about that magical season.

Way back in 1998, when my team was good, I was a sophomore at George Washington University. One of the main reasons I went to college in Washington, D.C., was because I was interested in history and politics, the hallmarks of the city. Unfortunately, college football didn't carry much weight around town. George Washington disbanded its football team in 1966, so it's safe to say college football wasn't very popular on campus, either.

Soon after I arrived in D.C., I started as an intern with Congressman Bob Clement from Nashville's 5th Congressional District. At that time Tennessee newspapers were not yet available online, so I looked forward to the daily arrival of the local Nashville papers to 2229 Rayburn House Office Building each morning.

Ostensibly the newspapers were being mailed to the office so that the congressman could keep tabs on the stories affecting his constituents. But for at least two of us, they offered an opportunity to satisfy our Vol fandom. Looking back now, with the advent of the Internet, it seems incomprehensible that only 10 years ago sports fans couldn't follow their teams anywhere at any time. In 1998 local newspapers provided a tangible connection to my home state and my home team. I was terribly homesick for most of my freshman year, and the articles about UT football made Nashville not seem so far away.

Alex Haught, Congressman Clement's chief of staff, was also a huge Tennessee football fan. Alex was a double UT graduate, both undergrad and law school, who at 33 was already a skilled political operative. He'd worked on Al Gore's presidential campaign in 1988 and assisted in Bill Clinton's presidential campaigns in 1992 and 1996. Now he was biding time with Congressman Clement until the 2000 Gore presidential campaign got under way. Our friendship developed based upon a mutual affinity for the Vols, a good-natured duel over who could be the first to read the sports section when the newspapers arrived.

In 1998 CBS affiliates split their SEC football telecasts with the Big East and the Pac-10. Due to this triplicate of the regional television feeds, D.C. residents could never be sure whether the local CBS affiliate would be carrying the SEC game, the Big East game, or the Pac-10 game. With its location directly between the SEC and the Big East, the game of the week in Washington was notoriously difficult to plan for. On many Fridays I'd arrive at the office to do my bidding for democracy. "Keep calling WUSA-9," Alex would say, "until you get somebody who sounds like they know what they're talking about to tell us what game they're going to have on this weekend."

I attacked this assignment with an ironclad will. Other interns were buzzing around the Capitol attempting to sign up co-sponsors for pending legislation on energy policy, welfare reform, and NAFTA; I was trying to reach the WUSA programming director to nail down which football game the local CBS affiliate would be carrying on Saturday. Regularly, Alex would show up at my cubicle. "Anything?" he'd ask, glasses perched on his nose, drumming his fingers on the cushioned cubicle walls.

Alex had tried to solve this telecast problem by attaching a satellite dish to his townhouse on the outskirts of Capitol Hill. This way he got CBS games from several regions of the country. On many occasions during the fall of 1998, Alex invited me to watch games with him at his house. It was there that I watched UT narrowly win 17–9 against Auburn at Jordan-Hare Stadium. At the end of the game I was anxious over how close the game had been and Alex disabused me of that notion. "Never," he said, "be upset when you get a win at Jordan-Hare."

Later on that season I arrived to watch the UT-Arkansas game with him. The Vols were 8-0 and playing an 8-0 Arkansas team. On Friday the WUSA director had promised me that they were going to be carrying UT-Arkansas in Washington. Thanks to delayed weekend Metro service, I got to Alex's house just as kickoff began. I stood on the front doorstep knocking for a minute before an upstairs window flew open and Alex stuck his head out the window. "They screwed us, Clay. We got UCLA. We gotta make a run to a sports bar in Virginia."

We climbed into Alex's old truck, left his Capitol Hill neighborhood, and sped off toward northern Virginia. I still don't know where the sports bar that was carrying the UT-Arkansas game was located. It seemed like we rode in his old truck forever, especially because both of us knew the game was progressing as we drove. At long last we squealed into a derelict hideaway off two back streets and raced inside. The undefeated and #1 team in the country, our Vols, were trailing 21–0 to Arkansas. We both cursed, pulled up chairs, and sat down in the dark and smoky bar in front of the television. The sound was off on the UT game. There were no other Vol fans in the sports bar. In fact, hardly anyone at all was there.

Together we watched one of the most remarkable comebacks in UT history. Our Vols stormed back from 21 down to cut the deficit to 24–22. Driving late in the game, the Vols faced a fourth down. Tennessee's quarterback, Tee Martin, a junior in his first season taking over for the departed Peyton Manning, threw an incomplete pass. Alex and I sunk in our seats. "That's it," Alex said.

I held out hope because we still had time outs, but there was only 1:47 remaining and Arkansas led 24–22. On the second play after we turned the ball over, Arkansas quarterback Clint Stoerner, a junior from Texas, took the snap and attempted to roll out for a bootleg. But UT's Billy Ratliff, a defensive tackle from Mississippi, who with his compact body and defensive crouch resembled a thick tree stump, sprang off the ball and drove back Arkansas center Brandon Burlsworth into Stoerner. As a result, Stoerner stumbled backward and fumbled the football.

Alex and I stood and screamed in the bar. For a tantalizing second or so the ball rolled on the Neyland Stadium turf. Then UT pounced on it. Every play after that was a handoff to Travis Henry, a sophomore running back from Frostproof, Florida, who rushed for over 4,087 yards in his final high school season. Before his career was over, the squat Henry, nicknamed "Cheese" because he was as tough as government cheese, would go on to claim the title of UT's all-time leading rusher. But on this day Henry gouged a stunned Arkansas defense for 43 yards and scored a touchdown on a rushing play with 28 seconds remaining. The Vols would go on to win 28–24.

Tennessee players collapsed in blissful joy on the sideline. Alex and I leapt to our feet and embraced in a northern Virginia bar. Somewhere on the Arkansas sideline center Brandon Burlsworth sought out Stoerner and apologized for tripping him. It was, and still is, one of the greatest UT football victories I've ever watched.

On the way home, Alex and I reconstructed the game, relishing every single miraculous moment. "Can you imagine what it feels like right now," he asked, "to be an Arkansas player?" We paused in contemplative silence for a few moments, then returned to celebrating.

A few days later Alex accepted the post of Tennessee finance director for Al Gore's nascent 2000 campaign. He was excited to be returning to his home city of Nashville to begin the new job. But before his move came the SEC championship game on December 5, 1998.

Three weeks after the victory over Arkansas the two of us gathered back in Alex's living room to watch our undefeated Tennessee team take on the Mississippi State Bulldogs in the SEC championship game. Since their victory over Arkansas, Tennessee had handily dispatched Kentucky and Vanderbilt by a combined score of 100–21. In the latter game, a 41–0 Vol victory over Vanderbilt, I was one of the tens of thousands of Tennessee fans who flooded Vanderbilt's football stadium with orange. That victory put Tennessee at 11-0 and set the stage for a potential national championship.

But first the Vols had to face off against a dangerous Mississippi State team. State, 8-3 on the regular season, scored first on a 70-yard interception return for a touchdown. Alex punched the couch and I kicked his ottoman.

"I was afraid of this," he said.

But the Vols regrouped and scored 10 unanswered points in the second quarter to take a 10–7 lead. During halftime, we passed our time anxiously eating a late dinner of barbecue and chips. My stomach was so tense I could barely swallow. It got even tighter late in the fourth quarter when Mississippi State returned a punt 83 yards for a touchdown. Suddenly, with just 8:43 remaining in the fourth quarter, Tennessee trailed 14–10. All the championship hopes, the SEC title, the 11 consecutive wins, all of it was at stake.

"I can't believe it," Alex said, head in hands, "I just can't believe it."

Tennessee took possession of the ball, their championship hanging precariously in the balance. Tee Martin methodically moved the ball up the field until he uncorked a 41-yard touchdown pass to Peerless Price, the most aptly named Volunteer wide receiver in the history of the program. Price streaked down the right sideline of the Georgia Dome turf and snagged the ball out of the air. Touchdown!

The Vols suddenly led once more, this time 17–14. Alex and I stood and screamed so loudly that his dogs, Truman and Scout, began to howl alongside us.

After a kickoff Mississippi State fumbled on their first play and Tennessee took possession once more. On the first play from scrimmage Tee Martin zipped a dart to wide receiver Cedrick Wilson in the end zone. Wilson, whose brother Ellix would later play for the 2008 Vols, snagged the ball out of the air and danced in the end zone. Just like that, Tennessee scored 14 points on two consecutive plays. The game was over; the SEC championship was ours. Tennessee was a perfect 12–0, headed to the first BCS title game to play Florida State.

Alex sank onto the couch and extended his hands while his dogs licked his palms. He spoke for the entire state of Tennessee with a single word.

"Whew." He sighed.

After the SEC championship game, Alex dropped me off on GW's campus. As I stepped out of his truck, Alex said that he would be leaving for Nashville soon but that he expected me to come to work with him that summer. I said that I would. I was 19 years old and Alex was 33. But when we watched football games, like many fans, we were both 11 years old again.

Less than a month later, on January 4, 1999, Tennessee took the field against Florida State in Tempe, Arizona. I watched the game with my dad from our Nashville living room. At kickoff my hands were trembling so much I couldn't hold a glass of water. Tennessee jumped out to an early 7–0 lead and then UT cornerback Dwayne Goodrich, who by 2008 would be in prison for criminally negligent homicide after a fatal car accident, intercepted a pass intended for Florida State superstar Peter Warrick and returned it for a touchdown. The entire state of Tennessee whooped as one. The Vols led 14–0, and in one glorious sprint down the Fiesta Bowl sideline, Dwayne Goodrich's life hit its peak.

Florida State scored 9 points before halftime and it was 14–9 as the second half commenced. Neither team scored during an agonizingly close third quarter. Tennessee, after 48 years without a consensus national championship, was only 15 minutes away from the ultimate prize in college football. Anticipation built. Tennessee took possession at their 21-yard line with less than 10 minutes remaining in the game, nursing a 14–9 lead.

Legendary Vol radio announcer John Ward, in his 31st and final year as the Voice of the Vols, explained what happened next better than anyone:

> With the clock showing 9:45 to go here at the Fiesta Bowl in Tempe. Florida State going to blitz this time. Here they come. Gonna throw the ball long, long downfield to Peerless Price. He makes the catch at the forty-five, he's at the forty, thirty-five, thirty, twenty-five, twenty. Just give it to him. Seventy-nine yards. Touchdown Tennessee!

Peerless Price, who would finish the game with four catches for 199 yards, was named the co-MVP, along with Goodrich, and the Vols attained perfection, a 13-0 mark and an undisputed national championship with a 23–16 victory. John Ward counted down the final seconds of his final radio broadcast, "Five, four, three, two, one. The national champion is clad in orange!"

Later, Phil Fulmer says he didn't enjoy that championship as much as he should have. "I regret not celebrating the victory more. We got up early and left the next morning and I got off the big airplane in Knoxville and got on a smaller airplane, changed clothes, and flew to Memphis to meet a recruit. I never even went home. Stupid, you know, I should have taken a couple of days, a day or two, to really enjoy the win with the people who helped me get there. But I didn't do it.

"I made up my mind that if we did it again, I was going to do it right, and in 2001, I thought we were going to do it. But we didn't."

In the wake of the national championship, Alex and I exchanged celebratory phone calls about the victory. It was the last UT football game Alex would ever see. On March 3, 1999, a drunk driver ran a red light at the intersection of 20th Avenue and West End near downtown Nashville and slammed into his car. He was pronounced dead that night. Al Gore suspended his campaign and flew into Nashville to deliver the eulogy.

In the days after his death, I heard a lot of stories about Alex from friends and family. Alex lived with his brother and sister-in-law during the 1994 Tennessee Senate campaign. One day she received a phone bill with charges to 1-900 phone numbers. For weeks she stewed over them, unwilling to confront him. Then one night she decided to call the number, to find out exactly how Alex had been spending his after-work hours while he lived in her house. She rang the number and waited for someone to pick up. When she heard a voice on the other end of the line, she began to laugh.

Alex had been calling recruiting hotlines. In the days before the Internet made recruiting a madhouse of online information, Alex was trying to figure out who was in UT's next recruiting class for a mere $3 a minute.

In the summer of 1998 Alex took his dad, Max, a lifelong Kentucky basketball fan, to the White House joint ceremony honoring both the national champion Kentucky men's basketball team and the national champion Tennessee women's basketball team. As he and his father walked into the ceremony, they discovered that one side of the auditorium was designated for Kentucky's men, the other for Tennessee's women. Alex's dad attempted to sit on the Kentucky side. Alex grabbed him. "We're with Tennessee," he said.

The hearse that carried Alex to Woodlawn Cemetery in Nashville flew an orange Tennessee Vol flag.

Fifty-six days after Alex died, on April 28, 1999, Arkansas center Brandon Burlsworth died in a car accident just 11 days after he'd been drafted in the third round of the NFL draft. It was Burlsworth who tripped Clint Stoerner on the most memorable play in University of Tennessee history. I cried all over again and thought once more of my friend.

ON THE THURSDAY BEFORE the Auburn-Tennessee game, I speak to one of the countless Vol alumni groups spread across the country, the Birmingham Big Orange Club. The Vol alums are crushed by how the season has begun and at the end of my talk, I take questions. "Do you think Fulmer will be our coach next year? Or can he not keep up with Mark Richt and Urban Meyer anymore?" asks a bespectacled man in the back of the meeting room.

"I don't think the game has passed him by," I say.

A few fans nod in my direction, but many more shake their heads. The great war among the UT fan base, should Fulmer stay or go, is officially under way.

I spend the Friday before the game hanging out in a Birmingham, Alabama, radio studio with my friends Lance Taylor and Ian Fitzsimmons of *Roundtable Radio* on WJOX. With the Vols standing at 1-2, Lance makes the perfect suggestion for a possible subtitle for this book: "Kicked in the Vols." (Later my esteemed editor will pooh-pooh this decision. "That's way too sophomoric, Clay," she'll say.)

The next day the drive to Auburn passes without consequence, other than spotting a sign in Childersburg, Alabama, on State Route 110 that reads HAPPY 468TH BIRTHDAY, CHILDERSBURG. The Pilgrims arrived in Jamestown in 1620. It must have been quite a surprise to them to find out that Childersburg, Alabama, already existed, having been founded, according to the birthday wish, in 1540.

I'm watching the game in Auburn with my friend Rogers Rowder, a graduate of Auburn and a former law school classmate of mine. Rowder is a curly haired Alabama native with season tickets to Auburn that are in the next-to-last row of the upper deck.

During the early afternoon of September 27, I tailgate with Rowder's friends in the shadows of Jordan-Hare. The sky is overcast and it's warm but not oppressively hot. We spend the morning drinking beers and sliding down a small hill to relieve ourselves in a creek that runs through the Auburn campus. "We had a Porta Potti," says Bucky, Rowder's college classmate, "but they made us take it down because it violated codes. So now we just pee in the creek."

Rowder, a practicing attorney in Atlanta, is wearing his lucky Bo Jackson baseball jersey, and he buttonholes me on proper rooting etiquette in his seats. "Now I don't mind you rooting for your team, but you can't root against mine," he says. I nod.

On the walk to the stadium it's strangely quiet; for a 3:30 CBS afternoon kickoff, there isn't a lot of fire in the crowd. Neither Tennessee's nor Auburn's fans seem particularly excited about this game, probably because both teams lost home games to hated divisional rivals last week—Auburn to LSU and Tennessee to Florida. There are also a ton of seats for sale on the street, all for below face value.

On the hike into the sky to our seats I meet one of Rowder's friends who was behind the Web site keepmikeshula.com. The site was a hysterical parody of an Alabama fan site that ostensibly supported Coach Mike Shula no matter what the results on the field were. It was run by Auburn fans and I wrote about the site for CBS. Now we meet for the first time in the Nick Saban era. "I think the site was a little too successful," he says wistfully.

By the time Rowder and I reach the top of Jordan-Hare stadium, I've forgotten my rooting promise. I don't care how Tennessee wins and I'm not opposed to rooting against Auburn. If Jonathan Crompton gets under center, steps back from the line of scrimmage, removes his mouth-piece, and subsequently shoots Auburn defensive tackle Sen'Derrick Marks with a poison blow dart, I'm all for it. Anything to win.

As we sit down in his seats, it occurs to me that Rowder and I have just entered that zone of fandom that is not often traversed, watching a game with one friend when the two of you are rooting for different teams. What's more, this is a college football game, a war between rivals, the modern-day equivalent of taking a picnic basket and a carriage out to watch First Manassas. No regular-season games matter more in sports than college football games. If this were any other sport in America—college basketball, the NBA, NFL, Major League Baseball—watching the game with a rival fan wouldn't really be that difficult. You'd want your team to win, but it wouldn't consume every fabric of your being. But a college football game? This is dangerous territory, even for close friends.

Especially in the SEC. In fact, it's been scientifically proven that the only time Southern men bear grudges against other Southern men that last longer than 1 week is when they've watched a college football game with a friend who is rooting for the other team. Affairs with wives, intentional elbows to the face while playing basketball, urinating in a friend's beer when he goes to the bathroom and then letting him unwittingly drink the pee beer? All of it can be forgiven. But anger over SEC football games? It never dies.

Rowder knows all about this. He's married to an obsessive Georgia fan. Auburn and Georgia have the longest rivalry in the South. "Those games can get a little rough," he says.

From up in the top of the stadium we have a majestic view of the Auburn War Eagle taking off and landing on the field, a mascot tradition that began in 1892. Legend holds that during an 1892 football game an old eagle that had been nursed to health after being found on a

Civil War battlefield took flight. As the old eagle soared above the field, the football game turned in Auburn's favor. The eagle fell to the ground and died, but not before Auburn triumphed. Now War Eagle VII reigns. During War Eagle VII's entire flight, as the Auburn faithful stand as one and unleash a deafening cheer, I am thinking over and over in my head, "My team can't be as bad as they've looked in the first three games of the season, they just can't." My internal soliloquy is interrupted by the cheers of a shirtless man who is so drunk he can barely walk.

"I can't believe he made it up all these steps," Rowder says.

And there are a lot of steps. I ask Rowder if he's ever thought about taking advantage of his big-firm lawyer's salary and moving down to better seats. He looks at me as if I just asked if he'd like a Zima. "This is where the real fans sit," he says, pouring smuggled whiskey into his Coke.

Auburn and Tennessee are mirror images of each other so far this season. In addition to losing to their rivals last week, both teams are breaking in new offensive coordinators, Tony Franklin at Auburn and Dave Clawson at UT. Plus Auburn's Tommy Tuberville and Phil Fulmer are the two deans of SEC coaching. This is Tuberville's 10th season at Auburn and Fulmer's 16th at UT. No other SEC coach has lasted more than 8 years at their current school. So far Auburn's offensive futility has led to a quarterback controversy as well. The Auburn fan base is divided between two quarterbacks: Kodi Burns, the only black man in Southern history to have a name envied by nine-tenths of the sorority girls at Ole Miss, and Chris Todd, a weak-armed junior college transfer. Neither inspires abundant confidence.

Auburn sprints onto the field below us. Sen'Derrick Marks flashes onto the new Jumbotron. Rowder elbows me in the ribs, hard. "I believe in Sen'Derrick Marks with all my heart," he says. Marks is a 6' 2", 296-pound defensive tackle from Mobile, Alabama. He's a 21-year-old junior and, according to one of Rowder's friends, he tackled Aubie, the Auburn tiger, in the open field last year when the tiger escaped from his cage. (Note: I believe this story is apocryphal. Upon further research I discover that Marks merely stared at the tiger until it fled to the safety of the cage.)

As UT-Auburn commences, Florida is in a tight game with Ole Miss in Gainesville. Everyone around me is more interested in talking about this game. And everyone, Auburn and Vol fans alike, is rooting for Ole Miss. The only thing that unites the SEC in the regular season is hatred for the Gators. Midway through the first quarter of an awful Auburn-Tennessee slugfest the final score of the Florida game is announced: Ole Miss has stunned Florida 31–30.

My spirit soars. Maybe, after all, Tennessee does have a chance to contend for an SEC championship! If we win this game, Tennessee and Florida will be even in the loss column. Maybe, just maybe, Tennessee can recapture the momentum that carried them through 2007 after a horrible start.

Peyton Manning certainly thinks Fulmer can rally the team. In his 11th season as quarterback of the Indianapolis Colts, Manning has traveled to Auburn during his NFL bye week to support Phil Fulmer and the Vols. In 1994 Manning, the son of legendary Ole Miss quarterback Archie Manning, shocked the Southland by signing with Phil Fulmer and Tennessee. The consensus top player in the country, Manning started midway through his freshman season at Tennessee, went 39-6 as a starter, and set 28 school records at quarterback. In 1998 he was the number-one draft pick in the country. He and Fulmer have a special relationship, and Manning returns to Knoxville every offseason to work out with the younger Tennessee players. Now he's standing on the sideline, the highest-paid cheerleader in University of Tennessee history.

My enthusiasm over Florida's loss lasts for all of 5 minutes, because Auburn's Chris Todd hits a receiver on a 15-yard pass in the center of the end zone to give Auburn a 7–0 lead with 3 minutes left in the first quarter. Touchdowns are precious objects in this game, orbs of pure, sparkling golden sunshine so bright that they can't be looked at with the naked eye. The Auburn fans around me shield their eyes.

"All right," Rowder exults. "Great play call. We got a touchdown."

"Nice defense," I say.

"That was a great throw," says Rowder.

"We're awful," I say. "Just awful."

We watch the replay on the Jumbotron.

"You're right," says Rowder. "That was pretty awful defense."

UT's offense answers the bright and golden orb of a touchdown with a field goal to slice the lead to 7–3. Then the defense stiffens, and Tennessee adds another field goal. The score is 7–6 halfway through the second quarter. I'm feeling cautiously optimistic. Rowder, sitting beside me, has gone quiet.

"This game is going to make one of us feel awful," he says quietly.

Tennessee takes over inside their own 5-yard line. Then the inexplicable happens: Arian Foster and Jonathan Crompton mishandle a handoff. The ball caroms backward into the end zone, where it's recovered by Auburn's defense. Suddenly, just like that, my snakebitten Vols are down 14–6. Rowder exults beside me. Jordan-Hare Stadium, which had been eerily quiet for about an hour, is boisterous.

"I'm not sure I would go for a car ride with Arian Foster," CBS announcer Gary Danielson says on the telecast. Yet again, Arian Foster has fumbled at the most inopportune moment. Somewhere Bernadette Foster sighs. The Vol message boards are set to explode once more; let the Arian Foster fumble recriminations begin anew.

I don't know how much worse Tennessee's offense can get. The Clawfense, under the direction of offensive coordinator Dave Clawson, is incapable of tiny successes, such as completed passes, first downs, or handoffs. To say this is painful to watch is, perhaps, unfair to the word *painful*. I'd sooner bite on a minié ball and have my arm amputated without laudanum than watch this.

When the stadium finally quiets down, Rowder puts his hand on my shoulder. "Do you ever think," he asks, "that Arian Foster might not hear that well? Maybe he doesn't hear the audibles."

"I don't know," I say. "He's heard all my questions."

"You should have them look into that. He seems like he's going the wrong way an awful lot of the time. Like against UCLA when he and Crompton ran into each other."

This is what my team's season has become: Rival fans are concerned that our running back might suffer from hearing loss.

"I think he can hear fine," I say.

Rowder swigs from his Coke, unwilling to let the subject die. "It doesn't look like he can hear fine."

Both teams let the half run out and Auburn jogs into the locker room up 14–6. Rowder looks out over the Auburn band covering the field. "If it's any consolation," he says, "last week I watched our band play at the half and I thought they looked better coached than our offense."

"Maybe we should make our band director the offensive coordinator," I say.

"You'd fumble less," Rowder says. "No one in the band ever drops their instruments."

The second half of the Auburn-Tennessee game just might be the worst half of offensive football I've ever seen in my life. How bad is it? Tennessee punts on fourth and 2 from the Auburn 34. The Vols stand a decent chance of netting *14* yards on the punt. Miraculously the ball is downed at the 3. This is when the Chris Todd quarterbacking experiment for Auburn goes horribly awry. Every pass he throws floats across the sky like a gentle butterfly being chased by playful children. On one pass in this series from the Auburn 3-yard line, two Tennessee players run into each other going for the interception and the pass is somehow completed over their heads. But shortly after that Todd floats another pass downfield that is intercepted by Dennis Rogan of Tennessee. Rogan returns the ball to Auburn territory and Jonathan Crompton jogs back onto the field.

In the first half Crompton played terribly. In the second half he's atrocious. Each of his passes seems to move at the same rate of speed, 299,792,458 meters per second, the speed of light. Crompton has no touch; it's almost as if he's simply decided that he's going to throw the ball hard no matter what. One 3-yard slant pass by Crompton zooms by at twice the speed of light. Later NASA scientists working in Huntsville will flag the atmospheric readings for Auburn, Alabama, and note several Crompton passes, thanks to their rate of speed, as potential alien aircraft. It's this bad—midway through the third quarter, Crompton completes his final pass of the day.

Sitting high in the stands, I decide that Crompton is Tennessee's own version of Rick "The Wild Thing" Vaughn from the movie *Major League*. Crompton isn't just throwing the ball hard and in the general direction of no one; he's also throwing the ball specifically where his receivers are not. Straight fly pattern down the field, Crompton throws the eight yard out. Receiver runs an eight yard out? Crompton throws a fly pattern down the sideline. On at least half of Crompton's throws no receiver is within 10 yards of the ball when it lands. For the past 3 years, Crompton prepared to be the starting quarterback at Tennessee and now that the moment is finally here, his play is a spectacular failure.

I picture a conversation between Crompton and former Vol superstar quarterback Peyton Manning going something like this:

Peyton: All right, Jon, tell me what you're seeing out there, what's the defense doing? Are they shifting before the snap, giving you a false front, dropping back into a zone, blitzing a safety? What are you seeing out there?
Crompton: You're supposed to look at the defense before the snap?

At long last Crompton, trying as hard as he can in a futile offensive system, does make a play. Facing a third and 14 late in the third quarter, Crompton, playing on a severely sprained right ankle that was reinjured in the first half, takes off running for the first down. I tense up in the stands. As he nears the first down marker Crompton doesn't slide. He takes a sickening shot to the head at the same time he's hit from below. It's a first down!

The fourth quarter begins with UT facing a third and goal from the

Auburn 2. In a game where offense is nearly absent, a touchdown would be huge here, particularly in light of UT's failings inside the 10-yard line already this year. Crompton takes the snap and pitches to backup running back Montario Hardesty on the sweep. Hardesty has the angle on the Auburn defense and rushes into the end zone. I'm gleeful in the stands, the only cheering UT fan in our section. It's 14–12 Auburn.

"Nice call," Rowder says, drinking from his cup of whiskey.

We go for 2, but the 2-point conversion fails in that way that always drives fans insane: on a completed pass that's outside of the end zone. I'm not certain, but I believe it may be the Chris Cutcliffe rub play that is the manager's go-to play and one that his father, David Cutcliffe, has made famous. The receiver makes the catch but has no shot of scoring. Instead he's dragged down 3 yards from the goal line. In a slugfest of epic proportions, Auburn has now put up 189 total yards of offense and Tennessee 177.

The Auburn offense goes nowhere on the ensuing possession and Tennessee's sophomore wide receiver, Gerald Jones, playing one of his best games for the Vols all season, returns a punt 40 yards to put the Vols in great field position at the Auburn 38. Tennessee doesn't even need to get a first down to attempt a field goal to take the lead. They only need 7 or 8 yards. That's all. But then the Vols lose 2 yards on three plays and are forced to punt.

Kodi Burns enters at quarterback and Auburn loses 9 yards on their first two plays. On third and 19 the Auburn crowd lets loose with a torrent of boos. Rowder is stunned. "I've never heard Auburn booed here before," he says. Prior to this season I'd never heard Tennessee booed before, either. It's an interesting observation; as the salaries of SEC coaches have increased and the national profile of the programs has grown, fans' expectations have become more in line with professional sports: win now or else.

As a kid I remember my dad saying that people didn't ever boo Tennessee players because they were college kids. "They aren't making money to play," he explained. In my life as a college sports fan I've cursed opposing teams, players, and coaches to high heaven, but I've never booed my own team. Other Southern fans have generally followed the same code of fan behavior. Prior to this season, when people asked me why I loved SEC football, I pointed to the fans' support. "The fans care more about football than anywhere else, but they're also the most respectful of the players," I'd say. "They don't boo the home team. Ever." Now, this is no longer the case. The winds of college football change have reached the SEC.

Rowder looks a bit taken aback. "I can't believe we're booing," he says again. "We stink. But we stink and we're winning." He stands with his hands on his hips looking out over Jordan-Hare Stadium. "Are we really booing?" he asks rhetorically.

As Auburn lines up to punt, the intensity of the game finally gets to me. After three and a half quarters of rooting for Tennessee but not against Auburn, I can't help myself. "Snap it over his head," I yell. Rowder glares at me.

"You can't cheer against Auburn," he drawls through gritted teeth.

Immediately I apologize.

"We're not going to score unless we get a safety on defense or special teams," I say.

Rowder stares at me. Then, finally, he relents. "You're probably right," he says.

Three more times Tennessee takes possession with great field position, needing a single first down or, at most, two first downs to get into field goal range. Instead the Vols fail to convert on three consecutive drives. In fact, on the final 12 offensive plays of the game Tennessee gains 12 yards. I could go through my cycle of emotions on each play, explain how I stand (we are all standing now) with my palms clenched so tightly into fists and with my heart beating so hard that I worry I might pass out. I keep thinking, believing, that this is the drive, this is the time, this is the play when the Vols will take control of our season and prove we're not a bad football team. Twelve times they line up needing but one play to put them in position to win. And 12 times they fail.

Five of those failures are Jonathan Crompton passes; every single one falls to the ground incomplete.

Tennessee center Josh McNeil later tells me that this was the worst quarter of the season. "We had so many chances and they just . . ."—he pauses, clenches his fists—"didn't happen. It just didn't."

With 2:59 remaining Tennessee punts once more to Auburn, whose offense in the fourth quarter is even more futile than Tennessee's. On the three previous drives Auburn has failed to gain a first down. What's more, they've gained –2 yards combined on those three series. Now they're pinned back on their own goal line. Get a first down and they win; fail, and once more Tennessee's offense will trot onto the field with one final chance for victory.

On third and 5 from the Auburn 10, Tennessee takes a time out. There is 2:14 remaining on the clock. Auburn's quarterback is Kodi Burns. He takes the snap and rolls out to his right. Everyone is standing, and an oddly hushed stillness settles over the entire stadium. One of UT's defenders is close, achingly close, to dragging Burns down in the end zone for a game-tying safety. But Burns eludes the defender and zips a pass to a wide-open receiver in front of the UT sideline. First down, Auburn.

Ballgame.

I sink down to my seat. Rowder doesn't cheer very loudly.

"I guess that'll do it," he says, as if we've both just witnessed an execution. "We choked you out. There wasn't anything pretty about it."

"There's not going to be anything pretty about my book, either," I say. I drop my notepad down on the hard metal of the Jordan-Hare Stadium bleachers and lean over. For a minute, I think I'm going to be sick. My foe, the extremely drunk, shirtless Auburn fan, is standing now, twirling his shirt above his head as the final seconds tick off the clock.

"Go to hell, Tennessee!" he screams.

I stare at this Auburn fan. Anger courses through me. This guy gets to be happy and I don't? This guy who arrived at the game with a blood alcohol level approaching .3? This guy who is over 50 and shirtless in the upper deck of a football stadium? I stare at the field where the clock has run out and the teams are meeting at midfield. I can't find him, but I'm looking for Jonathan Crompton. Why have you forsaken us, Jonathan Crompton, why?

I walk down the spiral concrete ramps of the stadium, which are quiet. Everyone leaving the stadium, even the victorious Auburn fans, looks like they've just watched a baby kangaroo get run over by a bulldozer. Rowder does his best to console me.

"You've played the toughest part of your schedule," he says.

If only; we still have Alabama and Georgia and South Carolina on the road. How much worse can things get? My BlackBerry won't work, so I can't review Jonathan Crompton's statistics from the game. We leave the stadium and trudge in the fading light in the direction of our tailgate. I've got to drive all night from Auburn, Alabama, to Nashville, Tennessee, accompanied solely by my nightmarish memories of the game.

Outside the stadium my BlackBerry gets a signal, and my fingers tremble as I click on the game statistics. They're as bad as I feared.

Jonathan Crompton, blue-chip stud quarterback from Tennessee, who told his father at the age of 2 that he wanted to be an NFL quarterback, has gone 8 for 23 for a grand total of 67 yards passing. His team, my team, the Tennessee Vols are now 1-3, 0-2 in the SEC—the worst start to a season since 1994. Rowder gives me his condolences as I recount these stats.

"Your team will get better," he says.

I nod and climb into my car.

"Watch out for deer."

As I begin my 335-mile drive, it's already pitch-black and the temperature is dropping. I turn my headlights on bright and scan the underbrush for deer, expecting at any moment to slam into Bambi's mom in the darkness. On the radio, Alabama has traveled to Georgia to play. I don't want to hear any more football today.

I want to be alone with my anger at Jonathan Crompton—a man I hate with every ounce of passion in my body tonight. How could he fail me like this? First against UCLA, then against Florida, and now, this latest indignity, against Auburn?

I sit staring at the open road, thinking about how I'm in the exact same situation I was in 2 years earlier, driving back home from Auburn after a gut-wrenching defeat. Then it was a televised loss in the midst of the Dixieland Delight Tour—Tennessee had just lost 21–20 to Florida in 2006. As I move on through the Alabama night, I ask myself why I keep putting myself in this situation, ruining an otherwise perfect fall Saturday night in the South watching my team lose. Why, why, why do I do this to myself?

After a while I start talking to myself, having an imaginary conversation with Jonathan Crompton that goes something like this:

Me: I hate you, Jonathan Crompton.

Imaginary Jonathan Crompton: Why do you hate me?

Me: Because you suck at football.

Imaginary Jonathan Crompton: But you don't know me. (Crompton is very logical in our conversation.)

Me: That makes it easier to hate you. (Someone honks at me because I'm sitting at a red light too long.)

Imaginary Jonathan Crompton: It doesn't make it right.

Me: Don't argue with me. (I'm getting heated now) I hate you! And your stupid passes and your stupid buzz haircut and that argument you got in with the Michael Jackson impersonator in Los Angeles. I knew it, knew you'd ruin things for me. You're everything that's wrong with the world.

Imaginary Jonathan Crompton: No, I'm not. But I hate you too. I hate your stupid jokes and your stupid beard and your stupid hating me.

Me: Why couldn't you complete a pass in the fourth quarter?

Imaginary Jonathan Crompton: Why couldn't you?

Me: This isn't about me. You're the one with the golden arm.

Imaginary Jonathan Crompton: I think this is about you.

My phone rings. My wife is calling. "What are you doing?" she asks.

"I'm getting into an argument with an imaginary Jonathan Crompton in my car," I say. "I hate him."

She's silent for a moment. I hear her sigh. "That's weird, Clay," she says.

I hang up and continue driving through the Alabama night. Eventually I turn on the radio and listen to the Crimson Tide radio broadcast. Alabama is destroying Georgia, which makes me feel better. I want everyone else's team to lose tonight too. In a college football first, I want there to be no victors in any game this evening, only losers. Not only that, I want Jonathan Crompton elected governor of every losing team's state.

It's eerie on the interstate, late and quiet. There are no cars. A dull fog steals across the roadway, encircles my car until it seems possible I'm floating in a boat along a deep and dark river. After midnight I cross the state line and return once more to Tennessee. I feel slightly better, being back on my home ground. Arriving in Nashville, I get off at West End Avenue. I stop at a red light at 20th and West End, near the Amerigo Restaurant. This is the intersection where my friend Alex Haught was killed on March 3, 1999. His parents, who live in Nashville, have still not driven past this intersection in the 10 years since Alex died. The road is empty and I sit through a cycle of the light. The light goes green, then yellow, then red again.

In 2000 Al Gore lost the state of Tennessee 51–47 percent by 80,229 votes. In the wake of the election, many figures in the state of Tennessee said that Gore got wrapped up in the national focus of his campaign and forgot about his home state, taking it for granted. Some national columnists wrote that if Alex Haught hadn't been killed by a drunk driver Gore would have listened to his Tennessee field director and would have spent the time and resources on his home state; that he would have won Tennessee and, in so doing, would have won the 2000 election outright.

The drunk driver who killed Alex Haught served a little less than 10 years in prison. When he drove through a red light on West End Avenue and killed Alex he had a blood alcohol level of .34. In November 2008, almost 10 years to the day after the UT-Arkansas game we watched together in 1998, Alex's mother, Joy Haught, will appear before a parole board. She doesn't object to the defendant's being released from prison early. "It's what Alex would have wanted," she'll say.

Later still, I'll ask Alex's parents whether they still watch Tennessee football games. His father nods. "But winning and losing doesn't seem that important anymore," he says.

CHAPTER 9

THE FRONT LINE OF THE REVOLUTION: VOLQUEST.COM

FOLLOWING THE AUBURN LOSS, THE TENNESSEE Volunteers stand at 1-3 overall and 0-2 in the conference. The Internet message boards come alive with countless aggrieved fans spewing forth angry threads at the Tennessee coaches, at the Tennessee players, and, in particular, at quarterback Jonathan Crompton. In this modern era of rapid-fire communication and instant opinion-making Crompton has become hated more quickly than any athlete in Vol history. For his part, Crompton does his best to ignore the criticism. "I don't read them. I don't listen to sports talk radio. I don't even know how to get on the message boards," he tells me.

All of the message boards bear venom for Crompton, but the most far-reaching and powerful of these sites is Volquest.com. Volquest is a member of the Rivals.com sports message board network and offers a cyber-gathering place for the most diehard Tennessee fans. It's also a lucrative business—the most hard-core Vol fans, myself included, pay $9.95 a month to subscribe and receive the most up-to-date news about our football team.

As the season goes down the tubes, I can't avoid the siren call of the message boards. With their second-by-second updates, excessive reactions, and meltdowns, the Volquest message boards offer a searing look into the heart of the fan base. No matter how unique you think your own pain is, the message boards prove that there are thousands of fans who share the exact same misery. And like no time before, you can connect with these other fans in an instant.

It used to be that losing a game on Saturday meant commiserating with your close friends and listening to other fans complain on talk radio come Monday. But, for the most part, your team's losses and the way they made you feel was a private affair. You weren't really sure whether anyone else felt like you. Being a fan was something we all did in our spare time, and even if we were obsessed, it was relatively hard to connect with similar obsessives in between games. No longer. The Internet makes connecting easy. And fans' addiction seems perfectly normal. When it comes to Volquest I'm always looking for my next hit, for the next bit of information. Until I get it, I'm jittery and uncomfortable, nervous. Yep, Volquest is my crack.

The head of Volquest is 34-year-old Brent Hubbs, a thin man with blue eyes, dark hair, and a buzz cut. Prior to taking over Volquest in January 2000, Hubbs worked in radio, and before that he attended the University of Tennessee. A lifelong fan of the Vols who can trace his fandom to the 1985 Sugar Bowl win, Hubbs used to visit team offices and meet players because his aunt worked at the football complex.

When Hubbs took over as the editor-in-charge of the site, Volquest was a free message board. But in 2001 the Rivals business model changed and the network began to charge customers for premium site content. Hubbs was terrified. "All I could think was, if I can just get fifteen hundred paying subscribers we'll be okay. And if I could ever get three thousand, good grief." Volquest now has 6,000 Vol subscribers and a staff of three full-time and one part-time writers. Rough math demonstrates that the site brings in revenue of around $700,000 a year, a hefty sum when you consider how low the overhead for an Internet site is.

The same year that Rivals switched to a pay model, Tennessee lost to LSU in the SEC championship game. Hubbs stayed up until 5 in the morning following the night of the game deleting trash-talking threads from LSU fans. "I'd just hit refresh and then delete, refresh and then delete, all night long and into the morning." Later Hubbs will trace this loss as the beginning of the end for Coach Fulmer. "Before that LSU game there weren't that many anti-Fulmer posters. After that game there started to be a lot."

As the number of Volquest subscribers grew, so too did the site's influence and journalistic credibility. "I'll put our information up against anyone," says Hubbs, "and being right has paid off. When we beat other places, more people sign up."

This is why Hubbs is quick to dismiss any suggestion that Internet sites have lesser journalistic responsibility. If anything, Hubbs believes they have a *greater* responsibility. Because if he's wrong about the Vols, people have no reason to pay for his content. As such, Hubbs never rests in his pursuit of UT news. In fact, he lives in constant fear that he won't be able to bring enough news to justify his subscribers returning, especially in the offseason.

Due to his and the staff's work ethic, Volquest has beaten the local newspaper, radio stations, and sundry other media sources with Vol news on a regular basis. As a result, Volquest is one of the 10 most lucrative sites for Rivals on the net. Six of the ten biggest sites are from the SEC, and Alabama, with 11,000 subscribers, is the largest pay site in the country. Those Alabama fans aren't paying over a million dollars a year for nothing; the Rivals site broke the news that Nick Saban would be the next coach of the Crimson Tide at midnight on January 2, 2007. Newspapers didn't catch up to the story until a day later.

The uncertainty regarding Coach Fulmer has been good for business. Hubbs is adding subscribers rapidly. Most diehard fans feel they have to subscribe to a site like Hubbs's. Otherwise, by the time the news reaches them it has been discussed and digested by everyone else. It's not just media competing against other members of the media for the big story; it's fans establishing their fan bona fides by being constantly in the know, the first to shoot an e-mail to their fellow diehards.

But some in athletic offices have been slow to realize this paradigm change in the way that fans consume their sports news. In 2006 Volquest sent a reporter to San Antonio to cover UT's basketball game in the Sweet 16. To several members of the UT athletic department the reporter's presence was eye-opening. Says Hubbs, "One of them asked, 'How in the world do you have the money to pay for this?' I think that was the first time they realized that we'd gotten pretty big."

Indeed, the business model of Volquest represents the future of sports reporting: lean, pared down, accurate, focused on a particular beat, and fast. Really fast. Before joining Volquest, Hubbs was a big sports fan. Now he acknowledges that he couldn't name four players on the Atlanta Braves. But he covers Tennessee in intimate detail.

Not only has the Internet made immediate news available about your team; so too does it make minute-by-minute news available about other teams. The result is that many fans are constantly obsessed with the status of their program in relation to other rival programs. "When we were kids," I say, "I had no idea where we ranked on a minute-by-minute basis. Now all we talk about is not just Tennessee football but what Florida and Alabama are doing. That's hurting Fulmer." Hubbs nods, pauses to check his iPhone to see if any new e-mail messages have arrived, and says, "That's because your local newspaper didn't tell you much about other teams except for the week you were playing them. We didn't know anything about Pat Dye's Auburn team in 1985. Now in thirty minutes of hopping from one fan site to another on the Internet, you can know everything about every team. And when your team isn't winning and your rivals are . . ." Hubbs shrugs his shoulders, pauses, thinks for a moment, and then says, "Well . . . people get upset."

And when fans are upset, they go to the message board and vent. At any given moment on Volquest seven or eight players are the subject of front-page discussion, as well as coaches (and not just head coaches; the Internet has made the assistant coaches celebrities as well) and recruits. Generally there is at least one angry debate between posters that involves name-calling. As a group these posters tend to be fairly well-educated and have the disposable cash to pursue their hobbies, in this case Volunteer football. Sometimes Hubbs is shocked to see what a doctor or a lawyer he knows from outside the Volquest arena will write on an anonymous message board.

Other times he marvels at a player's parent, like Bernadette Foster, being an active member of the community. "I wouldn't do it because I think it would be too tough," he says, "but she does and she has that right."

When Phillip Fulmer began coaching there were no message boards. Now, 16 years after he assumed the helm of the Volunteer program, the message board community is convinced he has to go. Each day the anger seems to build. The few public defenders of Fulmer on the message boards are quickly shouted down and ridiculed. The Volunteer football revolution is already in progress online.

The big question, of course, is how representative of the fan base at large these anti-Fulmer online ravings are. It's a question that the UT athletic department wrestles with, particularly when less than a third of the 6,000 diehard pay subscribers on Volquest ever post.

Athletic director Mike Hamilton acknowledges occasionally monitoring the board. "I check it. Not every day, but occasionally. But you have to keep in mind that's a small percentage of our fan base." Hamilton isn't alone; other Vol officials, players, coaches, and family members also monitor the message boards. And when these people check the board they can see that the Volquest community wants Phil Fulmer to go. This revolutionary football tide isn't unique to Tennessee; many schools have been through it before.

Members of the more "mainstream" media frequently rip apart the message board community for being so quick to adopt a negative posture. But Hubbs discounts those critics. Hubbs believes message boards are merely a reflection of the era we live in—not a huge departure from the world at large. "No one buys anymore. Everyone leases. You never pay off your fifteen-year mortgage, no one pays off their cars, we all see our neighbors with the new car and we want one too. Well, Bob's new car is Nick Saban. That upsets a lot of Tennessee people because Bob's new thing is better than our old thing. And then we go and start picking the scabs off our old guy and nothing heals."

Each hour on Volquest another scab is ripped anew. The subtext of every post is the same: Will Phillip Fulmer survive the season?

CHAPTER 10

THE MAC ATTACK COMES TO KNOXVILLE

THE BIGGEST NEWS TO COME OUT of the disastrous offensive effort against Auburn is that Jonathan Crompton has been replaced at starting quarterback by redshirt sophomore Nick Stephens. On the Thursday before the Northern Illinois game, at the end of practice, Coach Fulmer calls Crompton into his office and informs him that Stephens will replace him as starting quarterback. Crompton, whose ankle was severely reinjured in the first quarter of the Auburn game, doesn't hide his dismay. "I was disappointed. Especially after the ankle flared up against Auburn and I kept going. I didn't think it was the right decision," he confesses.

Now Nick Stephens, a native of Flower Mound, Texas, who has only attempted four passes in his college career, holds the distinction of being the first redhead to start at quarterback for the University of Tennessee. His hair color is probably insignificant, but when your team is 1-3 you look to any fact as a potential positive. Although, to be fair, I am concerned that Stephens will sunburn if he's out in the sun too long.

I'm driving across Tennessee for the Northern Illinois game by myself. When you're driving alone you have time to notice how much land you pass on the trip from Nashville to Knoxville, to take note of the gradual rise in elevation as the rolling hills of middle Tennessee become the mountains of the East. It also makes you realize that Tennessee is a long state, 440 miles straight across. You can drive from Nashville to Canada faster than you can drive from Bristol in the northeastern corner of Tennessee to Memphis in the southwestern corner of the state. Every Tennessee elementary school student learns this piece of trivia, that and the fact that Tennessee borders eight states, more than any other in the country. Our neighbors are Missouri, Arkansas, Mississippi, Alabama, Georgia, North Carolina, Virginia, and Kentucky.

Congratulations, place this handy knowledge under your beaver-pelt hats; now you're all honorary Tennesseans. Just to clarify, you can only marry *second* cousins here.

If you happen to be one of the Vol fans driving from the muddy banks of the Mississippi to Knoxville in the east, you'd cross the three major divisions of the state of Tennessee—west, middle, and east. The three stars on the red, white, and blue Tennessee state flag represent the three grand divisions of the state. These divisions aren't just geographical. Much of East Tennessee stayed loyal to the Union during the Civil War because the mountains weren't conducive to large-scale farming that required slave labor. Indeed, Tennessee's Andrew Johnson, who succeeded Abraham Lincoln after his assassination in 1865, was the only Southern senator from the thirteen states of the Confederacy who never resigned his Senate seat. Traveling west through Tennessee, the farms become more rolling and then flat, and the land becomes more fertile for large-scale farming. These regions, the middle and western portions of Tennessee, were strong adherents for the Confederacy and led the push for secession—a push that would ultimately make Tennessee the final state to join the Confederacy in April 1861.

Tennessee's history is embedded in the symbols of the Tennessee football team. The University of Tennessee's teams are known as the Volunteers, or Vols for short, because Tennessee gained the nickname the Volunteer State in the War of 1812, when Tennessee sent more soldiers to fight the British than any other state. This volunteer spirit continued during Texas's war with Mexico from 1846 to 1848. When the Alamo fell there were more native Tennesseans killed inside the walls of the old Spanish mission—including former Tennessee congressman Davy Crockett—than citizens of any other state.

As a result, one of the Vols' mascots on the sideline, a Davy Crockett look-alike, is dressed in brown buckskin and a coonskin cap and carries a musket. The other Vol mascot, Smokey, a bluetick coonhound, was introduced in 1953. That year the pep club held a contest, and at halftime of the Mississippi State game, several dogs were introduced to the crowd as potential canine mascots. Smokey howled upon his introduction and won over the students. Now Tennessee has Smokey IX, all lineal descendants of the original coonhound. The weakest link was Smokey VI, who in 1991 made the Volunteer football injury report—he'd suffered heat exhaustion during the UCLA home opener.

When I was a boy my dad would point out the stars on the state flag, or Davy Crockett on the sideline, and quiz me about Tennessee history. It was, after all, important that I knew where I came from. When we'd drive to games in East Tennessee my dad would also entertain me by pointing to large hills looming on the interstate. "The world," he would say, "ends at the top of that hill." It was a game his own parents had played with him when he was a boy growing up outside of Nashville, only it had more significance then because the horizons of my dad's childhood did not provide much in the way of an expansive view. My dad, Norm Travis, grew up on a farm in Goodlettsville, Tennessee, and visited three states before he left for college: Kentucky, Georgia, and Florida, only one of which didn't border Tennessee. He did not fly on a plane until he was interviewing for jobs after college.

His father, Henry Clay Travis, was born in Kentucky and received an eighth-grade education. When my grandfather was young he worked in the Kentucky coal mines, a job that provided the slimmest possible view of the earth's horizons. During the Depression he moved to Nashville and took a job at DuPont, where he labored in a cellophane plant until he retired. In 1944 my dad was born in Nashville. The city's population at the time was just 140,000.

Since then the city of Nashville and its surrounding area has grown to over 1.5 million residents. And in my dad's life the state of Tennessee has doubled in population from 3 million to over 6 million—20 percent of whom have been born outside the South. Even still, fewer people live in the state of Tennessee than live in the metropolitan area of Dallas, Texas. So it doesn't take very long on your drive to Knoxville to leave behind the big city of Nashville and enter the rural backcountry of Tennessee.

Off the interstate two-lane roads roll through darkened valleys and trees stand sentinel over empty farmhouses where crops no longer grow and barns sag at the joints and fall under the weight of their collapsed roofs. I drive past old plantation homes sitting far off long-since-abandoned dirt roads, shaded by large oak trees lined up in ancient rows, decades since their fireplace hearths were last warm. I pass shirtless men mowing their lawns for the final time before fall arrives, elderly men sitting in their yards watching small brush fires send smoke spiraling into the autumn afternoon. Old tires rest by the sides of roads, and double-wide trailers are parked on lots with overgrown grass and no trees directly adjacent to newly built mansions that crown small hills at the bend in the road.

Making my way through some of these small towns, places like Carthage, Cookeville, and Monterey, I can feel what Tennessee football means to their residents. It is a point of pride, a common connection in a world of disparate and strained alliances. Volunteer flags are flying on cars everywhere—on brand-new black Cadillac Escalades and care-worn rusty brown pickup trucks, at the local grocery stores and outside Mexican and Chinese restaurants. As I wind through the rural roads, I pass old gas stations sitting back off the road selling Tennessee T-shirts and old Southern-style meat and three restaurants sitting next to white clapboard churches with GO VOLS ON SATURDAY, GO TO CHURCH ON SUNDAY spelled out in black letters on the signs that front the road.

In fact, the only thing more prevalent than UT flags are churches. Everywhere I look, I see churches. Eighty-two percent of Tennesseans are Christian. Most Tennesseans, my family included, are still Baptists—a full 40 percent of the state's Christians (the next closest are Methodists at 10 percent). So it's no coincidence that Southern football is cloaked in religion. Being a football fan and going to church unite more people in the state of Tennessee than any other activity. It's no surprise to me that before every game there's an invocation or that the Tennessee football team still drops and prays as one before and after every game.

Religion suffuses every act in the South. In the Baptist churches of my youth, football games were often referenced from the pulpit. After a Tennessee loss to Alabama the pastor at Goodlettsville's First Baptist Church might take the pulpit and intone, "I see some loooong faces out there in the congregation today. But not so loooong as the faces of the unsaved will be on the day of the Rapture." We were instructed, time and again, that a UT football loss was one of many things in life that was momentary; the battle for our soul's salvation, on the other hand, was a struggle an eternity in the making.

But this rationale didn't stop the griping after losses. Heavenly life may be everlasting, but losing to Alabama every year made life on earth feel like an eternity already. Even then, as a young child, I remember being troubled by the concept of eternity.

"Wouldn't you get bored?" I asked my dad.

"It's like a football game every week," he said.

JONATHAN CROMPTON, WHO HAS gone from hero to Antichrist in the space of the month, has been kicked to the curb. The entire state of Tennessee is behind Nick Stephens, our new savior at quarterback. Crompton is living in football purgatory—banished to toil in infamy on the sidelines and be ripped to shreds on Volquest. Brent Hubbs acknowledges that he has never seen a player become as universally despised online as quickly as Crompton has. "It's pretty unbelievable," Hubbs says.

I feel a twinge of guilt about how quickly we've all blamed Crompton for the team's failings. But I'm also tired of losing; 1-3 is tied with 1994 for the worst start in the Phil Fulmer era. The Vols have yet to *lead* in any SEC game this season. It's time for a change. In announcing the decision to bench Crompton, Fulmer is direct and to the point: "We need a lot more production from the quarterback position."

The change to Nick Stephens offers a small window of hope for Phil Fulmer to get the season turned around and stave off the online rabble that would strip him of his job. The Georgia game looms next weekend; win and the season can be saved, lose and the SEC season is effectively over. Vol fans are hoping that today represents a new birth in the season—a return to offensive competence and dominant defensive football. Maybe, after all this, our only problem has been the newly hated scoundrel, Jonathan Crompton.

At 7 on Saturday evening, Nick Stephens emerges to delirious cheers from the comparatively empty stadium. Attendance will be announced at 99,539, but that's the number of seats sold; fewer people are here than that. Stephens, who prior to this start has taken just eight snaps as a Vol quarterback, is fair-skinned, with tiny freckles spread across his face and a lower jaw that juts out a bit as if he's doggedly attempting to accomplish something no one else believes he can. At 6' 4", 215 pounds, Stephens weighs less than Crompton but is listed at the same height. Alarmingly, the UT defensive backs have their own nickname for Stephens, "PicNick," because Stephens throws so many interceptions in practice.

The weather is a bit cool but comfortable, a night game in October in Knoxville, and on the first offensive possession for the Vols against Northern Illinois, Stephens completes two consecutive passes for 7 and 14 yards. The applause raining down on him is nearly deafening. Fans want to believe that Stephens will cure the season's offensive futility. But on his third pass completion, Tennessee's Josh Briscoe fumbles and Northern Illinois recovers. In the resulting drive Northern Illinois kicks a field goal to go up 3–0. As the first quarter ends, a dull murmur of discomfort sweeps through the crowd, an uneasy suggestion that perhaps Jonathan Crompton hasn't been to blame for Tennessee's football failings. This fact, more than any other, is the most disquieting. Crompton is the scapegoat, the reason the Vols are failing. If he's replaced and the team is still losing, there is no easy fix.

With 6:50 to play in the second quarter, Tennessee adds a field goal. At halftime the two teams are tied at 3. There's suddenly a very real possibility that Tennessee might lose to a team from the Mid-America Conference. At home.

During halftime every member of the crowd is an offensive coordinator. "I think we need to throw the ball down the field more," someone suggests. Another voice rises up. "We got to pound the damn football. Run it." There is no consensus on the remedy, but everyone can diagnose the problem: Our offense under new offensive coordinator Dave Clawson sucks. As the man who hired Clawson, Phil Fulmer bears the brunt of the fans' criticism for the offense's failure.

Early in the second half Tennessee takes their first lead on a 34-yard field goal by Daniel Lincoln. The score is 6–3 Vols. For the first time since the UAB game back on September 13, almost an entire month ago, Tennessee has the lead. Having a lead after trailing so long is an amazing experience. I'd forgotten what it feels like to play with house money, to have the potential to make a bad play and not find yourself in an even more tremendous hole. Perhaps buoyed by the feeling of having a lead, Nick Stephens uncorks the biggest offensive play of the Vols' season thus far—a 52-yard touchdown pass to sophomore wide receiver Denarius Moore. Suddenly, with 9:49 remaining in the third quarter, the Vols have their biggest lead of the season, a gargantuan 13–3 advantage. We're up 10 whole points!

The crowd reacts not so much with excitement as with relief. They cheer, but the applause has an undercurrent of despair, like receiving a deferment on your execution date. Why are we only beating a team from the MAC conference by 10 points? As the minutes pass by, we do not increase our lead. Instead, Northern Illinois whittles away at the deficit, first with a 24-yard field goal and then with a 25-yard field goal. As we begin the fourth quarter, the Vols lead just 13–9.

On their first possession of the fourth quarter Tennessee gives the ball to Arian Foster on seven consecutive runs. Foster gains 40 yards on these carries and on second and goal from the Northern Illinois 9-yard line finally gives way to Montario Hardesty, who promptly carries the ball to the 4-yard line. Facing a third and goal from the 4-yard line with 7:26 remaining in the ballgame, the Vol offense calls time out. Nick Stephens has not attempted a pass in the fourth quarter. He has completed just one pass, for a 7-yard gain, since his 52-yard touchdown pass early in the third quarter. At this point it is clear that Nick Stephens is not the second coming of Peyton Manning.

On third and goal from the 4, Stephens is sacked and loses 10 yards. Daniel Lincoln, whom I watched running through the water fountain in Los Angeles what now seems like 8 years ago, trots onto the field to attempt a 32-yard field goal that will give the Vols a 7-point lead. As usual, he misses.

My friend Junaid texts me. "If we lose to them, this seals it: Fulmer's gone." But our defense stiffens, and on two consecutive possessions UT does not give up a first down. The clock runs out and Tennessee hangs on for a 13–9 win over Northern Illinois.

Nick Stephens, the golden-boy replacement for Jonathan Crompton, has gone 10 for 17 for 156 yards. He has no interceptions, but he does have one fumble and is sacked several times in crucial situations. He completes just one pass in the final 25 minutes of the football game, and the Vol offense is only 3 for 13 on third-down conversions. Combining this with last week's game against Auburn, the Vol offense is now 7 for 29 on third-down conversions in the past two weeks. While the defense has played extremely well, the Vol offense has fewer first downs than Northern Illinois. Nothing about the game is extraordinary; there are no tremendous errors or amazing plays that have led to the 13–9 victory. I'm left with a sobering realization—we now have to play well to beat MAC teams at Neyland Stadium.

As I drive home, I listen to the Vol postgame report on Knoxville's 99.1. Fan after fan calls in to the show and undresses the current team. Frustration is building across the long length of the Volunteer State. Just 1 year removed from an SEC East championship, the Vols are 2-3 and facing an absolute must-win game at Georgia. In the wake of games, fan anger now mixes with player frustration. Junior center Josh McNeil confesses, "I listen to the radio shows on my way home too. I listen to the fans. Sometimes I want to call in and talk with them. I want to say, 'Oh, yeah, well, you think I suck? Well, why don't you come tell me that to my face? Here's my address, come meet me here and we'll talk about it. Just you and me.' I wouldn't ever do it, but I want to. Sometimes I want to real bad."

Driving back across Tennessee it's late, very late. Tennessee's won tonight, but unimpressively. I have little optimism that things will change against Georgia. All I can think as I drive in the darkness is my broken-record query: "Why do I care so much?"

I've recently talked to one of the foremost sports psychologists in the country, Dr. Edward Hirt of Indiana University, about fan obsession. He has a doctorate in psychology and has specialized in fan psychology for much of his professional career. Dr. Hirt, who grew up in Cincinnati as a huge Cincinnati Reds fan and has remained a committed fan throughout his 48 years of life, says he began studying the psychology of fans because he didn't believe the psychological studies that suggested most people became fans because they want to bask in the reflected glory of the teams they follow. The bask-in-reflected-glory theory holds that these fans experience an increase in self-esteem when their team wins.

"I knew that made sense for fair-weather fans, but it didn't make sense for fans who followed teams that constantly lost. If your team loses you don't feel better, you feel worse," Dr. Hirt says.

This correlation has been confirmed by science. A psychologist in Georgia, Dr. James Dabbs, tested the testosterone levels of Italian and Brazilian fans before and after Brazil's victory over Italy during the 1994 World Cup. (Why he didn't use Florida and Georgia fans before and after the World's Largest Outdoor Cocktail Party remains a mystery.) His results showed that Brazil's fans experienced a surge in testosterone of 28 percent after their victory and that, conversely, the Italian fans suffered a decline in testosterone of 27 percent.[1] When you and I feel sick after a loss, it's not just in our heads; our bodies are actually reacting as well.

Another psychologist, Charles Hillman, has studied the physiological responses of Florida Gator fans to game-winning plays (many of which, I'm sure, were against my team). Their level of arousal—measured via heart rate, brain waves, and perspiration—was comparable to the same fans' response when shown erotic photos.

And why wouldn't this be the case? Back to our friend Dr. Hirt, who has tracked the self-esteem of Indiana basketball fans after wins and losses. After games he showed fans pictures of very attractive men and women of the opposite sex and asked them to rate their chances of getting a date. After their teams won, fans were much more likely to believe that good-looking members of the opposite sex found them attractive. So if you're at a college ball game and your team loses, you haven't just lost a game, you're statistically less likely to get laid. As if you didn't already have enough to be upset about, not only is your team losing, the opposing fans are having more sex than you are that night.

So, what psychological benefits can I expect to derive from my team floundering through a season? What do I have to sustain me over the long haul of my losing season? "Statistically, sports fans are less likely to get depressed," Dr. Hirt says. "Plus you have a common bond, a connection, with lots of other people. That's of no small importance."

Awesome, everyone I know is miserable together. So when I log on to Volquest and read other message board posters who are clearly in the grips of great depression, I have tons of company. But it's tons of angry company. What psychological benefit is this actually giving me?

---

1. McKinley, James C., Jr. "Sports Psychology: It Isn't Just a Game: Clues to Avid Rooting," *New York Times*, Aug. 11, 2000.

Dr. Hirt explains that fans are drawn to sports because they provide a common language to talk to other fans. "Sports are unique in that people are willing to debate things. They aren't like politics, where most people keep silent if they disagree. Sports fans respect other sports fans' opinions in a way that rival political parties don't."

Sports also provide a tangible connection from one generation to another. Statistically speaking, if you're a huge sports fan the chances are your children will be as well. Which means my son, Fox, is in tremendous danger.

Finally, Dr. Hirt tells me that sports provide men, who tend to be emotionally reticent, an opportunity to express emotion and connect with other men. This last point rings especially true.

As I'm driving home from Knoxville through the darkened country roads, I think about a conversation I had with my dad this past summer. My dad came to my house and sat next to me on the couch, where I was feeding my 5-month-old son a bottle. He sat watching me feed Fox for a long time without saying anything. It was clear something was bothering him. Finally he turned to me and said, "You know, I read an article in the newspaper the other day about a dad's funeral. The son said, 'We never really talked unless it was about sports.' That's really sad, isn't it?"

My dad put his hand on my shoulder. I continued to feed Fox. "Yes," I said, "that really is."

We were both silent for a long time. While Fox drank his bottle my dad smiled at him and occasionally made faces. Finally my dad spoke again.

"I'm not as optimistic about this year's team as you are," he said.

He reached out and grabbed Fox's bare foot. "One day we're going to get this little guy to a game too," he said.

It occurred to me then that fathers and sons talk about a lot more than sports when we're talking about sports. And maybe in the end that's why most of us are sports fans.

CHAPTER 11

MEETING KEITH DAVIS

WHEN I WAS VERY YOUNG, I used to think football players weren't real people. I believed that football players showed up to play in games and then vanished between games. I couldn't imagine them driving cars or carrying backpacks to class or tying their own shoes. Football players were mythical gods, every bit as amazing and distant as the characters who populated the stories I read about in Sunday school. Tennessee wide receiver Eric Swanson, meet Daniel from the lion's den.

And then in September 1987, I met my first football player off the field. I was 8 years old and Tennessee had just beaten Colorado State 49–3 in their home opener. This was a big week not only because we'd won our opening game of the season, but because my friend Matt and I got to stay on the 10th floor, the suite level, of Knoxville's Holiday Inn World's Fair, named for the 1982 World's Fair that Knoxville hosted.

In the time we weren't scheming to get our hands on a *Playboy* magazine or watch naked movies on the hotel pay-per-view, our favorite thing to do was to ride the hotel elevator. You could go up, you could go down, you could press the hold door open button and wait for a friend, you could press the close door button and leave a friend stranded on a foreign floor. Riding in an elevator was as thrilling as life could get for an 8-year-old. The only problem with the Holiday Inn World's Fair elevator was that the 10th floor was restricted. In previous stays at the hotel, we could push the button but never go to the 10th floor. It required a key, and not one of those newfangled key cards that all hotels have today; an actual, physical golden key.

In previous stays Matt and I had constructed all sorts of elaborate fantasies about what the hotel rooms were like on the 10th floor. Generally these fantasies involved *Playboy* magazines, free Mello Yello, unlimited naked movies on television, and a hotel room that took up an entire floor. But during the weekend of the 1987 home opener, for the first time ever, we got to stay on the 10th floor.

And we found out what the mystical 10th floor had that no other floor in the Holiday Inn World's Fair had . . . a free morning and evening buffet. Still worse, most of the buffet was salad. After years of fantasizing about the 10th floor, I can't begin to explain how disappointed we both were by this revelation. Even Tennessee's win didn't allay our disappointment. It would take Keith Davis to pull us from the depths of our depression.

The Sunday after Tennessee ran their record to 2-0 with a home-opening win over Colorado State, we went to breakfast at the McDonald's on Cumberland Avenue. Just as we finished our hotcakes, my dad recognized Tennessee Vol running back Keith Davis. In 1985 Keith Davis, a Nashville native, was a hotshot freshman running back at the University of Tennessee. He was the leading rusher for the Tennessee team that won the Sugar Bowl in 1986, the first game I ever watched on television. That year he carried the ball 141 times for 681 yards. Included was a then-freshman record 141 yards rushing in a win against Alabama. After his freshman season everyone expected tremendous things from Keith Davis.

But Davis had bad knees.

In the season opener of the 1986 season, against New Mexico, Davis rushed for 89 yards on just 11 carries and had two touchdowns in the first half. On the 11th carry his knees failed him, and Davis crumbled to the ground clutching his knees. He would miss the second half and three entire games thereafter and gain just 204 yards for the remainder of the injury-plagued season.

After his freshman season Davis would continue at Tennessee until 1988, but he would never be the team's leading rusher again. In fact, after carrying the ball 141 times in the 1985 season, Davis would only carry the ball 181 times over the next 3 years.

On that September morning in 1987 Keith Davis was eating at a booth just on the other side of McDonald's from us. I was 8 years old and, wearing a Tennessee cap that was too large for my head, my hands were shaking with nervous excitement. Keith Davis! *The* Keith Davis! An actual football player. Here, in the flesh, at a McDonald's. Football players did exist in the actual world after all. Moreover, they ate breakfast at the same restaurants I did, and they didn't even wear their football pads and jerseys when doing so.

My dad gave Matt and me our ticket stubs from that game and told us to go ask Keith Davis for his autograph. (My dad has saved every ticket stub from every athletic event we've ever attended together.) Matt and I sprinted across the brown floor, but before we reached our hero my dad called out to Davis, "You've got some little fans coming your way." Keith Davis looked up from his breakfast and grinned, revealing bright white teeth.

Davis took our ticket stubs and signed his name and number, 28, with a flourish. Stepping back from him, I looked down at his knees— he had on sweat pants—and felt terrible for him. It was the first time I ever realized that football players had flaws.

"I hope your knees get well," I said.

"Me too, little man," said Keith Davis, "me too."

CHAPTER 12

GEORGIA ON MY MIND

IT'S FRIDAY, OCTOBER 10, AT 10:30 in the morning, and I'm early for the UT team bus trip to Athens for Saturday's game against #10 Georgia. This face-off will decide whether the Vol season has any hope of being a successful one. The Vols are 2-3. If we win this game, the SEC East title remains a possibility; if we lose, there is no chance at all. The stakes are tremendous.

I decide to go look at the BCS title trophy from 1998 before heading for the buses. I figure it will raise my spirits. And it does. As I gaze at the football-shaped crystal, resting gently atop its black base, I'm taken back 10 years, to when Tennessee ruled the college football universe. That 1998 season capped off a 4-year run for Tennessee during which the Vols went 45-5. Lose to Georgia this weekend and in just 6 weeks Tennessee will have lost four games, just one less than in that 4-year period.

Strolling farther into the museum, I head to where the wax statues of Peyton and Tee stand on a raised dais. I stop in front of the display and . . . they're gone. Missing! I look around to see if anyone else has taken note. None of the passers-by seem to have noticed. I walk to the front desk, where a lady in an orange jumpsuit is on the phone.

"Do you know where Peyton and Tee have gone?" I ask.

She covers the mouth of her phone. "Whaaaaat?" she drawls. Then she mouths, "I'm on the phone."

I nod and return to the museum, where a video montage showing this year's UT football highlights accompanied by the latest rap songs is playing on a midsize television screen. Already they've added scenes from the UCLA game (there were highlights?) and the UAB game. Jonathan Crompton, now displaced as starting quarterback, is shown in super slow motion completing a few passes. Arian Foster's long runs against UAB and UCLA are featured. Other than that there's a real dearth of offensive highlights from this season. The montage features no plays from the Florida, Auburn, or Northern Illinois games.

The beat of the rap music is so strident that it doesn't match the slow-motion highlights. I stand completely still and after a few moments the music stops, but the highlight reel continues to run in silence. I look up and see that there's a motion sensor on the highlights—the music only plays when the sensor detects someone watching. The metaphor is powerful; UT football only sells itself when it believes someone cares.

Incongruously displayed behind the sometimes blaring rap highlights is a UT football jersey and helmet from 1933—the final season my grandfather, Richard K. Fox, played for the Vols. The helmet and jersey apparently belonged to a player named Howard L. Stewart. The two men would have known each other well. Inevitably my grandfather was once in close proximity to this very jersey. Now I wear his old wedding ring, a golden band from 1938, on my left ring finger. I put my hand on the glass.

Then I stand looking at the jersey and try to picture my grandfather as a young man, younger still than me, before he ever thought that one day he might have a grandson, much less a great-grandson, named after him.

I pass the lady at the desk, who is still on the phone, and go to the bathroom near the indoor football field. For a moment I pause in front of the mirror. Writing a book about this season is exerting a visible toll on me. I'm heavier, at least 10 pounds, when nothing else in my life has changed other than being on the road and watching my team lose week after week for the past month and a half. Some men put on weight in their stomachs or legs or shoulders or arms. Mine goes to my chest. I turn to the side and look at my profile. Yep, man boobs have formed.

While I'm sitting outside the indoor football complex, UT's starting center Josh McNeil walks by. McNeil, a redshirt junior center with short brown hair and eyes that are set a bit wide on his face, arrived at Tennessee as the nation's top center recruit in the country and is on pace to start more games on the offensive line than any football player in Tennessee history. He pauses and looks at me. "Hey, you're the guy who wrote the book," he says, referring to my first book, *Dixieland Delight.* "My brother gave it to me and I've been hurt so I've been reading it in the training room."

One of the great things about writing a book is when people compliment you on it and then feel compelled to explain why they've actually taken the trouble to read it. In this case, McNeil read it because he was hurt and killing time on the training room table. Other people have read *Dixieland Delight* because they had mono, so their wives would have sex with them (one wife was so upset with her husband's bad example for the kids that she rewarded his reading with sex), and because they've been stationed as guards in Iraqi prisons and had nothing else to do.

I smile and nod. McNeil introduces me to Nick Reveiz, an undersized 5' 10", 225-pound backup linebacker from Knoxville. "This guy wrote a great book called *Dixieland Delight,*" he says.

McNeil was a top recruit from Collins, Mississippi, who picked Tennessee over Florida, LSU, and Southern Cal because he felt completely at home with Coach Fulmer—a man McNeil now considers a second father. I explain that I'm riding down with the team. Then, not content with just giving that information, I continue to talk. "We need to win some games so I don't have to jump into the Tennessee River. It's been tough."

"It's even worse when you get the shit beat out of you for seventy plays," McNeil responds, staring deep into my fan's soul.

Right. Of course it is. I feel like an idiot for complaining about how terrible losing makes me feel to a player, and for using the word *we* with him when I'm not the least bit involved with the team. I cover up this faux pas by discussing which team buses we'll be riding on. McNeil will be on Bus 1 with the rest of the offense and I'll be on Bus 3.

Next to arrive is Arian Foster, who has refused recent media interview requests unless they are conducted in pterodactyl. When asked by the Tennessee media to discuss the upcoming game against Georgia, Foster flapped his arms like wings and responded, "Veeeeek, veeeeek, veeeeeek." I sent Foster a text message saying that I spoke good pterodactyl and suggesting that if he scores against Georgia (the past two seasons he's scored six times against the Bulldogs) he should break out the pterodactyl in the end zone. "That would be really funny," Foster texted back. Now, he's just sleepy on the eve of the game. "I need a nap," Foster says.

At 11:35, I walk to the bus. It's scheduled to leave at 12:15, but the UT bus always leaves at least 5 minutes before the scheduled departure time. So I decide to grab my seat in advance. Outside the buses are sacks of food. I contemplate grabbing one but decide that would be too brash. Instead I climb onto Bus 3 and claim my seat.

There is only one other person on the bus now: Condredge Holloway, who was UT quarterback from 1971 to 1974. A tall man whose dark hair is slowly turning white, he was the first black quarterback at UT and led the team to three straight bowl appearances in the early 1970s. Holloway, who walks with a slight limp now, came to UT from Huntsville, Alabama, despite being the overall number-four pick in the Major League Baseball draft. Holloway's mother insisted he go to college instead of signing a pro baseball contract; he was only 17 at the time of the draft and needed her signature. Holloway dreamed of playing for the Crimson Tide. But Bear Bryant wouldn't recruit a black quarterback. "He told me up front," Holloway remembered, "and I respect him for that. On the other hand, Tennessee coach Bill Battle said, 'Hey, if you can play quarterback for me, you can play quarterback. If you can't, you can play wherever you can play.'"

After his college football career, in 1975, he was drafted in the 12th round by the NFL. He didn't latch on with any NFL teams but played in the CFL for over a decade, winning a championship for the Toronto Argonauts and being named the most valuable player of the league. He was inducted into the CFL Hall of Fame in 1998. Holloway is now an assistant athletic director at Tennessee, and he introduces himself to me as if I don't know who he is.

Holloway and I are the only two people on the bus, but we are kept company by six television monitors, leather seats, and wireless Internet. I sit down beneath one of the television monitors and then decide I should move because I'm too close to the screen. So I relocate to the other side of the aisle. In so doing I decide I should explain to Holloway why I've moved.

"I was too close to the screen," I say.

Holloway nods. "Good move," he says.

A former UT quarterback is impressed by my decision-making; maybe things are going to go well on this trip after all. While we wait, defensive tackle Walter Fisher, a giant of a man with a thick beard and a massive 6' 3", 275-pound frame, comes on the bus and puts his things in the seat in front of me.

"Satellite bus, dawg?" he asks me.

I have no idea what he's talking about and greet him with a blank face. "We don't always get that," he says, "sometimes we gotta watch DVDs."

Now his question makes sense. "No, it's a satellite," I say.

He nods appreciatively.

In an effort to stave off more awkward conversations, I leave the bus to go get food. Lenny's Subs has provided six coolers full of subs for the team. I grab one sack; inside are two full-length subs, a huge bag of chips (4.5 servings per bag), and a liter-size water bottle. I acknowledge to myself that eating a football player's lunch is not going to help reduce my man boobs, and then I dig in.

Some upperclassmen players have migrated to Bus 3 because it is less crowded than the others. Among them is Arian Foster, who is now spread out on his own row in the back of the bus. I'm not sure if he's speaking pterodactyl.

UT's team chaplain, James "Mitch" Mitchell, asks me what DVD we should watch.

"I've got *The Dark Knight*," he offers.

"*The Dark Knight*'s good," I say.

Mitch loads up the DVD player. A few minutes later the team managers walk through the bus confirming who is present and who isn't. We're only missing one player, fullback Kevin Cooper. Cell phones emerge and the Kevin Cooper search commences. A few minutes later, Condredge Holloway says, "There's K. Coop. 12:09, he made it."

At 12:10 a police escort leads us away from Gibbs Hall and we're off for the Georgia game with *The Dark Knight* beginning to play. "Property of Warner Bros." constantly flashes on the screen. I turn to a UT student trainer sitting across the aisle. "This movie's not on DVD yet, is it?"

"No, it won't be out until December," he says.

The now-deceased Heath Ledger makes his first appearance on the screen as we get on the interstate. We're driving to Athens for a must-win SEC showdown watching a pirated Batman DVD provided by the team chaplain. Things are going to turn out just fine.

WE'RE DRIVING IN THE left lane of the interstate with an escort provided by a Tennessee state trooper and at least one other police car. No one has passed us in an hour. Our route is taking us down I-75 through Chattanooga and into the state of Georgia. As we're driving I watch the countryside pass us by. Fall is coming to Tennessee. The leaves are just beginning to change color in the mountains, where cool nights have only just begun to arrive.

Many of the cars we pass on the interstate feature UT license plates or carry UT flags and stickers. Most of the fans we pass are oblivious to the fact that they're driving beside their favorite football team. UT's buses do not advertise that they are team buses and the windows are tinted.

I can't stop thinking about the way Josh McNeil reacted when I mentioned the team's losses, used the word *we* and admitted how badly *we* needed a win. For just a moment he looked at me like I was crazy and he pitied me. The closer I'm getting to the UT football program, the more insane my own fandom seems even to me.

I'm even starting to wonder whether the players aren't smarter than the fans. Watch as any college football game ends, and you'll see the way the players meet with their erstwhile foes at midfield and shake hands. Often the players will smile and make a joke or two before gathering and saying a prayer. Point being, football is just something these guys *do*. Wins and losses don't completely define them any more than losing a legal proceeding defines me as a lawyer. Indeed, I don't know any lawyer who wouldn't trade a loss in a legal proceeding for a big win featuring his favorite football team. Why? Our professions are just something we *do*, a football win or loss is something we *feel*.

Football matters to me in a way that's entirely illogical. I've never played the game, never worn pads or a helmet, yet, right now as we're driving south for the latest must-win game of the year, I'm already nervous in the pit of my stomach. And that's when it hits me: Sports are becoming more popular year after year because games are one of the few remaining things in life that can be resolved in 3 hours and change.

There's a winner and a loser, a hero and a goat. In an age when everything else seems steeped in artificiality, sports are real. You can fake a bank's balance sheet or a home value or a résumé, but you can't fake a win or a loss. You can't fake football talent or football speed. Put a guy on the line, grab a stopwatch, and see if he can run a 4.5 for real. When you get right down to it, almost everything else in today's life can be faked. But football in its primal urgency, in its captivating narrative and fickle stars, is real to us all in a way nothing else is.

Even if, in reality, we see a very small picture of the truth. On some level, despite all the attention they receive on TV, the radio, and message boards, these guys are just kids riding a bus to a game. And suddenly, shockingly, I'm faced with my own struggle: Could seeing everything up close, turning players into people, kill the fan inside me?

Now we're driving through the east side of Chattanooga, my grandfather's hometown and the place where he's buried. Anytime I come near Chattanooga, I'm taken back to a time when the 120-mile drive from Nashville to Chattanooga represented a journey into a foreign world. Now 120 miles is nothing to me, but as a child it was a seismic departure, a visit to my grandparents who lived in a different time zone with different terrain and, perhaps, even a different way of life. To my grandparents a movie was always a *show* and life was filled with stark lines, the difference between being saved and unsaved, rich and poor, black and white. Only one question really mattered: What day would the rapture at long last arrive?

The answer didn't come in their lives. When my grandfather died in 1994 he hadn't purchased a cemetery plot because he was so convinced Jesus was going to return before he died. He'd entered into voluntary knee replacement surgery to help repair an old football injury from his days at the University of Tennessee. Complications arose from the surgery, and he died on July 31, 1994, his 81st birthday. I was 15 years old.

My grandfather and I disagreed about some things—when he heard that I was attending Nashville's Martin Luther King Jr. High School he remarked, "They must have run out of a lot of names to end up with that one"—but we always shared a love for Tennessee football. UT football removed the age difference between us, made us both, eternally, 11 years old.

At 1:49 E.S.T. we cross the state line of Tennessee and enter Georgia. No one on the bus notices. The terrain has not changed, the hills still roll into distant mountains in North Georgia just as they did in southeast Tennessee. Heath Ledger as the Joker is onscreen burning a large pile of money at the same time I receive a stock price alert text message.

The stock market is tanking, down beneath 9,000 in an epic slide that only comes once in a generation. Some say we might be entering the second Great Depression, yet tomorrow over 90,000 fans will arrive to watch Tennessee's game and millions more will watch on CBS's national telecast. Even as the world buckles around us, SEC football does not change.

As the afternoon wears on we arrive on the outskirts of Atlanta, where our police escort splits the Friday rush-hour traffic. Cars pull to either side of the road to allow our buses to pass. Forty-five minutes later, we arrive at our destination—Berkmar High School near Duluth, Georgia. Our buses pull up in front of a football field surrounded by 20 rows of iron stands. The team disembarks and heads for the high school locker room, where the managers have already set out the players' helmets, shorts, and cleats.

Phil Fulmer walks onto the field where a cluster of waiting media immediately engulf him to ask questions for their nightly news telecasts. Among them is my friend Mark Nagi, a Knoxville sports anchor for ABC's WATE. He's in his 7th year of covering the Vols. After he's finished speaking with Fulmer, we talk.

Nagi reiterates what I've already gathered from message board chatter, from listening to sports talk radio, including callers to my own *ClayNation* show in Nashville, and from talking with my own Vol friends: Coach Fulmer's job has never been in greater jeopardy during his tenure with the Vols. After 16 years fans are clamoring for him to be fired. It's a drumbeat that intensified during the disastrous 2005 season—when the Vols started 3-1 and then collapsed, with a home loss to Vanderbilt and the first losing record in over 19 years at 5-6. The 2006 and 2007 seasons during which the Vols rebounded and went 19-8 offered some respite, but now with the team standing at 2-3, the proverbial knives are being sharpened. Phil Fulmer is a college football coach in winter.

He needs his team to perform well in this game, needs them to prove that they can still be a force in the SEC. He needs to show that he still has what it takes to compete with a new generation of mercenary coaches, that the game has not passed him by.

Phil Fulmer's team emerges from the high school locker room and jogs onto the field. Fewer than 100 players and coaches are on the field. Surrounding this group is maybe 50 other people—a few fans wearing orange, media, and onlookers from the high school. The players stretch on the green grass, appearing loose as they do a ball drill where they rapidly pass the football to one another in an effort to make a team-mate drop the ball. Arian Foster forces tailback Montario Hardesty to drop the ball and the two men laugh, mocking each other as they argue whether it was a bad pass from Foster or a bad reception by Hardesty. Recently replaced starting quarterback Jonathan Crompton warms up, tossing 20-yard passes, to his replacement Nick Stephens. No tension is evident between the two of them. After these drills the team breaks into offense and defense, and the coordinators, Dave Clawson with the offense and John Chavis with the defense, go over their game plans. Fulmer moves from the defense to the offense and then fixates on the offensive line.

Offensive coordinator Dave Clawson is marching his receivers through the routes. "They're going to play man and we're going to get you isolated," he says to wide receiver Gerald Jones. From the sideline, I sit and watch the team and marvel at how small the number of people associated with a football team truly is.

Practice ends with the offense running through the victory forma-tion, the kneeldown play. I close my eyes for an instant and pray that this is how tomorrow's game will end. Then the players stream off the field and into the high school locker room to get changed.

Clawson approaches one of the managers. "Do they need to bring their helmets with them?" Clawson asks. The manager laughs. "No, we take care of that stuff here," he says. Clawson remains a recent arrival at the top division of college football, and the managers say he still seems surprised by all of the details that the UT support staff manages.

When we arrive at the hotel, all of the players' and coaches' keys are already laid out for them to grab. I walk to the front desk and check in on my own. I had the option of adding my room to the UT team rate, but I was terrified that UT athletic director Mike Hamilton would see me next week and say, "Clay, we know you're responsible for *Backdoor Housewives 28*." When I turn around, Clawson is standing in line behind me with his room key. Another clerk arrives and Clawson steps forward: "I'd like to get my Marriott Rewards points," he says.

Dave Clawson makes $400,000 a year, and from my own experience it takes an awful lot of Marriott stays to get anything for free. This is a man who knows the value of a dollar, and isn't sure when the next one might arrive.

The night before a game the team has a curfew of 11. The strength coaches are in charge of doing the bed checks. They're accompanied by some of the police officers traveling with the team, including Vince Kanipe, a gray-haired, soft-spoken man with gentle eyes who is in his 16th year of traveling with the UT football team. When he's not traveling with the team, Kanipe is a member of the Tennessee campus police force. Kanipe's role is to accompany Fulmer and his family when they travel. In particular, he escorts Vicky Fulmer to and from her seat in the athletic director's skybox. Kanipe says he got the assignment by chance. "I was in the office when Gus Manning [former UT senior athletic director] called down and said they needed another officer." In addition to Kanipe, two other police officers travel with the team, a Tennessee state trooper named Dennis Murray and a Knoxville police officer named Sam Graham.

Kanipe says that Fulmer's wife is sometimes harassed by opposing fans. In fact, the triggering incident that led to Kanipe's assignment to the Fulmer family was when a Florida fan spit on Vicky in 1993. Kanipe says that generally the coach and his family are fairly safe in opposing stadiums. The most dangerous time is when students storm the field. While we're talking, Fulmer's youngest daughter, Allison, who just turned 22 and is a softball player for the Tennessee women's team, sits down across from us. She's wearing a dress and her long brown hair drapes over her shoulders.

"Hey, Vince," she says. Then she offers us each a piece of gum.

The next day the team has breakfast beginning at 8 and then meetings starting at 9. Shortly after noon, the players pour out of the hotel carrying their black Adidas bags, prepared to depart for Sanford Stadium. Most are stone-faced, listening to their iPods or texting on their cell phones. A few smile, but the majority are quiet as they stand in line waiting to board the bus that will take them to the game that will decide their season's fate.

We ride to Sanford Stadium watching Illinois-Minnesota on the bus satellite. Our trip from the Duluth Marriott takes about 45 minutes and during this time there is no sound other than the television broadcast on the bus. We drive through rural Georgia on a two-lane highway, passing old plank-boarded homes and empty land covered in the red clay dirt of Georgia. For miles and miles of rural country roads no one notices our passage. Even so, my stomach is so tense I can barely swallow.

Near the outskirts of Athens, we begin to see a few Georgia fans, who pop their Georgia Bulldog shirts and shake their red pom-poms in our direction. One man shoots us a bird outside a Shoney's; eventually I'll count 21 Georgia fans who flip off the bus, but I'm sure there were many others I didn't spot.

On we drive until we pull up through Athens and then make a left turn and pass down the side of Sanford Stadium nearest to the cemetery and railroad tracks. The buses stop and we all disembark. Many UT fans are waiting alongside the barricades, our very own orange army, cheering and yelling encouragement as the players walk past them down a long ramp into the recesses of the stadium. It's 1:15 and kickoff is still 2 hours and 15 minutes away.

Despite a forecast that called for a sunny and warm day, it's overcast, cool, and windy. There is no visible blue sky anywhere on the horizon. By the time the first Georgia students arrive and sprint down to the first row of the stadium's student section, Jonathan Crompton jogs out of the tunnel and begins to warm up with a football. Just over a month ago Crompton was universally beloved, but in four games he has managed to drive an entire state crazy, myself included. And why, exactly?

For playing quarterback poorly? For appearing too cocky in answering media questions after losses? For throwing the football as hard as he can and rarely connecting with his targets? His sins are not legion, but the passionate hate he's aroused among UT fans is substantial. And now as I'm watching him warm up on the field, I'm left wondering, how much more does UT fans hating Jonathan Crompton say about us than it does about him?

As I watch Crompton warm up, I talk with Andrew Haag, a junior Vol manager who walks using two arm braces as crutches. One of his jobs on game days is to go onto the field and grab the tee after Vol kickoffs. Chances are, if you've attended a UT game you've seen him racing across the field, crutches waving wildly. He's a 21-year-old from Hendersonville, Tennessee, and he's the second member of his family to be a Vol football manager, the first being his older brother Eric.

As we stand on the sideline I ask Andrew whether he still gets as upset about UT losses as he did before he was a manager, before he saw the team every day. "Well, yes and no," he responds, "because I see how hard they work and I don't want them to lose. But I also see things on a broader level now than I used to. I see behind the scenes more, see what Coach Fulmer does that doesn't have anything to do with football. Like what he did for me and my family."

When he was 8 years old, on December 24, 1995, Andrew Haag climbed into a car with two of his brothers and his dad for a trip to church. It was 9 in the morning and his mom stayed behind to take care of Christmas details. He was riding in the middle seat, in the back row, with his brother Brent to his right. Up front his dad was driving the family's Oldsmobile Silhouette with his older brother Eric sitting beside him. They were driving on a two-lane road. Andrew says he remembers looking out the window at the passing trees and houses. But he doesn't really remember the accident.

Another car, driven by a teenager, was traveling in the opposite direction at 65 miles an hour in a 30-mile-an-hour zone. The teenager lost control of his car and hit Andrew's family's car head-on. Andrew's father and his brother Brent died within minutes of the accident. The force of the accident broke Andrew's back and severely damaged his spinal cord. He spent the next 3 months at Vanderbilt Hospital in Nashville.

Andrew's mother and father were both University of Tennessee graduates. Word of the accident reached Coach Fulmer, and on the day before UT played Ohio State in the 1996 Citrus Bowl, Andrew received a telephone call in his hospital room. His mom brought him the phone. "Peyton Manning's on the phone and he wants to talk to you," she said.

"No, he's not," Andrew said.

But the 19-year-old Manning was. Andrew talked to both Peyton and Coach Fulmer on that day as he lay in his hospital bed. "You're going to get better, hang in there," Fulmer said. Then he invited Andrew and his brother to the spring game that April. The boys attended the game, and rather than do one good deed and vanish from their lives, Fulmer stayed in contact with the Haag family. Andrew's older brother, Eric, who was not as badly injured, went to Fulmer's football camp, and eventually Fulmer extended an offer to Eric to become a student manager. After 3 years Eric became Fulmer's personal assistant. Now Andrew has also become a student manager. Of the 16 managers of the UT football team, Andrew believes that every one of them has a similar story. "Coach Fulmer doesn't have to do things for people like my family, he just does," Andrew says. "Most of the time no one hears anything about it."

"My mom still comes to the games," Andrew says. "You know, one of the last things we did as a family was go to Knoxville and watch the UT-Vandy game in 1995. It was an ugly game, something like twelve–seven."

More of the UT players are beginning to warm up now and Andrew stands, braces himself on his legs, and prepares to go help out. "I love football," Andrew says. "I don't like my team to lose. But you know what? It's a game. Just a game."

Coach Fulmer, wearing his orange coach's polo with white stripes on the arms, is standing alone in the shadows of the field's entrance. There is no one near him in the tunnel. Above him the Georgia fans haven't even noticed him and aren't yet pelting him with insults and catcalls. Fulmer stares out at the field, lost in his own thoughts. As I pass he extends his right hand and we shake. I feel bad for breaking his reverie.

"Sun's about to come out," he says.

No one talks to Phil Fulmer for at least 5 minutes. Then the Vol tight ends arrive to enter the field. They pass him at a jog and Fulmer joins the players as they enter the field. It's still cloudy in Athens.

OUTSIDE THE VISITING LOCKER room at Sanford Stadium are two training tables where players are being taped up and stretched for the game. A manager is affixing T eyeblack stickers under UT linebacker Ellix Wilson's eyes.

Inside, the visitors' locker room is small. Lockers line the walls, and the UT managers have affixed orange stickers with the players' numbers on them at the top of the metal lockers. Above the lockers is a low ceiling laced with steel rafters. Metal chairs are pushed together in front of a blackboard, where General Neyland's Maxims hang. Unlike the expansive Rose Bowl locker room, there is not enough room here for all the players to sit in front of the coaches, so many players are crouched in front of their gray metal lockers. Many are leaning forward, staring down at the old, stained blue-gray carpet. Twenty-five minutes remain until kickoff.

Student managers walk around the locker room offering eyeblack, Pedialyte, and Gatorade. One of the UT graduate assistants, Kevin Simon, a former linebacker for the Vols, is walking around the outskirts of the seated players. "It's time to shock the damn country," he yells. Josh McNeil, eyeblack already streaked down his cheeks with the sweat from his warmup, nods. UT strength coach Johnny Long grabs Arian Foster by the arm. "You can only be stopped if you want to be stopped," Long says. "Take that shit to heart!" Otherwise the locker room is silent.

(right) Future University of Tennessee head coach Phillip Fulmer arrived in Knoxville in 1968 as a 17-year-old freshman after picking UT over Alabama. As a player, Fulmer's Vols went 30-5 and captured an SEC championship.
(UT Sports Information)

(left) General Robert Neyland addresses his team in the postgame locker room. Neyland's 173 lifetime wins as a coach placed him 26 ahead of Coach Fulmer's 147 as the 2008 campaign dawned.
(UT Sports Information)

(right) My maternal grandfather, Richard K. Fox, is third from the right in the back row in this photo of the 1933 Volunteer football team. Fifty years later, doctor's orders would forbid him from watching UT games live.
(UT Sports Information)

(above) Heralded recruit Jonathan Crompton scans the field during the 2008 season opener at UCLA. Tennessee fans anticipated that Crompton would follow in the footsteps of great Volunteer quarterbacks of the past, such as Heath Shuler and Peyton Manning. *(Elizabeth Olivier / UTsports.com)*

(below) Josh McNeil, who considers Coach Fulmer to be a second father, prepares to snap the football against UCLA. McNeil bears much of the responsibility for recognizing defenses in Dave Clawson's highly touted offense. *(Elizabeth Olivier / UTsports.com)*

(above) The Vols run through the T for the home opener against UAB. The tradition, which dates back over 40 years, signifies that it's now football time in Tennessee. *(Elizabeth Olivier / UTsports.com)*

(below) Neyland Stadium, the nation's third-largest football venue, gleams at night. As the weeks pass by and the losses pile up, more and more empty seats reveal themselves amidst the orange. *(UT Sports Information)*

(left) The student managers prepare the players' equipment 2 days before the Tennessee-Florida game. They'll break for only 20 minutes tonight, during which they'll dine on gator. *(Clay Travis)*

(right) Junior center Josh McNeil enters the field at Neyland Stadium, experiencing a rare solitary moment in a frenzied season. *(Elizabeth Olivier / UTsports.com)*

(left) Quarterback Jonathan Crompton and Coach Fulmer react to one of many disastrous plays during a 30–6 home loss to archrival Florida. *(Elizabeth Olivier / UTsports.com)*

(above) Brock Lodge, former UT cheerleader, displays his prized possession, a Heath Shuler–autographed megaphone, at his tailgate. *(Clay Travis)*

(right) As the 2008 season progresses, UT's 1998 national championship, just 10 years ago, begins to seem further and further away. *(UT Sports Information)*

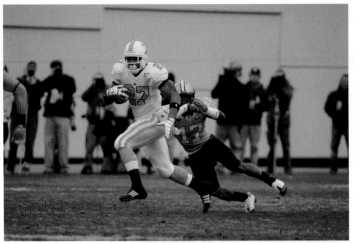

(left) Arian Foster, bedeviled by fumbles and not receiving anywhere near as many carries in 2008 as he'd hoped, breaks into the open field against Vanderbilt. *(Elizabeth Olivier / UTsports.com)*

(right) Arian Foster's grandmother, Lucy Maez *(left)*; mother, Bernadette Foster *(middle)*; and girlfriend, Romina Lombardo *(right)*, pose outside Neyland Stadium before the Alabama game. The women are hopeful this will be the day Arian and the Vols' luck turns. *(Clay Travis)*

(left) The most electric defensive player in the SEC, Eric Berry, presents the game ball to Coach Fulmer in the postgame locker room after the victory over Vanderbilt. *(Elizabeth Olivier / UTsports.com)*

(above) UT offensive coordinator Dave Clawson, who arrived in the summer of 2008 intent on revolutionizing the Volunteer offense, confers with quarterback Nick Stephens, who replaced Jonathan Crompton after four games. *(Elizabeth Olivier / UTsports.com)*

(above) "Good Time" Charlie Harris, the Vols' equipment truck driver since the 1999 Fiesta Bowl, shows off the fresh paint job the UT big rig received in 2004 after Coach Fulmer sized up the opposition's gear carrier. *(Elizabeth Olivier / UTsports.com)*

(above) Tennessee graduate assistant Inky Johnson, who suffered a career-ending injury as a junior in a game against Air Force, coaches from the sideline during practice. *(Elizabeth Olivier / UTsports.com)*

(above) Coach Fulmer, victorious over Kentucky, is carried off the field after his 152nd and final victory as UT head coach. *(Elizabeth Olivier / UTsports.com)*

(below) A new era dawns in Knoxville: Mike Hamilton *(left)* introduces Lane Kiffin to the Volunteer faithful. *(Elizabeth Olivier / UTsports.com)*

Across the locker room Phil Fulmer is huddling with his coaches in front of a drab white wall. As the digital clocks tick down to kickoff, Fulmer steps in front of the team. "I like you quiet if you're about your business and your focus." He lifts his hands and runs them over his chin and pauses. "Let me see the captains and kickers," he says.

Fulmer has enjoyed many successes at Sanford Stadium, winning here in 1992, 1994, 1996, 1998, 2004, and 2006. He's 6-2 in his career at Sanford Stadium. Considering the quality of the opponents and the intensity of the rivalries, Fulmer has had his best success as a head coach against Alabama and Georgia.

Above us 92,000 fans are alternating chants of "Georgia" and "Bulldogs." Their voices are just barely audible in the bowels of the visiting locker room as the team endures the final moments before kickoff. Phil Fulmer returns from meeting with his captains and kickers and begins to speak.

"You know, I'm really proud to be going into my two hundredth game with this football team. It hasn't been the easiest year, but I'm proud of y'all." The team is still silent. Fulmer, hands clasped together in front of his khaki pants, continues to speak.

"I have some unbelievably fond memories from this locker room, of singing in this locker room. If we can do that again it will damn well be worth it . . . We're a good football team, let's just make sure we show it."

Fulmer says he's not going to talk very long, but he wants to make sure to go over a few key reminders. "In big games like this a few plays will make a difference. Be prepared because you don't know when they're going to happen. There will be all kinds of opportunities for big plays out there."

Then he zeroes in on matchups. "Our d-line is better than those guys on offense. You're better. Show it. Get some pressure on their quarterback. He will throw it to you if we give him a great pass rush. Offensive front, you're better than their d-line, show us."

Fulmer asks for the wide receivers to get good releases on offense and for the linebackers to help the safeties with the underneath passes.

Then he says, "God has given all of you something that not everybody has: a strong body, an opportunity to compete. Now let's compete. Do all that and we'll be singing in the locker room if we play our game for sixty minutes."

With that the team begins to recite General Neyland's Maxims. On the seventh maxim the team stands and rushes to the door. The sign in the shape of Tennessee that says I WILL GIVE MY ALL FOR THE STATE OF TENNESSEE is affixed above the exit to the visitors' locker room. The players slap the sign on their way out and then form a line in the tunnel just off the field. Once outside the locker room the noise from the stands is powerful, all-encompassing. "Sun's out," yells a coach nearby. And it's true, the sun has broken through the clouds for the moment.

I'm standing near the back of the team, alongside Jonathan Crompton, who is calm, stretching his head from one side to the other, while continuing to face forward. In all of his dreams about football for the past 21 years, I'm sure none of them has included being benched for one of the biggest games of the season.

The T unfurls on the flag in front of us, and as a group the team explodes from the shadowed tunnel and onto the sunlit field, where they are greeted by a cacophony of boos from 92,000 Georgia fans.

I stand beside the girls distributing Gatorade and water from a stand. Right now I don't want to get too close to the field because I'm afraid of getting run over like Notre Dame's Charlie Weis earlier this year. This fear is echoed when a student manager walks up to me and says, "Keep your head on a swivel, Clay." The last thing I need is to get wrecked on the sideline and then have my phone start buzzing with text messages from friends who have seen me flattened by a Bulldog.

But even that would be preferable to somehow influencing the game. This is the fear of every fan, turning into Chicago Cubs antihero Steve Bartman. Being penalized for standing too close to the field, accidentally tripping our new quarterback Nick Stephens and causing him to sprain his ankle, leaning over and picking up a live fumble before it's actually left the field like Mack Brown's son-in-law did at Texas, or just tripping over a cord on the sideline and tumbling forward onto the field. You name an egregious error that could be committed on the sideline and chances are I'm worrying about messing up and doing it.

Across the field from us, Georgia is ranked #10 in the country and needs this win almost as badly as Tennessee does. After beginning the season ranked #1, the Bulldogs were humiliated by Alabama on September 27. The Crimson Tide came into Sanford Stadium and leapt out to a 31–0 halftime lead, before cruising home with a 41–31 victory. Now 5-1 on the season, Georgia is just 1-1 in the SEC. If they lose this game, the Bulldogs will be 1-2 in the conference and, with two homes losses, in dire straits in the SEC East. Georgia is led by yet another coach with no connection to the school, Mark Richt, a former quarterback from the University of Miami.

Richt, 48 years old with a boyish face, is in his eighth season at Georgia after a coaching career that began at Florida State in 1985. He announced his arrival in the SEC with a 2001 victory at Neyland Stadium over Fulmer's highly ranked Tennessee Vols, finishing 8-4 on the season. He also beat Fulmer in 2002 and 2003, before Fulmer finally won a game against him in 2004. Since Richt's first year with the team, Georgia has won 10 games in all but one season, 2006, when they won 9. He's also won SEC championships in 2002 and 2005. In total he's beaten Fulmer four times and lost to him three times. Fulmer's teams have performed better against Richt's than any other rival of late, winning 51–33 in 2006 and mauling the Bulldogs 35–14 last year in Knoxville. If Fulmer wins this game he'll even the lifetime score against Richt and, most important, his team will have a chance in this year's SEC. If he loses, he may not get the opportunity to coach against Georgia again.

Tennessee loses the toss and will receive the ball first. Meanwhile, I realize it's really hard to actually see the field when giant football players are in front of you. In cleats and pads even a player who is smaller than me, for example UT wide receiver Gerald Jones, is suddenly transformed into a large man. Put cleats and pads on someone who is already large, say defensive tackle Walter Fisher, and he becomes a giant, adding at least 2 or 3 inches to his height and expanding his bulk by half.

I miss the first Tennessee offensive play and can only tell the play has been a success when I see Gerald Jones running with the football through gaps in the UT players. Ultimately he gains 26 yards, and the players, coaches, and managers are jumping up and down on the sideline. No one is sitting down on the benches behind me right now, and I have no idea what's going on for the next play. Plainly this won't do.

So I start to walk down the sideline searching for the best view. UT is near midfield and I post up outside the initial row of players where I have a nice angle on the line of scrimmage. For one play this vision is perfect. But then UT defensive coordinator John Chavis strolls directly in front of me. I can hardly tap him on the shoulder and tell him he's obstructing my view. So I keep moving. UT's first drive ends in a punt and Georgia takes over.

The sideline seems more alive when the opposing offense has the football. The defensive coaches and staff constantly scream out at the players. Several times, as the players line up, they're calling out play possibilities. "Watch the screen," yells Chavis. Several other players and coaches join in with the warning. Matthew Stafford, Georgia's junior quarterback, who has NFL scouts drooling, hands off to redshirt sophomore tailback Knowshon Moreno, who also has scouts drooling.

But eventually the screen Chavis warns his defense about arrives. On third and 8 from their own 38, Georgia dials up the screen pass for a gain of 37. I catch glimpses of this gain, see that the first down is made, and then lose the runner into the mass of UT players. But I can tell things aren't going well based on the roar of the crowd. It's a building roar. On offensive plays you can tell what happens on the field just based on the home fans' reaction. There's a mild cheer for a 4- or 5-yard gain (applause that dies rapidly), the no-gain cheer (complete silence), the loss on a play (extended groans leading into silence), the first-down cheer (cheering leading into the next play), the big-gain cheer (cheering that builds in intensity for several seconds as the play continues to gain yards and then ends with a rousing crescendo), and the orgasmic touchdown cheer (a cheer that extends for a minute or more, dies down for the extra point, rebuilds to a height not quite as loud as the one right after the touchdown on the made extra point, dies down once more, and then returns with a vengeance for the kickoff after the score).

Georgia's third-down screen pass is a near-touchdown, so it elicits from the crowd a mix between the big-gain cheer and the orgasm cheer. I suspect this is because some drunker fans have trouble telling whether Georgia has scored a touchdown and give us a premature orgasm cheer while the more sober fans tell them to tamp down a bit.

After the first score to put Georgia up 7–0, the UT sideline remains fairly calm in spite of the maelstrom of sound around us. Fulmer claps his hands furiously as his kickoff return team gathers around him. He doesn't scream or yell. In fact, I'm learning that the sideline is one of the calmest places in an otherwise crazy environment, the proverbial eye of the football hurricane.

The Georgia student section is behind us, and its occupants are making fun of UT defensive back Brent Vinson for his Mohawk and UT senior punter Britton Colquitt for the fact that he has been arrested several times for alcohol infractions since arriving on campus.

Standing on the sideline you realize even more than sitting in the crowd that there's lots of time during a football game when nothing is really happening, particularly for the majority of the players, who are dressed for this game but won't play. These guys just walk around from one area to the other and try to look busy. One of these young players sidles up to me. "You were right about the cleavage on the girls," he says. In my last book I called Athens the cleavage capital of the South.

Tennessee's offense fails to move the ball, and shortly thereafter Georgia's new superstar freshman wide receiver, A. J. Green, drops a touchdown pass from Matthew Stafford that you or I could have caught. Georgia settles for a field goal to go up 10–0 with 3:12 left in the first quarter. UT's offense fails to gain a first down yet again and punts.

Georgia returns the punt to the Vol 36. The first quarter ends with Georgia driving.

The Vol defense stiffens and forces a third and 10 from the UT 36, but Georgia gains 28 yards to the Vols' 7-yard line. Facing an early blowout, the UT defense holds at the 3-yard line and Mark Richt settles for a field goal to go up 13–0. During the ensuing television break I turn around and look for the orange in the crowd. I've been to UT-Georgia games in Athens in 1998, 2002, and 2006, and this is the smallest crowd of UT fans I have ever seen make the trip. Back on the field, the Vols punt once again and Georgia takes over.

On third down UT's linebacker swats away a Matthew Stafford crossing pass in a perfectly timed jump. But the referee doesn't see it that way and throws a late flag. The UT sideline reacts to the questionable call the same way fans do: with indignation, cursing, and barely restrained suggestions of referee cheating. "They giving this game to 'em," yells a huge, angry player beside me. He looks down at me, smacking his gloved fists together. For a moment I think he might want to kill me.

"Fuck, yeah," I say, "cheaters."

He glowers at me. "Cheaters," he says.

"Cheaters," I say again, but he's already gone. I breathe easier.

On the next play, Tennessee defensive coordinator John Chavis still has not let go of his anger. "Look at them holding," he screams at the ref, "right damn in front of you." Brazenly, the UT staff member in charge of monitoring the sideline to ensure that the coaches don't get on the field steps forward and pulls Chavis back by his brown belt. Then, as if to confirm his status in the sideline hierarchy, this small man turns to face all of us. "Get back now!" he screams. He yells at the players and staff dozens of times during the game; keeping coaches off the field on game day is an eternal struggle that requires great vigilance. Just as quickly as they've been remonstrated to keep their distance, they begin edging forward again, trying, with all their might, to get as close to their players as they possibly can.

Georgia is driving again. Already up 13–0, if they get another touchdown this game is over. The Vols need a miracle. And, amazingly, we get one. Defensive end Robert Ayers blows up a screen pass and, in the process, picks off Matthew Stafford's pass. The sideline in front of me erupts in cheers, and 2 seconds later I see Ayers trucking up the sideline surrounded by a small convoy of teammates. I know something good has happened for us because for the first time all game long the Georgia crowd is completely silent.

Robert Ayers, interceptor, returns as a conquering hero to the sideline. He's swarmed by teammates. Defensive back Eric Berry bounces on his shoulders. "Yeah, big man, yeah!" Berry exults. A new energy has ignited the sideline. UT needs to do something on offense. Right now the Vols have 39 yards of total offense in the game. Of that total, 26 yards came on the first play from scrimmage. So in the ensuing 20 minutes, the team has gained 13 yards.

With 4 minutes and 30 seconds remaining in the second quarter, for the first time in what seems like eons, the Vols string together more than one big play in close succession. Denarius Moore, the explosively fast wide receiver, who caught a 52-yard pass for a touchdown the week before against Northern Illinois, breaks into the open field and runs underneath a perfectly thrown Nick Stephens deep ball.

As the ball arcs through the air I'm involuntarily running alongside it. Seeing a deep ball thrown from the sideline gives you an agonizing appreciation for how long the ball hangs in the air. Time seems to stand still; from the moment the ball leaves the quarterback's hands, all that matters is: catch or don't catch.

Moore makes the catch and is dragged down at the 3-yard line. Bedlam erupts on the UT sideline—a big-play catharsis of sorts. After months of futility the UT offense is close to making this a ballgame. Latrell Scott, the tall black UT wide receivers coach Dave Clawson brought with him from Richmond, sprints down the sideline to greet his wide receivers as they come off the field. "That's what I'm fucking talking about!" Scott screams, slamming Moore's helmet with his large hands. "I told you guys you'd get your chance to make plays today!"

Now UT is facing a first-and-goal situation—on the doorstep of success once more. Players on the sideline must stand between the 20s on the field. So on goal-line plays a crowd of players gathers on the 20-yard line closest to the goal line. On second down UT's pass is incomplete. Several players react angrily. "Why can't we just run the fucking ball?" a defensive player screams. On third down, as the roar of the Georgia crowd crests, Nick Stephens throws a quick pass to Gerald Jones. Touchdown Tennessee!

The sideline is an orange mosh pit. We're all jumping around, arms and legs flailing in every direction. Amidst the celebration on the sideline it feels like we're winning by 30. It's 13–7 and the Vols are hunkering down and giving the Bulldogs a fight.

For the first time all game, Sanford Stadium is eerily quiet.

As if that weren't good enough fortune, Georgia mishandles the next kickoff and takes possession at their 3-yard line. Anticipation builds on the Vol sideline. Every player is glued to the action, standing on the benches, crowding up close to the edge of the field to watch the plays as best they can. On two consecutive running plays, UT's defense is a stone wall. The Vols take a time out with only 1:33 to play in the half and Georgia pinned back deep. Offensive coaches hand out new wristbands for the players featuring the 2-minute offense. A graduate assistant, Jim Bob Cooter, distributes most of them. "Get the Zebra formation," he calls, "get the Zebra formation."

Arian Foster and Gerald Jones rush to put the Zebra formation bands on their wrists or attach them to their waistbands. It's third and 8 and it's looking like Georgia will be punting from their end zone. But then Matthew Stafford scampers away from a pursuing rusher and throws back across his body to Knowshon Moreno for a first down.

"Damn," Arian Foster curses, slapping his hands on his thighs. "Damn!"

Damn indeed. It gets worse. Vol safety Demetrice Morley makes a clean hit on Georgia wide receiver Mohamed Massequoi near the sideline. The hit is so solid—dislodging a pass and knocking Massequoi to the ground—that a referee throws a flag for helmet-to-helmet conduct. Replays clearly show this is not the case, but Georgia gains 15 yards on the penalty.

The UT sideline is indignant. "That's bullshit!" screams defensive coordinator John Chavis. Former quarterback Condredge Holloway, a veteran of many ballgames, walks the sideline clapping his hands. "Bad call," he says, clapping harder. "Bad call."

Now past midfield, Georgia pounces. UT is called for another 15-yard penalty for hitting a receiver out of bounds and suddenly the Vols are facing near-disaster. Georgia takes a time out with 9 seconds left. It's third and goal. Hold them here and the Vols can escape only having given up a field goal.

How badly are things going this season? The Vols have played the percentages perfectly. They had to take the time out with 1:33 remaining in the half and Georgia facing a third down from their own 5. Otherwise Georgia would have run the clock all the way down and been content to enter the half with a 6-point lead. Yet in taking that time out, the Vols have given Georgia the opportunity to put points on the board late in the half. To his credit—and aided by at least one bad call by the refs—Mark Richt has put the ball in his quarterback's hands and attempted to score. Even still, in this situation, with this amount of time remaining, the odds of Georgia scoring a touchdown beginning a drive at their own 3 are minimal at best.

But, unfortunately for the Vols, percentages don't govern individual circumstances. Stafford drops back to pass and hits a wide-open Massequoi in the end zone. 20–7 Dawgs. As quickly as momentum has found the 2008 Volunteer football team, it is gone. UT heads to the locker room trailing by 13 once more.

Inside the locker room the players are still upset about the Morley call. "I ain't seen that called all year," says running back Montario Hardesty, slapping a white towel on the chair in front of him. "That's straight bullshit," says another to muttered assent.

"Who gets the ball?" asks Hardesty.

After a few moments of silence, a manager quietly replies, "They do."

Hardesty shakes his head. "Fuck," he mutters.

Other Vols are taking shots at Georgia players now. "Fuck A. J. Green. He got one catch early. And fuck Moreno too with his goofy-ass arm-swinging. Somebody needs to break his legs."

A few players laugh in agreement. The coaches, stern-faced and grim, return to the locker room.

Offensive coordinator Dave Clawson gathers the offense. "We're taking more shots down the field. Wide receivers, we've seen you running past them, you're doing a great job. We're going to take a shot at them early with either a reverse or a deep ball." Then Clawson begins to speak to particular formations they're going to change for the second half. His instructions sound like a foreign language. "Okay, we're going to run razor forty-eight shuler bingo wings tecmo thirty-six bukkake at them," he seems to say. "Got that?"

The players nod.

"And if they counter with bama bangs micro machines full down forty-two blue, then you know we've got to counter their counter with blade gonzo vampire bgid pink dolphin sixteen, right?"

The players nod again.

"We're also going to run the football."

The first and last quotes are valid. The other two are completely inaccurate representations of the complex instructions Clawson gave the offense. I've watched football all my life and I feel like I'm watching Japanese sumo wrestling instruction—in Japanese. I literally have no idea what the terminology means. Clawson dismisses the offensive players to meet with their position coaches. Then he walks over to where Jonathan Crompton and Nick Stephens sit, side by side, arms resting on their thighs, in front of the gray lockers. The running backs go to Stan Drayton, and Latrell Scott takes the wide receivers to another area of the locker room. As the position coaches address them in the cramped locker room, the players are quiet, sitting with their eyes downcast. After the players have met with their position coaches for a few minutes, Coach Fulmer returns to talk to the team.

"The defense has got to get a damn stop," he says, striding in front of a chalkboard. "As bad as we've played, this is still a damn game. Let's go get this thing." Then Fulmer claps his hands furiously and the team stands and files back out of the locker room. As we exit I see defensive tackle Walter Fisher, right foot bare, on crutches outside the locker room. With Tennessee's lack of depth up front I fear that Georgia is going to pound us with Knowshon Moreno and the running game.

The Vols get their damn stop on the first possession of the second half, but the offense does nothing in turn. On the ensuing punt, UT's punter, Britton Colquitt, gets a personal foul for a late hit, and Georgia takes over in good field position. As soon as Colquitt's number 47 is announced as the offending party, Fulmer yanks off his headset and spins in the punter's direction. There is fire in his blue eyes. The players part before their coach and Fulmer storms toward Colquitt.

"Britton!" Coach Fulmer seethes, before turning back to the field. For a moment he faces the field, but then, as if he suddenly remembers something else, he wheels back toward Colquitt. Mercifully, for Colquitt's sake, someone upstairs is talking to Fulmer on his headset and the confrontation fizzles. Within seconds Colquitt is gripping the neck of his shoulder pads and laughing about the scene.

Walter Fisher is off the crutches and taped back up. He's attempting to jog on his foot to see whether he can go in for the second half. Wincing, he attempts to make a quick cut on the foot. He's in too much pain to return to the game. "Fuck," he mutters.

Georgia drives all the way down to the goal line before Matthew Stafford makes his second big mistake of the game, throwing an interception that UT's Eric Berry picks off. Once more the sideline comes alive as Berry, making a case for himself as the best pound-for-pound defensive player in college football, sprints down the field. He has only Matthew Stafford to beat and a 100-yard interception return will be his. But Stafford gets ahold of his foot and trips him up.

Nevertheless, Berry's teammates mug him on the sideline. UT's most dynamic playmaker on either side of the ball has taken points off the board for Georgia and given the Vols yet another opportunity to make a game of it. Nick Stephens comes alive now, throwing accurate and timely passes on this drive, converting one third and 9 and then, having moved the team down the field, facing a third and 8 from the 13. Stephens trips coming out from under the center and rolls left. He fires a pass to the back corner of the end zone and finds senior wide receiver Lucas Taylor there wide open for a touchdown. It's suddenly 20–14 and that fickle mistress, momentum, is back on the Vols' sideline.

Lucas Taylor is swarmed on the sideline. "We're back in it!" he yells. "Got that play." Nick Stephens, hero of the moment, arrives back on the sideline aglow with joy. He takes a congratulatory phone call from offensive coordinator Dave Clawson, hangs up, stands still for a moment, and then says, "I gotta pee."

He takes off at a full sprint for the locker room. If UT gets a turnover at this moment, Jonathan Crompton is going to have to come in to take a snap and the television audience, the message boards, and all the world is going to believe that there's a quarterback controversy or something is wrong with Stephens, when the reality is that the quarterback just has to pee.

"Hey, we gonna win this motherfucker," barks strength coach Johnny Long, strutting by with his chest out. One of the policemen, Sam Graham, agrees. He claps his hands. "We got 'em where we want 'em, boys, we got 'em where we want 'em."

Yet, once more, Georgia's offense converts on third down. Eventually, the drive stalls, but Georgia bangs home a field goal on the first play of the fourth quarter, and the Vols are now down 23–14. On the ensuing drive the Vols punt after facing a fourth and 1 at their own 45. The ball will not return until the game has already been decided. Georgia puts on a methodical, draining drive that features the same toss sweep to the left over and over and over again. After each play the defense slowly climbs to its feet. As first down after first down comes, the offensive players slink back from near the field and sit down on the benches. Slowly, the realization spreads along the sideline that this game is going to end as three of the five games this season have already ended, with another loss. At 0-3 Tennessee will be off to their worst SEC start since 1988, the disastrous season when Johnny Majors's Vols began the season 0-6. Many players, eyes half-lidded, gaze morosely at the ground beneath their feet. Eventually the Vols get a stop, even tipping the ensuing field goal attempt, but the ball still crosses the uprights. The score is 26–14 Georgia and now it would take a miracle to win.

Anger and frustration flare on the sideline. A few defensive players stand together and complain about the offense. "They ain't done shit all game," says Demonte Bolden. His defensive comrades agree. The storyline of every season is that the offense and defense win and lose together. But this is a figment, a paper-thin rationale that players recite to the media in time-worn clichés. Now, in the fresh moments of defeat, they are honest. "We been on the damn field all day," says another defensive player. And it's true. By the end of the game the Georgia offense will have had possession of the football for a staggering 42 minutes.

Arian Foster, seated on the bench, is approached by a UT fan. Today Foster has carried the ball just three times for 3 yards. It is his worst-ever healthy performance in an SEC game. Tennessee has managed just 1 yard of rushing offense. The fan, who is wearing orange from head to foot and appears to be in his thirties, dog-cusses Foster to his back. "You ain't worth shit, you fucking quitter. You fumbling asshole, you quit on this team. I wish you'd left." Foster does not bat an eyelash, pretending not to notice the fan, and eventually a member of the Georgia security staff leads him away from the fence behind the bench. It's come to this—Georgia security guards are protecting Tennessee players from their own fans.

Later Foster claims the fan's hateful rant did not affect him. "I've learned that I'm always going to be the scapegoat," he says. "No matter what happens in the game, it's my fault. I've just got to accept that. There's nothing I can do." His answer is breezy, nonchalant, the type of answer most players give when asked about fans. But it's only part of the story. Later still his mother, Bernadette Foster, will say, "Arian won't tell anyone, but that really upset him."

The game ends and the players head to the locker room. "Jog off, men," yells a coach. But only a few players are jogging now. As the team heads into the locker room, an older Georgia fan in his fifties hangs over the rampart above us, yelling down at the players, his Georgia Bulldog jersey rounding amply over his gut. "We gonna be back in Knoxville to whip that ass again next year!" he screams. Most of the players ignore him. I can't.

Instead, I stop and look up at him, pausing for a moment to marvel that a single fan, a man old enough to be a grandfather, would rather taunt college kids leaving the field in defeat than celebrate his own win. None of the players take notice because they're angrier with themselves than about anything a fan could say. But I look at that man for a minute or so and wonder, is that what all fans become—old and embittered with age? The further away from college age you get, the angrier you become with victory or defeat? What if we're so busy scratching at the scabs of our lost seasons that we can't even enjoy actual victories anymore?

Back in the locker room, wide receiver Gerald Jones is angrily unwrapping the gloves from his hands. He sums up the first six games of the season—the Vols are now 2-4, the worst start of the Phil Fulmer era—in only five words: "Shit just don't go right," he says.

The team drops down to a knee on the worn blue carpet and Coach Fulmer leads them in a postgame prayer. When the prayer is finished Fulmer stands—blue eyes fierce as ever—and glares about the room. Players begin to move but he silences the movement with a sentence. "Stay right where you are," Fulmer intones.

"It's gonna be worse than it's been yet about me, about this staff, and about the team. People are going to pile on now. But I want you to hear it from me: I ain't quittin' and I'll look every one of you in the face and say the same thing." His voice is dripping with a barely restrained anger, his shoulders holding the tension of a large bear suddenly trapped on a ledge. He raises his voice as he says, "I damn well don't want to see anyone with that quittin' look on their faces either!" Here his intensity grows to another level. He practically shouts. "If I don't see your ass in class, in study hall, or practice, then long as I'm here you're gonna be on a short stick!"

Now he backs off. "I'm sorry. I can do a better job," Fulmer says, softer now. "We can all do better jobs. And if we all do better jobs we can get this thing turned around."

Mike Hamilton spends a short time in the locker room before retiring to the team bus, where he sits alone in quiet contemplation. Hamilton is wrestling with his attempt to separate the person, Phil Fulmer, a man he truly respects and likes, with the position, head football coach at Tennessee. Hamilton allows himself a negative thought: "This season has a chance to go in a direction it doesn't need to go. It could be Fulmer's last." By the time the team buses arrive in Knoxville, Hamilton's BlackBerry inbox contains 89 e-mail messages regarding Phillip Fulmer. Every single one is negative.

CHAPTER 13

CARRY ME BACK TO TENNESSEE

IN THE WAKE OF THE GEORGIA loss, I'm riding back to Nashville on a luxury bus filled with Tennessee fans. I meet up with Doug Tackett, a 37-year-old in-house attorney from Nashville, shortly after Fulmer's postgame speech. Doug shakes his head. "We're awful," he says. He leads me through a cavalcade of celebrating Georgia fans outside the stadium to a large black bus in a parking lot.

"We've got ten cases of beer, so drink as much as you need."

"I might need a lot," I say.

Doug nods. "We all do, man, we all do."

In just 10 minutes, I've moved from the eye of the football hurricane inside the Tennessee Volunteer locker room to the stormy exterior of Vol football fandom. Inside the luxury bus are 13 Vol fans from the ages of 25 to 55. Ten, including Doug, left Nashville at 6:45 in the morning. Two were picked up in Murfreesboro and another man joined the bus crew in Atlanta. All are wearing orange and have been drinking since early in the morning. They've rented the bus for an entire day for the cost of $2,600, and as I enter the bus, passing the two drivers employed for the day, all are watching the postgame show on satellite television.

"We fucking suck," says one middle-aged man, shaking his head as highlights of UT-Georgia are playing.

The two 40-inch flat-screen televisions, one in front and one in the back, each come with their own DirecTV receivers so passengers can watch two different games at the same time. Earlier in the day, Tennessee fans hoped that the Vols would beat Georgia and LSU would beat Florida. If this had happened, then each SEC East team, Florida, Tennessee, and Georgia, would have two SEC losses and the Vols wouldn't yet be eliminated from SEC East contention. But now those hopes are dashed; we're 0-3 in the SEC.

What's more, Tennessee hasn't just lost to Georgia; the Bulldogs have humiliated the Vols. Georgia racked up 458 total yards to the Vols' 209, 148 rushing yards to 1, 29 first downs to 10, and held the ball for 42 minutes on offense. Tennessee is lucky the score wasn't worse. Even more alarming, the Tennessee defense, the only reliable component of the Vols this year, played its worst game of the season. The Vols' season is collapsing on all fronts.

I make my way to the back of the bus and take a seat. There are three granite tables for eating, and right now everyone is helping themselves to the 6 pounds of barbecue brought for the trip.

My hosts are Doug Tackett and Jake Stribling, a 31-year-old mortgage broker from Nashville who graduated from Tennessee in 2000. During his time in Knoxville, Jake worked in the athletic department and was in charge of making sure that football players went to class. Each weekday his boss gave him a list of players and class times and he was responsible for walking around to the classrooms and checking them off. Believe it or not, some players had less than stellar attendance.

The mood on the bus is angry and pessimistic. Every single Tennessee fan on the bus believes Phil Fulmer has to go. In fact, instead of arguing about whether he should stay or go, talk has moved on to which coach should replace Fulmer. Jon Gruden, Mike Leach, Lane Kiffin, and Butch Davis's names are all discussed in detail. Well, at least in drunken detail.

"Did you know," Doug asks, "that we're the only team in the SEC without a conference victory?"

This silences my section of the bus. All of us sit quietly, staring straight ahead, replaying the season's failures in our minds. Finally Jake speaks up with a word of consolation. "No, Kentucky doesn't have a win either," he says. "It's us and Kentucky."

The bus begins to move. It can't move fast enough for me. I just want to be back home.

"Us and Kentucky," I say.

"And we ain't talking about basketball," says Jake.

As we wind through the postgame Georgia traffic, I'm peppered with questions by the other Vol fans. Has the team quit? What halftime adjustments are the coaches making? What do I think the problem is? What's the solution? Is Fulmer done?

Every fan on the bus feels the need to understand what's going on with the Vols, why our season of promise has collapsed so rapidly. LSU and Florida are coming on the television now, a rare CBS night game. LSU enters the field and the Florida crowd boos lustily. Jake stares at the television. "Remember back in the day when watching a game like this mattered to us?" says Doug.

He cracks open a beer. "It seems like a long time ago," Jake replies.

And it does. Already this season, just six games old, seems to have lasted a lifetime. Florida jumps out to a 17–0 lead as we travel through the outskirts of Atlanta. With five seconds left in the half LSU scores a touchdown to slice the lead to 20–7.

Doug decides this is a sign to double down his bet on LSU. So he calls his bookie and does so. Florida surges to a 51–21 victory. By the end of that game the bus has become quiet. Anger at Fulmer and the Vols gives way to silent resignation. We flip the channels around from one Pac-10 football game to another and even check out the baseball playoffs. It's late now and we're driving through the Tennessee night en route to a drop-off point just outside of Nashville.

As we near Nashville, Jake leans across to me and asks, "Be honest, Clay, is this really it for Coach Fulmer?"

CHAPTER 14

TACKLING DAVID PALMER

ON OCTOBER 14, THREE DAYS AFTER the Georgia loss, the *Knoxville News-Sentinel* interviews Mike Hamilton about Phil Fulmer's future at the University of Tennessee. Until now Hamilton has refused to publicly comment on Fulmer, although privately he has begun to discuss the future of the program. Indeed, while Hamilton asserts that he didn't begin to seriously contemplate replacing Fulmer until after the Georgia game, several UT boosters assert that Hamilton asked them hypothetical questions about firing Fulmer in the wake of the Florida game. "How would you recommend I fire Phillip?" Hamilton asked, according to multiple boosters who didn't want to be quoted by name.

Hamilton's public silence ends the moment his newspaper interview hits the Internet. Emblazoned beneath the sensational headline, "Hamilton Not Afraid to Make Coaching Change" is this subheading: "AD Aware of Fan Apathy; Finances Won't Stand in Way If Fulmer Leaves."

Hamilton's words rocket across the state of Tennessee. He's not just considering firing Fulmer, he's considering firing him before the season is even over.

"Our traditional model at the University of Tennessee is that we evaluate these kinds of things on a year-end basis," Hamilton says. "That doesn't preclude you from doing something different. But our typical model is that you let the seasons play out and then you evaluate them appropriately and give the student athletes and coaches their best chance to be successful in any particular year."

When pressed on Fulmer's future with Tennessee, particularly whether a 6-6 record is enough to save his job now that the Vols are sitting at 2-4, Hamilton bristles. "Our goals are not to be a five-hundred ball club."

The Vols have six games remaining. And even though it's mid-October, Hamilton said he's heard from concerned boosters and realizes that the school might start losing donations if the Vols don't improve. "That's always a risk, particularly in a year with economic situations being as they are," Hamilton tells the newspaper.

When he reads the interview, Fulmer is irate. "That was stupid," he says, "that cut the legs right out from under me."

In their private conversations about the state of the program, Fulmer will later say Hamilton was indirect with him. "He tells me, 'Some people are concerned. We need to fix things.'" More frustrating to Fulmer, Hamilton continually emphasizes the business side of the football equation, the falling home attendance numbers. Fulmer, who has always been leery of Hamilton's background in the business side of football, disagrees with Hamilton's position. "I tell him, so we've lost ten thousand people at a game? You've got to give me another year to fix this. If we win, they'll come back; those fans will be there again."

Hamilton has not yet made his final decision, and Fulmer knows he needs to beat Alabama or South Carolina to give Hamilton reason to believe he can turn the program around. In Mike Hamilton's words, "I need a win I can hang my hat on."

I read the Hamilton article back home in Nashville while my son, Fox, plays with a gift he recently received, a miniature brown football. Of late Fox's favorite game is taking any object, be it a Smurfette action figure or a building block, and tossing the object out the door of his nursery onto our dark brown hardwood floors to see if it rolls. Fox's default position is that every object is a ball. If the toy rolls, he's confident that he's found another ball; if it fails to roll, he understands that the object is not a ball.

Now he grabs the football and quickly crawls to the doorway. He hauls back his left hand and sends the football off onto the dark hardwood floors. But the football does something strange. It rolls straight ahead for a few feet and then makes an abrupt and sudden turn to the right. Then it waddles back in our direction, coming to rest just outside of Fox's reach. He looks at the football quizzically. Then he sits himself up and turns to look at me. He grins.

Fox is mesmerized by the football.

He throws it twice more in succession. At times it appears to be a ball, rolling straight and true, and at times it doesn't, turning haphazardly in any direction. Eventually Fox grabs the football and crawls back to me. He drops the football into my lap and then stares up at me. Fox has just learned his first lesson about football: You never know which way it's going to bounce.

FOUR HOURS BEFORE THE UT-Mississippi State game, I'm lying down in the front seat of my Mercury Mountaineer parked in downtown Knoxville. Lara and Fox are shopping in the Market Square area, and I've just taken two Advil and am attempting to sleep. My team is awful, I feel nauseous, I can't stop coughing, and I have a fever. Usually my wife doesn't believe that I have a fever.

"You don't have a fever, Clay," she'll say. Often when I say I'm ill she produces a thermometer and stands by me to ensure that I don't artificially inflate my temperature. Today she knows I have a fever. I feel like complete and utter shit, because I have whooping cough. Seriously, whooping cough. The strange thing about whooping cough (aside from the *w* being silent) is that once you realize you have whooping cough there is nothing that can be done for you. Zero. You're not contagious anymore and all you can do is wait for the symptoms to disappear. My cough is debilitating and appears without warning. One moment I feel blissfully healthy, the next I'm doubled over in pain, coughing up a storm, convinced that at any moment my lung is going to come flying out of my mouth. As if my team's collapse weren't bad enough, now I've got a communicable disease that was deadly in the 19th century. Pretty soon I'm going to have a nasty case of smallpox mixed with cholera. If you'd told me before the season that Tennessee would be 2-4 and I'd have whooping cough, I'd have bet my house and car to the contrary. But it's true; my world is crumbling.

And when you're sick and your team is bad, this means you feel 10,000 percent worse than normal. This is a scientific fact, proven by dozens of reputable scientific research laboratories. Such as the Clay Travis Center for Feeling Shitty When Your Team Sucks Laboratory.

The game is kicking off at 7 P.M. Fox is dressed in his UT orange outfit and we're carrying him in our brown Baby Bjorn. The Baby Bjorn was invented by Swedish people who are so industrious they believe that they should carry a baby and whittle a harpsichord out of tree bark at the same time. Consequently Fox is facing forward as we walk down University Avenue. Everyone wants to stop and say hello to him, even people who are clearly going to spend the rest of their lives in hell because they are completely evil, such as the two Alabama fans whom we pass on the street, enemy combatants who've arrived in Knoxville a week early. Fox grins at everyone. At the intersection of James Agee Drive and Phillip Fulmer Way, we take a left. We're en route to Brock and Amy Lodge's tailgate.

In 1993 Brock Lodge was a male cheerleader for the University of Tennessee. He stood on the sideline at the UT-Alabama game and watched as Alabama's David Palmer lined up under center to attempt a game-tying 2-point conversion in Birmingham. UT led #2 Alabama, the defending national champion, 17–15. The Vols had not won in the series since 1985. Every single UT fan knew what was coming next: The football gnat known as David Palmer was going to take the snap and attempt to score by running the ball. Everyone, that is, except for the UT defense.

As the ball was snapped Palmer ran right—racing toward the UT cheerleaders in that corner of the field. I was 14 years old at the time, sitting in an upstairs loft of my grandfather's West Tennessee farmhouse near Hohenwald with my cousin Steve—a UT graduate—and my dad. We were all gathered around a small black-and-white television with an antenna climbing toward the ceiling. We were sitting on a ratty green-and-white couch, all crouched forward as closely as we could to the flickering screen. Occasionally our signal would disappear for an instant and my dad would spring forward and adjust the antenna. As Alabama scored to tie the game, the three of us exhaled in anger.

"Well, shit," said my dad. It was one of the few times in my life I would ever hear him curse. "Unbelievable," said my cousin Steve.

Me? I didn't even know what to say. I'd never been more devastated by a tie in my life. Which put me in the same camp as a male cheerleader at UT I did not then know but would later befriend. Brock Lodge was speechless on the sideline. "For a long time," says Lodge, a cherubic-faced man of 36, "I've wondered what would have happened if I'd come onto the field and tackled him. I could see him so well, he would have never seen me coming."

He slaps his hands together to simulate the longed-for contact. Brock Lodge, UT cheerleader, has still not escaped that autumn day in Birmingham. "Later I looked up the rules to see what would have happened," he tells me. "They would have probably rewarded him the score. Refs can do that."

Lodge is good friends with Brad Lampley, a top-rated guard from Louisville who played on UT's football team from 1993 to 1997 and later experienced his proudest moment as a father when he moved his son Jackson's Florida Gators pennant to above the pooper. Brock and Lampley often travel to games together. Occasionally (often) Brock pretends to have been a former Vol offensive lineman as well. Brock is 5' 9" and 190 pounds. "You don't remember me?" he'll ask. "I was the pulling guard."

Then he'll lean over and pantomime a block.

"You must have been quick," a Vol fan will say.

"I was quick," Brock will respond.

"Oh, hell yeah, I remember you," the Vol fan will say.

Now Brock Lodge sells rocks for a Birmingham-based company, Vulcan, and is hosting my family and me for a tailgate in the parking lot across the street from Phillip Fulmer Way. Neyland Stadium looms in the afternoon sunlight across from us.

"I'll be honest, Clay, I'm thinking about staying out here for the tailgate tonight," Brock says.

Brock is not alone in being pessimistic about the outcome of tonight's game. The primary topic of fans' conversations this evening can be summed up in four words: "Will this do it?" If UT loses this game, will this be the final nail in Fulmer's coffin? Fulmer's haters have been emboldened by the 2-4 start. By the woeful offensive performances put forth against UCLA, Florida, Auburn, and Georgia, and the 13 pathetic points that UT scored 2 weeks ago against lowly Northern Illinois of the MAC conference.

My 8-month-old son, Fox, has no clue that his first UT football game is a deathwatch. Instead, he's attempting to take the beer out of my hand and dancing on a curb behind fold-out chairs. He's not yet old enough to sample the finer delicacies at Brock's tailgate, but he is already a fan of certain other finer culinary delicacies. Such as leaves. Last week he yanked a leaf off a passing tree and tried to eat it before I noticed. My wife turned in time to see Fox throwing up the leaf and me attempting to catch his puke.

She was not pleased with me.

Now Fox is trying to eat some leaves again. But I'm on to his game. To distract him, I remind him that he was named for his great-grandpa who played on the field that we'll see tonight and that it will be loud and crazy and exciting in the stadium. Fox nods contemplatively.

"Pffffff," he says.

This is one of Fox's favorite words. Another is a motorboating sound that does not lend itself well to the page. Lara comes to take charge of Fox, and I join Brock beside his tan SUV, where he's adjusting the playlist on his speaker system. The list is varied, including tunes from Johnny Cash to Skee-Lo.

"Is the megaphone here?" I ask.

Lodge switches to Journey's "Don't Stop Believing." "You know it," he says.

We walk over to the ample spread of food, which features Chick-fil-A chicken, deviled eggs, cookies covered in UT orange-and-white frosting, barbecue, and everything else a Southern man might want to eat. Brock leans down underneath one of the tables and stands up, holding the white megaphone from his cheerleading days at UT.

Other than a bloodstain from a tailgating injury before the Georgia game in 2005, the megaphone looks just as it did in the early 1990s when Brock Lodge prowled the Tennessee sideline. In 2005 Lodge cut his hand while moving a tailgating tent and the megaphone caught his blood. He thought the blood added character to the megaphone and never tried to remove it. Now Lodge lifts the bloodstained megaphone and points it in my direction. "Go Vols," he says into the hole.

Then he lowers the megaphone.

In addition to the bloodstains, the megaphone features a signature that reads, HEATH SHULER #21. For Vol fans of a certain age, and I'm one of them, Heath Shuler, a rocket-armed quarterback from the tiny town of Bryson City, North Carolina, is still a god. So seeing Brock's megaphone in conjunction with Shuler's signature carries with it an almost totemic power.

I vividly remember showing up at my dad's office after school one January day in the winter of 1994. I rode the city bus to downtown Nashville and walked up to Nashville's L&C Tower each day, up five flights of stairs to my dad's cubicle. I'd sit at a table there and do homework, or my dad would take a break and we'd go up to the 17th floor and have a snack while we looked out over the city. On this particular day, we were debating whether Heath Shuler would leave school a year early or return for his senior year. In the previous year, his junior season, Shuler finished second in the Heisman voting and many Vol fans held out hope that Shuler would return and become the first Tennessee player ever to win the Heisman Trophy.

My dad said, "Well, you know, Shuler just looks like a Greek god."

My dad's co-worker, a fellow Vol fan, said, "A what?"

As it turned out, Shuler went pro a year early and embarked on a state autograph tour that winter. He came to my local mall, Rivergate, and charged $14, a princely sum, for his signature. "Fourteen dollars!" my dad gushed when he read the ad for the event. "Fourteen dollars is a lot of money!" Even for a Greek god, evidently. Dad made sure to convey his disappointment—we were 10 minutes late for the autograph session.

That March day in 1994, my dad and I dutifully stood in line with hundreds of other Tennessee fans and waited for our opportunity to reach Shuler. His table was in the center of the mall, the same place where Santa had set up shop a couple of months earlier. Now the crowd was even larger. As we stood in line I thought of all the interesting things I might tell Heath Shuler. Maybe I'd mention the biographical speech I gave at Nashville's Martin Luther King Jr. High School about him. My speech focused on his dad being a mailman and his winning three state championships in North Carolina, but I'd use these details as a vehicle to convey how much I'd read about him. Surely no one else knew the Shuler biography as well as I did, and he'd be stunned. "I've never met a truer fan," Schuler might say, beaming up at me as he signed my glossy 8 x 10, whose purchase price was an additional $10. I also thought about telling Shuler that I planned to become a fan of whichever NFL team drafted him. Instead, when the moment finally arrived and I stood before my idol, I said nothing at all. For the first time in my life I was completely starstruck. I simply smiled for a picture. Looking at it today, I notice that my smile is genuine, ebullient. Shuler looks distracted as if he wasn't sure which of the cameras he should be looking at; the dimples in his cheeks are strained.

Fourteen years later, I hold the Heath Shuler–signed megaphone in my hand. The sun breaks out and shines on the tailgate. For a moment, in the late-afternoon sunshine, I allow myself to relive the magical glory days of UT in the 1990s. I feel a bit like Moses looking over into the Promised Land of Vol SEC dominance. We'll never be there together again, we fans. I hand the megaphone back to Brock, who cradles it in his arms like a baby. Now Heath Shuler, just 37 years old, is North Carolina's congressman from the 11th Congressional District. He played only four seasons in the NFL and retired at the age of 26. But to a certain generation of Vol fans, myself among them, Heath Shuler will always be a Vol, the perfect quarterback link to Peyton Manning and a decade of dominance.

In his suburban brick house outside Knoxville, Brock Lodge has two prized possessions: one is the Heath Shuler–autographed megaphone, the other is the final ball used in the UT-Alabama game in 1995, when Peyton Manning finally vanquished the Crimson Tide and led the Vols to a 41–14 road victory. The victory was sweet redemption from 2 years earlier when he'd almost tackled David Palmer on the 2-point conversion play. Lodge scooped up the ball and hid it inside his megaphone as soon as the game ended. Manning has since signed the football, which looks old and shrunken now.

Last year before the Georgia game, a contest the Vols won 35–14, Brock broke out the megaphone and used it to cheer on the band because he didn't think they were showing enough energy. Today, he's more circumspect.

"I think it's time for a change," he says.

Brock's wife, Amy, who recently had their second child, earlier admitted to me that the biggest hindrance to her marrying Brock was the male cheerleader angle. "I was like, he's a what?" Now the UT grads live in bliss outside Knoxville. Except for when it comes to the megaphone. "That megaphone," she says, rolling her eyes, "he wanted to put it on the mantle in our house."

The sun is beginning to set, and as we stand at the tailgate a Mississippi State fan pulls me aside. "I don't know if y'all are going to lose, but I know we're both bad football teams." We clang beers, the mutual sign of fan resignation.

Everyone wants to know what the mood of the team is and what I think is going to happen. I tell them I have no clue, that divining the mood of a football team with 100 players is almost as hard as divining the mood of an introduction to biology class. As fans we have a way of projecting one emotion onto an entire team, which is often artificial. Players, like each of us, are all unique in the ways they handle their wins and losses, their small victories and their small defeats.

I confess to Brock that I'm feeling really sick.

"At least you're not Dave Clawson," he says.

Lara scoops up Fox and we head across the street, tickets in hand. For the first time in my life, I'm a dad taking my son to a UT football game. I'd be lying if I said I didn't feel a swell of pride in my chest. Twenty-three years after my own first game, I'm back with another generation. This pride lasts until we reach the ticket-taker.

Fox is 8 months old and riding on his mother's chest, tiny orange legs dangling out in front of him. The ticket-taker accepts our two tickets but puts his hand across the entrance in front of me.

"Do you have one for him?" he asks.

No, I don't. Because it had never occurred to me that an infant might need a ticket. Previously Fox has been on airline flights and attended a Tennessee Titan football game without tickets. If airlines and the NFL, two of the most money-grubbing entities to ever exist in the capitalist era, allow infants free passage, why doesn't Tennessee?

The ticket-taker, a kind man with glasses and a dark mustache, grabs me by the arm. "I'll get him in," he says, looking both ways to make sure the coast is clear. Then he reaches into his apron and tears a ticket. "You're good," he says, waving us into the stadium.

Fox, Lara, and I walk down the aisle and then outside into the lower concourse of Neyland Stadium. Night games in Neyland are special, and Fox is amazed at the spectacle. He motorboats his lips in delight. The lights glisten on the bright white helmets, power T's shimmering in the light. We climb up to our seats and sit down, but Fox doesn't want to be still. He rapidly makes friends with an elderly woman behind us and with a blond woman next to us with three blond sons. "We brought him when he was nine weeks old," she says, gesturing to the 5-year-old on her lap. On my lap Fox squints up at the lights bathing the green field in light as bright as day. He kicks his feet and grins.

But not everyone is delighted by the prospect of a night game. As kickoff nears, Neyland Stadium hosts fewer fans than I've ever seen. The end zone beneath the scoreboard is nearly empty. Tons of student seats remain unfilled. Most ominously, many of the expensive donor seats around us are empty as well. It appears that Vol fans are beginning to send a message about their opinion of Phil Fulmer by not showing up for the game. Befitting the poor fan attendance, UT begins the game slowly.

Watching a game with an infant presents its own unique challenges. For instance, you sometimes make happy faces even when your team is doing badly. Other times you can't stand up for a big play because you are feeding him a bottle. I'd like to say that I care less about the outcome of the game because of the added maturity brought on by having a child in my lap, but I don't. I care just as much.

Mississippi State completes their first four pass attempts, but other than that nothing very impressive takes place on the field tonight. Two bad teams are throwing tentative jabs at each other. The entire first quarter is scoreless.

Early in the second quarter UT kicks a field goal to go up 3–0. It's October 18. Half of the football season is now over, and this field goal is UT's first *lead* of the SEC season.

Later on Mississippi State answers with a field goal to tie the score. But UT closes out the scoring with what qualifies as an offensive on-slaught, another field goal, with 1:09 left in the second quarter. The score is 6–3 at the half.

As the UT band plays at halftime, I hold my son in my lap and think about how special the threads of life can be. My grandfather, Richard

K. Fox, was born in a July summer in 1913 and grew up to play football in Tennessee under General Neyland. Ninety-five years later, his great-grandson, born 14 years after he died and named in his honor, is watching a football game on the same field and inside the same stadium. I realize how impermanent the actual games are. They're going to come and go and we'll win some and lose others, but what endures is the generational connection, something that is distinctively Southern: a college football game in fall.

I find myself fantasizing about Fox having a son one day and then about that son having a son and what Tennessee's stadium and this beloved football team might look like 95 years from now. I am moved by the sense that something is immutable about the game. Come what may in the world at large, football will return every fall. When you're a fan, seasons are timeless and no single season stands alone. As we watch a game, we're young and we're old and we're with the people who are still with us and we're with the people who will never be with us again. When a ball rises into the air on a football Saturday, a game is about to take place on the field, but we're all experiencing every game we've ever seen in our minds. And we're sharing them with everyone we've ever shared a game with in the past.

So, right now, I like to think that I'm Fox's link to a man he'll never know whose name he shares. A man who played football in a leather helmet, wore an orange sweater jersey, and lived in a dorm in Neyland Stadium. Fox will not remember this game, but when he gets older he might read this. And at first he'll be too young to know what exactly his daddy means, and he'll probably be mad because Tennessee just lost to Florida in 2018. But, I think, as he gets older, he'll come to know and feel exactly what I mean. We come to watch college football games and root for our teams not because we need to see them win but because it's part of who we are. In the South, college football is in our blood.

Back on the field the second half is as close to sublime as UT's season has been thus far. On their opening drive of the second half, the Vols score a touchdown to go up 13–3. For the first time all season Neyland Stadium comes alive with that old-time feel, dominance and swagger and excitement all mixed with a fervent fan roar. The sky above the stadium is alight with bright yellow fireworks.

For an entire quarter the two teams trade possessions until, with 10 minutes left in the fourth quarter, sophomore safety Eric Berry, the son of James Berry, a former running back for the Johnny Majors–era Vols, picks off a deflected pass and returns it 72 yards for a touchdown. Just like that, the Vols are leading 20–3 and Berry is the all-time SEC leader in interception return yardage. I jump up and down a bit and Fox lets go of his bottle, screws his eyes open, and looks quizzically at his dad. Then he's back asleep, dead to the world as all of Neyland Stadium rocks around him.

Not quite 2 minutes later Demetrice Morley, who lived in his car for part of last season after being booted off the football team for academic ineligibility, returns his own interception for a touchdown and UT leads 27–3. For one night at least, all is well on Rocky Top.

My family and I exit the stadium before the final whistle blows. I've never left a Tennessee game early, but I've also never had a sleeping baby with me, and I feel confident of the outcome. We arrive at our car in time to hear the final few minutes of the game on the radio. While we drive Tennessee tacks on a late rushing touchdown to go up 34–3. An old-fashioned SEC rout! I want to party like it's 1998. My heart soars with pride and relief as we drive through the Tennessee darkness in near silence.

UT is now 3-4. Alabama week is here and the Vols have a chance to win and erase much of the pain and frustration of the first part of the season. I'm buoyant with optimism. One win can do this to any fan. This is not a bad football team after all, I think. Phil Fulmer is not finished yet. No, he's going to finish out the season 8-4. I'm certain of it.

Somewhere outside of Cookeville my wife looks up and catches me smiling in the passing lights of a car.

"Why are you so happy?" she asks.

"Because," I say, "the Vols are going to beat Alabama by double digits next week."

CHAPTER 15

THE CHARGE OF
THE BOOSTER BRIGADE

IN THE WAKE OF THE NEWSPAPER interview where he discussed firing Fulmer, John "Thunder" Thornton, a multimillionaire booster and best friend of Phil Fulmer whom ESPN has called one of the most powerful boosters in the nation, is furious with Mike Hamilton. "Un-fucking-believable," he says. "Why would he do that? Why answer questions like that?" Thornton continues, "This is a minority view, but I believe Mike Hamilton wants to be known as the greatest AD in the country. He's full of blind ambition. I love Bruce Pearl [the men's basketball coach], I think he's great, but I think hiring him is the worst thing that ever happened to Mike Hamilton. He wants to swing for the fences on every hire now. His blind ambition is driving him."

As the booster war intensifies over the future of Phil Fulmer at Tennessee, there is no one more firmly ensconced in the Fulmer camp than Thornton. Born in Maryville, a little more than 1.5 miles from where Fulmer would eventually settle with his family, Thornton didn't attend Tennessee but grew up a rabid Vol fan. "We'd all get together and listen to games on the radio. I'd go to games with a neighbor, Mr. Badgett."

Thornton graduated from Tennessee-Wesleyan in 1975. "I don't think I could have gotten into Tennessee: I didn't take a foreign language in high school and I was never that interested of a student. And if I had gotten in, I'm not sure I'd have ever gotten out if I had the Strip to contend with," he says. Thornton, a businessman who sold his carpet and rug manufacturing company for $100 million in 1993 and has since made tens of millions more through real estate and a variety of other business dealings, gave his first donation to Tennessee athletics in 1991. A year later he met Coach Fulmer.

"Coach Fulmer took me to the indoor football practice facility and said, 'John, I want you to look at all these students trying to study in here.' There were forty or fifty football players all scrunched up with books and things, baseball players and cheerleaders were trying to practice in there at the same time. Then Phillip took me up to an old dingy tutor room that was dimly lit and just awful. He said, 'We need to do better for these kids.' I committed a million dollars on the spot." As a result Tennessee built the Thornton Athletics Student Life Center to ensure that athletes received individualized attention with their studies and the best tutors possible. The next year Thornton received a note from the women's volleyball coach explaining that the team GPA rose from 3.3 to 3.6. He gave Thunder credit for the improvement. "I never was worth a damn as a student, I played a lot," says Thornton. "I just appreciate Phillip giving me the opportunity to help out."

Thornton, a brown-haired man with a quick smile, frequent joke, affable manner, and unforgettable nickname, declines to explain how he got the nickname "Thunder" in college. "It involves five girls, a lot of oil . . . I really don't want to share this with an author." When he hears Thornton's "explanation," Fulmer cuts in immediately. "Five girls? You don't even know five girls," he quips.

In 1993 Thornton purchased an old limousine, painted it orange and white, and drove to all home football games in the vehicle. "It only cost us about five thousand dollars and we did it kind of as a joke. But we won all the games when we rode up there in the limo. That offseason,

I told Phillip about it, and he looked at me and said, 'Thunder, you've got to drive out to UCLA. We open out there.' So I went back to my mechanic and I said, 'You think that limo will make it to California?' He said, 'Hell, that thing won't make it to the Mississippi River.' So we ordered a brand-new one from Lincoln, got it painted orange and white, and drove it out to UCLA."

The trip in the brand-new $55,000 limo took Thunder and two friends, Larry Johnston and Danny Mizell, 13 days. The three men drove themselves; Mizell and Thunder took the wheel until 3:30 or 4 in the afternoon, when they retired to the back of the limo to drink. "Larry didn't drink, so the two of us would drive in the morning and then drink in the evening," says Thornton. Along the way Mizell invented a new sport, limo surfing. "He'd open the sun roof and climb out the limo, then he'd brace himself like he was surfing in the wind."

The trio stopped in Jackson Hole, Wyoming, where they held a UCLA-Tennessee tailgate party at the Stagecoach Bar. They announced on local radio that anyone who wore orange drank beer for free. The bar was slammed with newly found Tennessee fans. "There were guys wearing orange life preservers inside," Thorton says. "That was a hell of a party."

The three men also toured famous sites, such as the Crazy Horse Memorial in the Black Hills of South Dakota. Pulling up in the Tennessee limo, they quickly attracted a crowd. "Whose limo is that?" the crowd clamored. "That is Wild Moose," Thunder said, gesturing to Mizell, "the great-great-great-great-grandson of Crazy Horse." At other stops along the way they claimed to be ferrying Tennessee's governor Ned Ray McWherter and country music singer Charlie Daniels.

Thornton now lives on a palatial 10-acre Chattanooga estate (nicknamed the "Thunderdome" by friends) with five children, a wife, and eight dogs—one of them a sister of Smokey the mascot, named Smokey as well. He's served as a trustee of the university and on many committees, including the committee that recommended Mike Hamilton as Tennessee's athletic director. Initially Thunder was a supporter of Hamilton's candidacy, having worked alongside him for 5 years as part of a major fund-raising initiative. Hamilton's selection took longer than Thornton thought was wise.

On the day of his daughter's graduation in 2003, Thunder and another major Tennessee booster, Jim Haslam, visited the home of then-university president John Shoemaker. "We sat down out on the back porch and said, 'Look, it's time to hire Mike. The committee has made their recommendation [endorsing Hamilton] and this thing [the search] is dragging on too long and making us all look bad.'" According to Thornton, Shoemaker was hesitant to act because he wanted a "big-name hire," someone with more name recognition than Hamilton, who had worked under the retiring athletic director, Doug Dickey, for 11 years. Thornton and Haslam were adamant that now was the time to make the announcement.

Shoemaker demurred. "Well, I leave for Jamaica at five," he said.

"Fine, then," Thunder said, "we can make the announcement here at two. We'll have the press conference on the front porch."

Shoemaker finally relented. "Fine then, I'll do it. I don't like it, but I'll do it."

With the wheels of the hire in motion, the committee located Hamilton in Gatlinburg and rushed him back to Knoxville. Later that day he was introduced as the next athletic director of Tennessee.

Now Thunder is leery of the man whose promotion he helped to facilitate. "He hasn't been supportive enough of Phillip," Thornton says. In addition to this fact, Hamilton and Thornton have also had a falling-out over Hamilton's selection of a new tennis coach in 2006. (Thornton's son played on the tennis team at the time, and the family supported another candidate.) Since late 2006, the two men have had limited contact. But in the summer of 2008, while his family vacationed with Fulmer's family in Hawaii, Thornton called Mike Hamilton to congratulate him on the statements he made when Fulmer's contract extension was announced. "I told him he did a fabulous job handling that. He said, 'I appreciate that, John, why don't you let me take you out to lunch?'" Thornton accepted Hamilton's offer.

But no lunch invitation ever arrived from Hamilton.

So far this season, Thunder has contacted Hamilton only twice, both times via e-mail to point out issues with difficulties leaving the club seats after games. He's heard rumblings from boosters who don't support Fulmer, but he knows everyone is aware of his allegiance to Coach Fulmer. "When you got a guy like Phillip, you fight for him," he says.

He believes that Mike Hamilton wants to fire Phil Fulmer and that there are only two people who can stop Hamilton from making that decision: university president John Petersen and major booster Jim Haslam. Thunder doesn't believe it's right for a booster such as Haslam to stand in the way of a firing. "No matter how much money you give, you shouldn't have the right to pick a coach." On the other hand, he believes President Petersen should protect Fulmer. But Petersen has told Thornton he believes in deferring to his athletic director. "He told me, 'I hire people and I don't micromanage them.' I said, 'Telling people how much money they sell Cokes for at the stadium is micromanaging, hiring or firing a damn football coach isn't micromanaging.'"

MANY OTHER MAJOR BOOSTERS feel differently than Thunder Thornton and are receptive to the argument that it is appropriate to discuss Coach Fulmer's tenure at Tennessee. Among these men is Bill Stokely III, a 68-year-old fourth-generation Vol graduate, whose family funded the since-replaced basketball arena on campus, the Stokely Athletic Center. Now Mike Hamilton's office is in Stokely Center.

Bill Stokely's ties to Tennessee football trace back to his own grandfather, William B. Stokely Sr., who was captain of the 1894 Tennessee football team. That Stokely was a senior transfer from Wake Forest. He captained the football team to two wins and two ties after the university disbanded the team at the close of the 1893 season. The 1893 team, which lost its first four games by a combined score of 250–0, was the final official team until 1896. In announcing their decision to disband the football team, university officials asserted they "wanted to put emphasis on academics." Consequently, the university does not acknowledge 1894's 2-0-2 record or 1895's 3-2-1 record.

By the time William B. Stokely Sr.'s grandson, Bill Stokely III, arrived on campus, Tennessee football, officially readopted in 1896, was flourishing. Bill Stokely played 3 years of football at Tennessee, finishing in the early 1960s. Asked his position, he responds, "Mostly hurt. I tell people I helped the single wing die." Stokely's lifelong involvement with the university continued after football, and in the early 1970s he chaired a fund-raising committee for the business school. The goal was $3 million. Says Stokely now, "It was like pulling chickens' teeth. No one asked for money like that before. You took it if people gave it to you, but no one asked." Since that initial effort at fund-raising Stokely has been intimately involved in fund-raising campaigns with goals of $250 and $400 million. Currently Tennessee is in the midst of a new fund-raising effort. Officially launched on April 17, 2008, the Campaign for Tennessee seeks to raise $1 billion for the university. Stokely's family foundation gave the first large donation, a $2.5 million bequest, on April 25. Stokely is the chair emeritus of the newest campaign.

A lifelong Tennessee football fan, Stokely likes Phil Fulmer personally. "I consider him a friend," he says, "and I have great respect for his body of work and record as head coach." However, Stokely believes Fulmer "took us to the mountaintop, but hasn't been able to keep us there." When asked a question that suggests Fulmer's problems mostly relate to the current season's failures, Stokely disputes this characterization. "Oh, no," he says, "I think the problems began in 1999, the year after we won the national championship. We returned all of our talent from 1998, and we didn't have a very good year [the Vols finished 9-3 with two SEC losses by a combined 6 points]. People quickly got upset." Indeed, Stokely believes that in retrospect, the 1998 national championship was a close call. "People forget we had five games go into the final five minutes," he says. "We had a lot of great luck that year."

Stokely believes the program's decline can be attributed to two factors: one, not enough talent, and two, other coaches and teams getting better. "We used to put eight, ten, thirteen guys in the NFL each year, now we're putting one, two, or three." He also feels that Fulmer has such a personal relationship with many of his coaches that he isn't adequately judging them. Stokely believes that of late the program's dominance has been nonexistent. "We're struggling against the Vandys and Kentuckys of the world, teams we've traditionally dominated."

"Fulmer has had plenty of time to make changes and turn the boat around," Stokely says, "but it's hard to do it if you don't realize the boat is askew. I think he's in denial; he's proud and smart, but if you don't think the program's in decline then you can't get things fixed."

Last season Stokely traveled to California for the opening game against the University of California at Berkeley and was unimpressed by what he saw. "We played an awful game. We were fat, sloppy, and uninspired. Punting to the best punt returner in the country? We played a soft defense and they threw under us all day. Right there out of the box, we were a long way from being a good ball club." He saw echoes of this poor performance this year at UCLA. "It was the same ole, same ole, the kids were just inept. We even had poor line play. Phil's forte is the offensive line; well, you've got a team that couldn't pick up a first down."

In the wake of the Georgia loss, Stokely has no confidence in the team's ability to turn things around. But he says he has not advocated Fulmer's firing and never got a call asking his opinion of whether Fulmer should be kept or replaced. Stokely also says he doesn't know of anyone who's called Hamilton and demanded Fulmer's firing. Instead Stokely offers his own hypothetical, "Had I been asked, I would evidence my distress over the state of affairs, and how it didn't look like we were making any forward progress." In Stokely's mind the key question to ask in regard to any coach is: "Are we fielding a competitive team?" He believes the answer regarding Tennessee is no.

While they don't have regular conversations, Stokely trusts Hamilton's ability to make the correct decision. "I believe he's consulting with the right people, probably twenty to thirty major boosters that he really needs to talk with." Asked whether he believes, as Thunder Thornton suggests, that Mike Hamilton is fueled by blind ambition, Stokely laughs softly. "No. Without debate, no, I don't believe that's the case."

Asked whether it matters if the Tennessee football team is coached by a Tennessean, Stokely, a fourth-generation Vol grad, says, "I don't think a smart coach is credentialed by his home state. I think you get a cushion because you are a homegrown boy. It's a national game, and you go wherever you need to go to get a winner. If the team is not winning, then it affects the perception of its alumni, its donors, and its entire constituency. I have been assisting the university in raising donations for many decades and I once told Dr. Ed Boling, past president of UT, give me a winning football team and doors open and wallets open and we can raise significant monies for the university."

Stokely acknowledges that every fan only sees one part of the story, but he believes he's seen enough to make a determination. "There are so many little things that go wrong. When all the fans can tell you what the next play is going to be, something's wrong."

CHAPTER 16

THE FOURTH SATURDAY IN OCTOBER

IT'S ALABAMA WEEK, AND IF Phil Fulmer wants to keep his job he needs the football to bounce his way.

On the Friday before the Alabama game, the University of Tennessee hosts the Perfection Gala for the 1998 national championship team at the Tennessee Theatre in downtown Knoxville. The party is the culmination of the season-long campaign to honor the 10th anniversary of Tennessee's 23–16 victory over Florida State. To accompany me I've brought one of my college roommates, Shekhar Kodali, who grew up in Connecticut wanting to be an astronaut.

The two of us enter the Tennessee Theatre, one of the oldest movie theaters in the state, originally built in 1927, and almost immediately run into Al Wilson, the starting linebacker on the 1998 national championship team. Wilson has just retired after a nine-year NFL career with the Denver Broncos. Drafted in 1999's first round, Wilson, a dark-skinned glowering menace of a man who looks much older than his 31 years, made five Pro Bowls playing middle linebacker for the Broncos.

"He's really not that big," says an unimpressed Shekhar of the 6', 240-pound Wilson.

UT-Alabama will be Shekhar's second game at Neyland Stadium. His first came when we were both sophomores in college and traveled down from Washington, D.C., for the UT-Georgia game. On that occasion we tried to sneak Shekhar, a 6' 2", dark-skinned, brown-eyed Indian man, into the stadium using a high school friend's UT student ID. This friend was 5' 2", blond, and female.

"All you have to do is look like you know what you're doing when you swipe the ID," my friend Jennifer Knight instructed him as we sat drinking beers in her off-campus house.

Shekhar nodded gamely. When the moment of truth arrived, Shekhar walked up to the entrance and accidentally swiped the card in the wrong direction—not once, but twice. An old white man with spectacles approached him and asked to see his student ID. Shekhar handed it over. The man scrutinized the blond, blue-eyed girl on the picture ID, looked back up at Shekhar, looked at the picture again, and then said, "Is this really your ID?"

"Yes," Shekhar said.

The man didn't let him in, and he had to buy a ticket outside the stadium. He sat in the top row of the stadium by himself and cursed me throughout the game. Jennifer was not pleased to find out that her ID had been confiscated. "He didn't look like he knew what he was doing, did he?"

Nine years later Shekhar makes a triumphant return to Knoxville. Then he was a baby-faced 20-year-old, now he's a grown-up 29—with the goatee to prove it. He's rocking the goatee to complement his Captain Jack Sparrow costume for Halloween. As a result he looks vaguely like an Indian man from 1975. (Full confession: For one semester in 1998 I had a goatee. I didn't shave it off until I was hired to work at Abercrombie & Fitch. They, much like the New York Yankees, had a no-facial-hair policy. As soon as I was fired for insurbordination, I grew back my goatee.)

When my friend Tardio arrives later that night he will have great fun with Shekhar's goatee. "Did you know," Tardio asks, "that if you get five men with goatees in the same bar you time-travel back to 1992?" But until then Shekhar gets to spend the evening hanging out with UT fans celebrating their championship from a decade ago.

The 1998 Volunteer football team, with nary a goatee in sight, is in the lobby of the theater swarmed by UT fans. Grown men clutch footballs close to their orange-clad chests and chase after linebacker Al Wilson, wide receiver Peerless Price, kicker Jeff Hall, defensive tackle Billy Ratliff, and other former greats as if their eternal fan salvation depended upon obtaining the men's autographs. Lines form as players stop to sign footballs, photos, and other paraphernalia. Every fan I see is smiling. We've all stepped onto a magic carpet ride to 1998—when our football team didn't lose and our biggest concern was whether computers would work when the magical and mysterious year 2000 arrived.

The theater is not sold out, but the crowd is boisterous enough to make it feel like a sellout. Before anyone is introduced, the UT marching band comes stomping down the aisle, past rows and rows of seated Vol fans, and plays "Rocky Top." Shekhar is surprised. "They brought the band here?" he asks.

Indeed they have. When Vol fans pay $50 a head, they expect the full accompaniment of Volunteer fandom. Thirteen hundred Tennessee fans, from ages 8 to 80, stand and sing along in the theater.

UT athletic director Mike Hamilton, wearing a suit and an orange tie, strides out onto the stage after the band finishes its rousing serenade. For one night at least, he does not seem stressed about the coaching situation in Knoxville. Hamilton welcomes everyone. "Tonight is a special night," he says, and then Phil Fulmer, Al Wilson, Peerless Price, Billy Ratliff, Jeff Hall, and legendary Vol announcer John Ward emerge to applause and sit on stools facing the Vol faithful. The current radio announcer for the Vols, Bob Kesling, asks each man questions about the 1998 season.

Kesling asks Fulmer what he remembers of the first game that season, the Vols' road opener at Syracuse. "I remember Al could never catch Donovan McNabb," says Fulmer to much laughter. Fulmer, wearing a dark suit and an orange tie, seems relaxed sitting on the stool at the front of the stage. His legs hang loosely just above the wood floor, he's quick to laugh, and his national championship ring sparkles in the bright lights of the stage. For an evening he's relieved of the albatross of the Vols' 3-4 record this season. He's just won an SEC game, and he's here to relive his—and every other Vol fan's—glory days.

A few moments later former Vol announcer John Ward brings down the house when he's asked about the memorable pass interference call that allowed the Vols to kick a game-winning field goal on the final play of the Syracuse game. "Great acting job," he deadpans.

Now a hawk-faced man with silver hair, Ward began broadcasting games for UT football in 1968, and his final season calling games was 1998. Along the way he became a Tennessee icon. Vol fans recognize him all over the world. Once, as he took a seat beside his wife on the Orient Express, a man walked past in the aisle. "Bottom!" he said, referring to Ward's signature call for a made basket by the Tennessee men's basketball team.

With his distinctive cadence and mastery of the English language, John Ward is the Shakespeare of Tennessee football. Prior to the 1998 season, Tennessee held a press conference to announce this would be his final season calling games. Ward, ever succinct, approached the microphone and stood before the assembled media. "I have a prepared statement, and I'm going to read it," he said. "It's time."

Then he sat down.

The final football game he ever called capped off the perfect 13-0 season, the Vols' national championship triumph in the Fiesta Bowl on January 4, 1999. Even 10 years later, Ward, who called games from the football press box with a blue towel draped around his neck, still possesses a perfect rhythm and timing to capture the ears of listeners everywhere. When asked about Billy Ratliff's huge play against Arkansas—which caused Arkansas quarterback Clint Stoerner to fumble late in the fourth quarter—Ward pauses for a moment. Then he slowly unspools a single sentence that looks like nothing in print, but will ring true for any fan who ever listened to him call a game on the radio: "It was a great, great moment for Tennesseans, Ratliff." Later, responding to a question about what it was like calling the Tennessee–Florida State game, Ward's brevity touches the souls of Volunteer fans everywhere: "The moon is orange. This is Tennessee's night."

When I was a kid, my dad often turned off the television announcers during games and pulled the radio next to the television so we could listen to John Ward's broadcast instead. We'd sit in front of the television and John Ward's voice would describe the game to us from the radio. It was like watching the game on your great-uncle's knee.

Ten years after the fact, the perfect national championship season seems even more remarkable. Three of the first four games, victories over Syracuse, Florida, and Auburn, came down to the final play. Against Arkansas, Tennessee managed one of the most miraculous victories in SEC history. No SEC team since the Vols has finished a national championship season without a loss.

Later, I'll ask Fulmer to reflect on those close games in 1998 and what they meant to Tennessee. "Look at history since," he'll say. "Who has done it [had a perfect season and won the national championship] in our league? It's very hard. Your most talented team doesn't always do it. Our 2001 team was probably our best team, and we got upset in the championship game, but in this league, the great competition, the bull's-eye changes. When I came in it was Florida, then it was us, then Georgia, then us again, Florida again. Right now it's Florida for sure."

When the questions, comments, and the laughter they provoke have passed, the room goes dark for the debut of the *Perfection* DVD, a special 10-year anniversary recap of the magical season. The highlight DVD begins with plays and reminiscences from the opening game against Syracuse. In that game Jeff Hall, a native of Phil Fulmer's hometown, Winchester, Tennessee, drilled a 27-yard field goal on the final play of the game. Just before he trotted out to attempt the kick, Fulmer grabbed Hall's helmet. "Make Winchester proud!" Fulmer hollered.

As soon as Jeff Hall's game-winning 27-yard kick splits the uprights on screen, the Tennessee Theatre crowd cheers. Next come highlights from the Florida game. Even 10 years later, the crowd hisses when Steve Spurrier appears on the screen. And when Florida's Collins Cooper misses the overtime field goal attempt wide left to award the Vols the 20–17 win, a colossal roar of delight explodes in the theater. My joy is no less now than it was on that day.

I have to leave before the DVD finishes, because I'm meeting Arian Foster and his family. As I stand and walk down the aisle in the direction of the exits I see four grown men openly weeping, Southern men who have been raised to conceal their emotions wiping their eyes in the darkened theater. It's altogether possible these men might not cry in public for the rest of their lives. But now, in the darkness of a Tennessee theater, as they watch 10-year-old film of their team winning, they can't restrain themselves. And I know exactly how they feel.

AT KNOXVILLE'S CROWNE PLAZA HOTEL, a team that isn't winning is gathered in the dimly lit lobby. The UT players are visiting with their family members. Arian Foster, wearing orange pants and a gray T-shirt, is sitting on a couch in the corner of the hotel bar. Next to him on the couch sits his mother, Bernadette, and next to her is his girlfriend, Romina Lombardo, a dark-haired and dark-eyed 22-year-old native of Germany who has come to the United States to pursue her pop singing career, and his maternal grandmother, Lucy Maez, an attractive older Hispanic woman whose unlined face makes her appear much younger than she is. Arian's father, Carl, is sitting on a chair across from him.

"I don't want to talk about football at all," Arian says.

I can't blame him, given that last week against Georgia, Arian had just three carries for 3 yards. This was the fewest carries he'd received in a game in 2 years. His inaction against Georgia was particularly galling because in the two previous seasons he had scored a total of six touchdowns against them. Worst of all, Georgia was just the latest frustration in a season of incredible frustrations for Foster. Thus far this season, in six games, he's only carried the ball 68 times for 341 yards, which means he's on pace to rush for half as many yards as he did last season.

Arian's ascendance to the top of the all-time rushing record at Tennessee, which seemed a mere formality at the beginning of the season, is now uncertain. In 2008 Foster has yet to score a single touchdown. Last year he had 17.

Instead of talking about football, Arian is regaling the group with stories about one of his UT classes—a police procedural class where he has learned Spanish slang words in order to better communicate with those who are arrested. Bernadette, born in New Mexico and of Hispanic heritage, is horrified.

"That's racist," she says.

"You have to know how to talk to the criminals," he explains. "They all speak Spanish." His mother slaps him on the knee. "Arian!" she squeals. Arian is joking; he's already moved on and is waxing eloquent on a variety of subjects. Within 5 minutes he has danced the robot, discussed the upcoming presidential election—he supports Obama, but isn't sure much will change—made fun of Bernadette for having a bad sense of humor that rarely converges with his own, explained that he loves dating his German girlfriend, Romina, even though every time he thinks of Germany he thinks of Adolf Hitler, and expounded upon his philosophy of race relations in the South: "It's not as bad as people think it is down here. Except for old people; they're bad."

Meanwhile, Arian's grandmother, Lucy Maez, pulls me aside and tells me about growing up on a 7,000-acre ranch in New Mexico. "You can't imagine what it was like to have so much space," she says. "Now people buy the land and break it up into smaller parcels, and they are from the East Coast and have no idea about the land. One woman said to me, 'How do you landscape that many acres?'"

Arian has been dating Romina since they met in Atlanta through mutual friends. Arian and Tennessee offensive lineman Anthony Parker, a 6' 3", 300-pound senior from Jonesboro, Georgia, were arguing about whether man had ever landed on the moon. Parker, who took the position that man has never landed on the moon—he believes it was a Hollywood stunt—made a point that Foster didn't consider very persuasive.

Enter true love. "I heard this guy yelling 'Congratu-fucking-lations' really loud and I wondered who it was," says Romina. Arian, whose mother has been telling him to watch his language, exults. "See, Mom," he says, "cursing pays off."

Indeed. Romina, who had never heard a word conjunction like this before in her native Germany, is now pregnant with Foster's first child.

At 10:30 P.M., the room curfew arrives. It's time for the University of Tennessee players to return to their hotel rooms for the night.

"Come on, Arian," says Bernadette, "you've got to get up to your room."

Arian walks slowly across the hotel lobby. "What are they gonna do," he grumbles, "give me one carry a game instead of three?"

THE VOL WALK LEAVES at 5:30 P.M. on Saturday afternoon. Today is the fourth Saturday in October and the UT-Alabama game has traditionally been played on the third Saturday in October. But in some years, such as this one, the game is played on the fourth Saturday due to scheduling issues. Late-afternoon sunlight filters through the trees alongside the Neyland-Thompson Sports Complex. The players' black Adidas bags are laid out on the sidewalk, an anthill of equipment. A few student managers stand idly alongside them, chatting in the crisp autumn afternoon. The doors to the complex open and the players, wearing suits of many colors, file out and line up in the shade.

I'm standing next to Vol superstar Eric Berry, a future multimillionaire. Berry is listed at 6', 210 pounds, but he looks shorter. Yet Berry's reputation for bone-jarring tackles, amazing interceptions, and all-around playmaking is enough to make him seem larger than life. All week long fans have clamored for Berry to play on offense, for Berry to return kicks, for Berry to be immediately cloned in a Knoxville laboratory. Anything to beat Alabama.

Today Eric Berry is wearing a faded olive-green suit that appears older than he is. One of his teammates is standing next to him rubbing lotion onto his hands. The teammate drops the lotion bottle, and lotion squirts all over Berry's olive pants. "Man, I told you, you don't need any lotion before the game," Berry snaps, his light-brown eyes flashing in the afternoon shade.

After cleaning off his olive pants as best he can, Berry puts his iPod into his backpack. Berry's hands are cracked and his fingernails are uneven and jagged—the hands of a much older man. The screen on his iPod is cracked; a long tremulous crescent runs from top to bottom of the display. Soon he will set out on the Vol Walk to play his second career game against Alabama. Already he is a Volunteer football legend whom Tennessee fans will never forget. Eric Berry is 19 years old.

The sun is setting behind us, and as the first players step out onto the walkway their shadows fall forward. As the team begins the walk, fans hurl suggestions to beleaguered offensive coordinator Dave Clawson. "Let's see some Berry on O, Coach," calls one fan. Another yells, "Put in Berry at quarterback, Coach Clawson."

"Appreciate it," he says, looking the fans in the eyes.

The team comes to a stop on Lake Loudon Boulevard. Vicky Fulmer is giving her game-day hugs to all the players and coaches. After half a season, I'm no longer a stranger; she sees me and stretches out her arms. What can I do but step into her embrace? Soon 106,000 fans will watch Tennessee play Alabama, but right now, on the Vol Walk, Vicky Fulmer is the de facto team mom giving love and support. This isn't a famous football team; these are just her boys on their way to play Pop Warner football.

On down the road, Eric Berry stops to sign a large poster that reads BERRY 4 PRESIDENT. This Vol Walk is more intense, more claustrophobic than the UAB walk. Fans seem even more eager to touch the players than they did then, to pound their shoulders and to clasp their hands, as if, in so doing, they can reverse the course of the season. Toward the end of the walk, the team passes a wild-eyed man wearing orange overalls and a camouflage Tennessee baseball cap who repeats to every player who walks by, "Fuck the Crimson Tide, fuck 'em up good, boys."

The team proceeds down the corridor and into the locker room, where student managers walk around distributing hand sanitizer to those who wish to use it. Eric Berry, icon at age 19, takes the hand sanitizer and stands rubbing his hands together in front of his locker. As quickly as they've bathed in the adulation of the fans, now they wash away all traces of their supporters. It's 5:45 P.M. and in just 2 hours the Vols will kick off for ESPN's night game.

I sit down in a row of fold-out chairs where the players will soon sit to hear the final speech before the Alabama game begins. My own stomach is churning. I take deep breaths. It's UT-Alabama week once more, and this time, for probably the only time in my life, I'm going to see exactly what it's like in the moments leading up to the game. As if that weren't enough, soon I'll be running through the T with the team.

Phil Fulmer walks through the locker room with recruits, including quarterback phenom Tajh Boyd. Boyd is ranked one of the top 50 players in the country, a Virginia quarterback whom many of the best football programs in the country are pursuing. Recruiting, if nothing else, is going well for UT so far this season. Fulmer has already rounded up the number-seven recruiting class in the country and has 21 commitments for 2009. He hopes to add Boyd this weekend.

Over his 16-year tenure Tennessee's recruiting classes have been the best in the SEC, and Fulmer's brought in talented players from across the country, players who've gone on to be NFL all-pros such as Peyton Manning, Albert Haynesworth, Jamal Lewis, Jason Witten, John Henderson, Travis Henry, Peerless Price, Leonard Little, Donte Stallworth, Jerod Mayo, and countless others. In 2007 Tennessee had more players on NFL rosters than any other SEC school. But lately, Fulmer's recruiting hasn't been as impressive.

After nearly a decade of consistent top-10 classes at Tennessee, in 2003 and 2004 Fulmer stumbled relative to his past success, corralling a class that Rivals ranked just the 18th- and 11th-best, respectively, in the country. In the wake of 2005's disastrous 5-6 season, Fulmer snagged the 3rd-best class in the country and this went a long way toward helping to paper over the failings on the field that year. But he followed that top-ranked class in 2006 with his worst class as a head coach to that point, the 22nd-best bunch in the country for 2007, behind seven other SEC schools. In 2007 Fulmer rebounded and signed the number-three class in the country, including the jewel of his class, Eric Berry. But that success would be short-lived. In 2008 the class that just signed in February, Fulmer finished with Rivals' 35th-best class in the country, a disastrous position made worse when Tennessee's three top rivals, Florida, Alabama, and Georgia, all finished among the top-seven classes in the country. Tennessee, at eighth in the SEC, appeared in danger of falling even further behind their rivals. While the NFL draft successes clearly demonstrate that Tennessee has recruited good players in the past, many Vol fans fear that Fulmer's best days as a recruiter have passed. That makes the on-field performance even more jarring; the gap between Tennessee and their rivals is widening and things might not get better, fans reason.

Most of the current Vols are wearing headphones now, listening to their own music, and occasionally one will sing out loud. Eric Berry is walking around in a T-shirt with BEAST written across the front of it. Some players are slowly getting dressed in front of their orange cherry-wood lockers while others are getting stretched out atop the six training tables in the center of the locker room.

At 6:13 P.M., Phil Fulmer walks to the dry-erase board in the front of the locker room. He spends 5 minutes gazing at the board now, deep in thought. No one speaks to him, and he picks up a black marker and begins to write on the dry-erase board in tight, clean print:

1. FAST START!
2. MAKE IT 9 ON 8!
3. DISCIPLINE—DO MY JOB!
4.

He steps away from the board and surveys his team during a lap around the locker room. Then he returns and unfolds a piece of yellow notebook paper. He writes on the dry-erase board:

TONIGHT

TENNESSEE

*FAMILY

RESPECT

Then he turns and stares straight ahead, toward the back of the locker room for a few moments, jaws tightly clenched, before turning around and adding these words on the dry-erase board:

*4. SHORT YARDAGE/GOAL LINE ORANGE AREA

5. KICKING GAME!

PROTECT AND COVER—"ARENAS" OPPORTUNITIES TO SCORE!

As Fulmer writes, occasionally the door to the locker room opens and the roar of the stadium crowd filters inside, a preview of the deluge to come. Otherwise the locker room is almost completely soundproof. As millions of fans across the South prepare to watch this game and expend ridiculous amounts of energy screaming, yelling, or talking excitedly, the locker room is calm and quiet. Soon all the attention these players could ever want—and more—will be beamed down upon them, but now, in the final hour before the game, they're alone with their thoughts and their leader.

Suddenly Coach Fulmer is standing in front of me, arms crossed over his orange sweater, looking down at me.

"How's the book coming?" he asks.

I stammer out a response. Fulmer nods. "You picked a hell of a season to write a book, son," he says.

Just then the referees calling the game enter the locker room and greet Coach Fulmer. They ask him how he's doing. "Nothing a good win wouldn't cure," Fulmer says, shaking each of their hands.

"Punters, kickers out of here in two minutes," strength coach Johnny Long yells.

The first of the players are fully dressed now in their orange jerseys and white pants. My hands are shaking now. I try to disguise this by keeping them busy and writing. In reality I'm drawing interlocking boxes on my notepad.

Coach Larry Slade claps his hands. "Let's go, returners, we're walking out right now." I look up. Eric Berry is not among the returners. I feel sad, as if I've lost something. Moments later, Slade pushes open the outside door and barrels back into the locker room. "Where's Eric?" he asks. "Eric needs to get out here and return some kicks."

At 6:47 the red digital game clock on the wall begins to count down the final hour toward the scheduled 7:47 kickoff. Coach Fulmer is back in the locker room, alone, standing with his arms crossed, taking deep breaths and staring at the ceiling as his players and coaches rush around him. I feel as if he wants to talk to someone, anyone.

"Is it harder to play or coach against Alabama?" I ask. He steps forward, sucks on his lower lip, and then answers, "Both. When you're a player you're worried about doing what you're dang-gone supposed to do. When you're a coach, you're worried about everyone else doing what they're dang well supposed to do as well as yourself."

He pauses as if he's going to say something more, thinks for a moment, and then concludes, "But I really like this series."

Vince Kanipe, the white-haired UT police officer in charge of Fulmer's security, enters. "That was a heck of a Vol Walk," he says. "I had to pull three women off of him." When asked if anyone said anything rude to Coach Fulmer, Vince responds, "Naw, nobody ever says anything bad to his face. Never." We may have entered a world where fan message boards enable fans to unleash all their negative thoughts, but face-to-face interactions remain as infused with Southern manners as they were in the days of General Neyland.

But his continued popularity as a person does not protect Coach Fulmer from the demand for wins. Unbeknownst to most, UT athletic director Mike Hamilton has begun conversations with a group of eight people that he trusts intimately—four from inside the university, including university president John Petersen, and four major boosters from outside the university—about whether Phil Fulmer will return as head coach next year. Hamilton is looking for a win "to hang his hat on"—a victory that will justify bringing Fulmer back for another season. So far he has found none. This game may be Fulmer's last chance for a win to stave off his firing.

Tennessee's running backs coach Stan Drayton, a short, powerfully coiled black man whom Fulmer hired away from Urban Meyer and Florida last season, calls out from the front of the locker room, "You got two minutes, running backs, two." Eric Berry returns from the field, pushes open the door, and the roar from the crowd pours into the locker room. "Oh, hell yeah, it's hype already," he yells, skipping on his toes to his locker. Strength coach Johnny Long jumps among the running backs. "If you don't hate these motherfuckers you got no business sitting in this locker room! And that's the truth!" he screams.

Defensive coordinator John Chavis stands silently, arms crossed in front of his chest, chin jutted sternly forward, while the linebacking corps gathers around him. "Linebackers," Chavis says simply. Then they're out the door too. Defensive end Chase Nelson slams his hands together. "Them motherfuckers tried to embarrass us last year," he says. "Fuck them!"

The entire team is out on the field, and I'm alone in the UT locker room. I pace slowly around the carpeted floor and realize how nervous I am. My stomach is trembling. I head to the bathroom, go into the one of the orange stalls, walls painted orange and white. I drop down to my knees and puke into the toilet. I hear the sound of my puke hitting the water and feel beads of sweat breaking out on my forehead. I stand, feeling better for an instant, and then drop back down and puke again. Leaning forward, staring at my own vomit in the toilet bowl, I shake my head. Never before have I ever thrown up before an athletic event, not even one I'm competing in. I want Tennessee to win so badly, my stomach can't handle the stress.

Finally I stand, open the stall door, and drink water from a dripping faucet, trying to erase the stench from my mouth. By the time I'm finished, the student managers have returned to the locker room and are giving out UT eyeblack stickers to the first returning players. For just a moment, I'm so fired up about the looming kickoff, I contemplate getting the eyeblack stickers myself. Right now if Coach Fulmer asked me to run through a brick wall, I would try to run through a brick wall. I want him to win, and need Tennessee to beat Alabama that badly.

Within minutes, the entire team has returned and the players are sitting in fold-out chairs before General Neyland's Maxims. The locker room is quiet while the players check one another's shoulder pads, fasten and unfasten their dark gloves, tighten their cleats, and tap their hands on their thighs, atwitter with nervous energy. Coach Fulmer is pacing, circling the team. Occasionally he pauses and runs his hands along his forearms to make sure that his white undershirt sleeves have been pushed up to his elbows. His eyeglasses are hanging from his orange sweater. He's everywhere now, standing behind his team, in front of his team, pausing and looking at the players from every angle, an orange lion in autumn.

In 15 previous seasons Phil Fulmer has won 10, lost 4, and tied once against Alabama (this 1993 tie was later credited to the Vols as part of Alabama's probation for cheating). It's the rivalry he most wanted to change when he became head coach at Tennessee. And he has. When Fulmer took over at Tennessee in 1992, Alabama boasted a string of seven straight victories. That first year, in 1993, he tied Alabama in Birmingham. The next year he lost 17–13 in Knoxville. But beginning in 1995 Fulmer ran off a streak of seven consecutive victories. After 2006's 16–13 victory, Fulmer's record against the Tide was 10-2-1. He'd not just triumphed, he'd outlasted *six* different Alabama coaches during his tenure. Gene Stallings, Mike DuBose, Dennis Franchione, Mike Price, Mike Shula, Joe Kines, all had come and gone. But now he's facing a new Alabama coach in Nick Saban, Alabama's lucky number seven. Saban is just one year younger than Fulmer but they represent different eras of football. Saban is a mercenary head coach, a West Virginia native who coached for nine different teams in both college and the pros before he received his first head coaching job in 1995 at Michigan State.

Saban coached at Michigan State for five seasons, running up a record of 34-24-1. In his best season, 1999, he went 9-2. But before he could coach in the bowl game that year he resigned and accepted his first job in the South, as head coach of LSU. At LSU Saban thrived, going 48-16 with two SEC titles and one national title in five seasons.

Then he left.

For more money and to coach the NFL's Miami Dolphins. After just two seasons with the Dolphins, during which time Saban compiled a record of 15-17, Alabama fired Mike Shula. Saban, still a Dolphin, treated all questions about his interest in Alabama with disdain. "I'm not going to be the Alabama coach," he said. But in January 2007 Saban was introduced as the 27th head coach in Alabama history. LSU fans reacted with outrage, Alabama fans with glee. Nick Saban, mercenary head coach at large, was back in the SEC.

Last year, in Saban's first year with Alabama, Fulmer's team was embarrassed 41–17 in Tuscaloosa. This season Saban's Crimson Tide is undefeated, standing at 7-0 and ranked #2 in the country. Fulmer knows he needs this win, has to have it.

Coach Fulmer stops pacing in the locker room, readjusts his orange hat, rubs his hands over his face. He stays still for just an instant and then walks all the way across the locker room and steps in front of his team.

With 13:40 remaining until kickoff, Fulmer speaks. "Let me see the captains and kickers," he says.

I'm leaning against one of the four pillars behind the team, recording the scene around me, when the captains return to their seats. Phil Fulmer walks to the front of his team, slowly brings his hands together in front of his body, and looks in my general direction. "I'm going to ask you to leave with that camera," he says, gesturing to the twentysomething brown-haired man beside me with the video camera, "and you as well," he says, looking at me. The entire team turns to look at the UT sports cameraman and me. I nod and feel a quick rush of embarrassment flush my face at being singled out in the locker room. The two of us make the orange walk of shame past the entire team and then out the double doors of the locker room, held open by Knoxville police officer Sam Graham, one of Phil Fulmer's security staff. All I can think as I make the walk across the locker room is, "Don't trip, don't trip, don't trip."

"I appreciate it," Fulmer says, nodding at us as we pass.

Later the appreciation comment will strike me as particularly emblematic of Coach Fulmer's generosity. He didn't need to say that to us at all. What was either of us going to do, refuse to leave? Chain ourselves to one of the locker-room pillars? Of course not; we were going to leave without saying a word, just like we both did. Even still, Fulmer spoke to us as if we were both doing him a personal favor and helped us save face in front of the team.

But that would be later. Right now, in the immediate aftermath of our exclusion, the camera guy is irate.

"He's never done that before," the camera guy says. "Ever."

Fulmer has never done this to me, either. This is the first time he's restricted my access to anything, and there's no doubt in my mind he's reacting to the increasing pressure of a season that's rapidly falling apart.

I lean against the brick wall in the tunnel. Above me, I can already hear the thunderous roar of Neyland Stadium at night. I'm nervous now and wonder whether I'll still be permitted to run through the T. Have I been barred from this too or just the pregame speech? Will I be tackled by a member of the security staff? Slammed into the tubas, impaled by a flag-bearer, or, in an ultimate undignified irony, crashed in the head by the guys on scholarship who play the cymbals? Suddenly the locker-room doors open and a fired-up Tennessee football team comes pouring into the tunnel.

The players are jumping, pounding into one another in the enclosed confines of the tunnel. I can barely see above me to the field and the open sky and the UT band moving in night-lighted formation. In a matter of seconds the band will split, the crowd will roar, and the T will be formed. I make my decision: Even if I'm going to be kicked out of the locker room, I'm going to run through the T.

Many Vol fans believe the Vols have always run through the T to begin games. In fact, it's a relatively recent tradition—arriving in 1965 courtesy of new head coach Doug Dickey, an owlish Florida grad who coached Phil Fulmer and won two SEC titles at Tennessee. This, then, is the 43rd year that the Pride of the Southland band forms the T as they march in the direction of the north end zone.

I still remember coming to my first game in 1985 and my dad telling me to stand up as the band made its turn on the field and spread open to form the T, the way the entire stadium roared as one, and how I'd covered my ears; this was and still is the loudest noise I'd ever heard. I've spent the past 23 years fantasizing about what it would be like to run through it myself. So too do many other Vol fans.

In fact, John "Thunder" Thornton is widely reported to have donated $1 million to the university for the chance to run through the T. He tells me this is inaccurate. "I made the donation and [then] President Joe Johnston called me. I said, 'Joe, you've been with the university for thirty-seven years and have never run through the T?' He said he hadn't. So I said, 'Let's you and me do it together.'" As the two men prepared to rush through the T at the homecoming game against Oklahoma State on September 30, 1995, the puckish Thornton turned to President Johnston."Joe," he said, "I'll give you another million if you run through naked."

Johnston declined.

Now, as the final moment arrives, the Tennessee orange flag with the white T unfurls and the team shoots forth onto the field. The sound is jarring, deafening to the eardrums, the kind of volume that seems to grab you and shake you until you feel its reverberation from the tips of your toes to the crown of your head, like 10 airplanes taking off at the same time.

But I expected it to be loud. What I didn't expect is the rapid transition from feeling claustrophobic to the freeing feeling of floating in space. One moment you're unable to move in a low-ceilinged enclosure just off the field and the next you're in the middle of an undulating sea of orange and the skies are clear as far as you can see, the fresh air a pleasant shock to your skin and lungs. Running onto the football field at night, as the T splits open before you, it seems possible that you could jump into the air and take flight on the roaring yells of the Tennessee faithful. This is as close to the gladiatorial experience as exists in modern American society.

Some players move quickly, others dawdle, turn, and wait for their teammates to run past and leap in a joyous greeting. I move at a slow speed, turning my head around me in wonder. I've spent my entire life watching the maelstrom from afar, and now, suddenly, I'm in the midst of the orange storm for a UT-Alabama game. It feels so unreal I halfway expect to awake and find myself staring at the ceiling of my childhood bedroom.

But I don't wake up. Instead I run on through the left side of the T to the Vol sideline and stand there. I'm out of breath and close to passing out. Somewhere along the way, without even realizing it, I've forgotten to breathe.

In my entire life as a sports fan I've never felt such an electric environment. The hairs on my arms are standing up, the team is bounding as one, the entire stadium, all 106,000 people, are on their feet and screaming as loud as they possibly can. No one sits on either sideline as Tennessee's kicker, Chad Cunningham, lines up the Volunteer football team, drops his right arm, and, rushing forward, boots the ball high into the night sky. Lightbulbs flash across the expansive orange face of Neyland Stadium, and the biggest rivalry game in Tennessee history is renewed for the 91st time.

Alabama takes possession first and moves the ball until they face a third and 11. At this point the UT crowd unwinds itself. I've been to every SEC stadium and this is the loudest I've ever heard it anywhere. Alabama is stopped and settles for a field goal. Less than five minutes into the game, Tennessee trails 3–0.

Eric Berry is announced as the kickoff returner after this score and the crowd roars anew. But he can't do much with the ball, gaining just 21 yards on the return. Nor can the Tennessee offense, taking possession at their own 27. On the ensuing punt, finally, after a season of tough luck, Tennessee gets a break. Britton Colquitt booms a punt to Alabama's Javier Arenas. The ball hangs so long in the air that Arenas should have called for the fair catch. Or he should have simply let the ball bounce and hoped it went into the end zone. Instead he does neither—Arenas attempts to field the ball without signaling for a fair catch. It's a mistake. UT crushes him just as the ball arrives.

The ball squirts free, and amidst the leaping Vol players on the sideline I can't tell exactly who has the ball for a moment. As the play unfolds the UT cheering continues to grow until the crescendo is almost overpowering. My ears are actually in pain from the hurtling of the sound, and before we can even see the actual result, the crowd's roar confirms it: Tennessee recovers the fumble. Later, at the hotel, two different Alabama fans say, "I've never heard a stadium louder than when Arenas fumbled." The sideline is a frenzied mosh pit of celebration; I bounce from one set of shoulder pads to another, unable to control where I'm going.

After seven games, Tennessee has recovered their first fumble of the year. Now we absolutely have to get a touchdown. Unfortunately, we get a 5-yard penalty on first down and squander the touchdown opportunity. The Vols settle for a field goal and we're tied at 3.

On the next series Eric Berry comes in on offense and catches a 4-yard pass. The crowd goes wild. In a fit of excitement and optimism I write on my notepad that Eric Berry is going to single-handedly win the game for the Vols. But the offensive drive fizzles and 'Bama kicks a field goal to go up 6–3 at the end of the first quarter.

Strength coach Johnny Long sidles up to me and says, "Hell of a game! Last year I got tossed from this game for cussing a ref!"

UT running back Montario Hardesty makes the next big play. As Alabama prepares to punt with 7:22 remaining in the half, he rushes through the middle of the line of scrimmage and lays out for a punt block. The ball deflects forward off his arm and comes to rest at the Alabama 32. The Vols have a golden chance to give Alabama their first deficit of the 2008 season. But the offense fails once again. The team actually loses yardage on three plays, and facing a fourth and 13 from the Alabama 34, Fulmer sends the punt team out onto the field. Then, at the last moment, Fulmer changes his mind and hurriedly calls time out on the sideline. His coaching staff gathers around him for a conference, and Fulmer decides to attempt the field goal. Daniel Lincoln trots out onto the field to attempt a 51-yard field goal that would tie the game. The resulting kick is no good.

Alabama takes advantage of decent field position and musters their first big drive of the game. The big play is a long completion from Alabama quarterback John Parker Wilson to freshman phenom wide receiver Julio Jones. On fourth and goal from the 3, Alabama's Glen Coffee rushes off the left side and scores to go up 13–3. The Neyland Stadium crowd goes quiet.

Tennessee has to have some points before the first half ends. And the offense strings together a series of big plays, but on two consecutive third-down conversions inside the Alabama 15, Tennessee receives penalties. The first penalty occurs because the offense only has 10 men on the field and lines up with not enough men on the line of scrimmage. The second penalty, a questionable offensive pass interference call, brings the bench to the point of mutiny. "That's bullshit," scream a half-dozen players in unison. Not to be outdone, several members of the coaching staff charge onto the field screaming at the referees. Later replays will confirm this was a bad call.

The resulting offensive pass interference penalty negates a first and goal and pushes Tennessee back to a third and 21 from the 34 with 11 seconds left in the half. The Vols gain 8 yards on a pass play, call a time out, and attempt a 43-yard field goal to end the half. Daniel Lincoln's field goal attempt slides wide left, and the half is over.

"This shit ain't right," says center Josh McNeil, jogging to the locker room. "We had ten men on the field." He spits in the grass. Daniel Lincoln's missed field goal has deflated the entire team.

Starting quarterback Nick Stephens seeks out Lucas Taylor in the locker room. The two narrowly missed on a deep pass to the end zone near the end of the half. "Hey, Lucas, Lucas Taylor, that's going to be a TD in the second half," Stephens says excitedly, extending his hand in greeting. Taylor merely nods.

The players separate and go to their respective position coaches in the locker room. Defensive coordinator John Chavis stands with a dry-erase board in front of him. "We're not going to allow their ass to run the football," he says. "They made a few plays, but y'all were great out there . . . Let's get it cranked up in the second half."

Phil Fulmer, wearing glasses, stands up in front of the team. "It's gonna be a four-quarter ballgame," he says. "Defense, that's a hell of a job. You're playing your asses off." Fulmer tells the team that they're in good shape because the offense gets the ball to start the second half and because "We got more yards than they do."

This is not actually true. I've got the stat sheet in front of me; the yardage total is close but Alabama has more yards. I wonder whether this is an oversight or a calculated attempt to make the players think they performed better than they actually did, or to help defuse the tension between the offense and the defense.

The team returns to the field once more. The intensity and emotion of the first half are gone; the players know they missed two golden chances to score. Despite starting one drive at the 32 and another at the 5, they produced only 3 first-half points. But once more they dive into the football breach.

Alabama sacks Nick Stephens on the first play of the second half and Stephens misses on his first two passes. Tennessee punts and Alabama kicks a field goal on their first possession to go up 16–3. It's cold now on the sideline, and the waning excitement of the team is evidenced by the growing number of players huddling in front of the heater or sitting on the sideline bench. Still, there's a friendliness on the sideline that's incongruous with the low spirits. Players come off the field after a series of violent collisions and apologize if they bump into one another, managers, or the staff.

Now, with Alabama driving late in the third quarter, this is the time when the UT defense has to make a play. And they do. An Alabama running back fumbles and, who else, Eric Berry is there to yank the ball up and race down the sideline for the touchdown. The UT bench explodes. The players are suddenly back on their feet, screaming, yelling, their cold hands the last thing on their minds. Defensive tackle Walter Fisher shakes his head. "He's a superstar, boy!" he screams.

But the play is subject to replay review. The Neyland Stadium Jumbotron replays Berry's run just once, and everyone on the sidelines cranes their heads to watch. The single replay is inconclusive. The wait for the decision is agonizing; the team knows the difference between a 16–10 one-score ballgame with an energized stadium and a 16–3 deficit with dwindling time remaining and an anemic offense. At long last the referee returns.

"The runner was down by contact," he says.

The UT coaching staff and sideline come undone. Curses fly, some coaches and staff members have to be restrained from rushing far out onto the field. All of the frustrations, angers, and pressures that have come with a 3-4 start boil over. It's as close to anarchy as a sideline can be.

Alabama quarterback John Parker Wilson completes a pass directly in front of us shortly thereafter. He's rolled to his right and after he throws, for just a moment, he turns to the UT coaching staff, looks them in the eye, and pumps his fist in their direction. "Fuck John Parker Wilson's untalented gay ass," says a player standing beside me.

Alabama scores another touchdown to go up 22–3 late in the third quarter. The worst Vol offense in recorded history now has to score three touchdowns in the final 16:38 of the game to avoid a fifth loss on the season. At this exact moment I receive a text message from my friend Junaid. "Regime change. I've seen enough," he writes. I look at the text message from a fellow fan and feel a bit like I'm cheating on my team, standing on the sideline reading an insult about their performance. I look over my shoulder, check to see if anyone else can see the words on my screen. No one is looking at me, not even John Chavis's grown son—who is playing with a yo-yo while wearing an earpiece and occasionally taking calls on the sideline. "Yeah, we think it's kind of weird too," one of the managers says to me. I bury my phone in the pocket of my fleece jacket.

For the first time all game, the "Roll Tide" cheers from Alabama fans in the stands are audible on the UT sideline. Mike Hamilton, needing a win to justify Phil Fulmer's continued employment, looks around at the rapidly emptying crowd. Some of UT's best seats are filled with fans in Crimson attire. He believes Tennessee fans are becoming indifferent to the team and giving up their seats to the enemy.

I stand behind Coach Fulmer and watch as he coaches through the final quarter. It's the 200th game of his career and Alabama is pouring salt in the fresh wounds of the Vol season. Another Alabama touchdown brings the score to 29–3.

Phil Fulmer runs his hands over his face and slowly pushes up his baseball cap. Then, just as quickly, he recovers and joins the special teams huddle, where he claps hard and slaps his players on the helmet.

Behind him the UT student section has taken up a new chant with their own clapping: "Fire Fulmer," clap, clap, clap, "Fire Fulmer," clap, clap, clap. All of the players can hear the chant and so can the coaching staff. But everyone pretends they can't.

I'm suddenly aware of how very cold it is on the sideline. I blow out my breath, and for the first time all fall the air is cold enough to see it turn to mist in front of me.

The UT offense scores a touchdown, and as they come off the field, Jonathan Crompton, who has kept his helmet on the entire game, congratulates every member of the offense. As I watch this, I think, not for the first time, about why I've blamed so much of this season on Crompton's failings. He's never done anything to me, never said a word to me on the sideline or in the locker room or in the hotel. Several times I've seen him look at me as I write things. I've thought that I should introduce myself. But I haven't.

Why not?

I think I know. Because it's easier to blame him for the season if I don't know him. The Jonathan Crompton of my fan's mind, the gun-slinging big-armed dolt who throws every pass as hard as he can, is not an accurate image. It's far too simplistic and probably not fair. I've made him a caricature. As I watch Crompton congratulate his teammates, including the quarterback, Nick Stephens, who currently has the job he wants more than anything in the world, I start to think that maybe I'm the jerk in the Jonathan Crompton–Clay Travis relationship, that what I write about Crompton reveals far more about me than it does about Crompton. And maybe that makes me the kind of guy who wouldn't stand on the sideline in the fourth quarter of a loss, wear my helmet the entire game, and congratulate my teammates as they come off the field after scoring a meaningless touchdown. Without realizing what I'm doing, I raise my hands to my face and run them over my eyes, squint, bare my teeth. It's not until after the movement is complete that I realize what I've done. In my unconscious moments of self-criticism on the sideline, I've aped the mannerisms of Coach Phil Fulmer.

On the next failed defensive series, when Alabama converts a first down on third and 3 with 7 minutes to play, graduate assistant and former backup quarterback Jim Bob Cooter slams down his headset on the ground with such force that I'm amazed it doesn't break. Even the players gathering around the heater to stay warm take note. "Damn," says one.

It's quiet enough in the barely half-full stadium that I can hear the chains being dragged along the sideline. They remind me of Dickens's *A Christmas Carol*, the Ghost of Christmas Past coming after Mr. Scrooge. Now the Ghost of Alabama Games Past is returning. I think about the game in 1990 when I cried while watching it with my grandfather. I recall the tie ballgame in 1993 when Brock Lodge dreamed of tackling David Palmer as he scored to tie the game. All the years of losses come flooding back, and I can't remember the wins at all.

Alabama runs the final 14 plays of the fourth quarter. All but one of these plays is a run. Four yards, seven yards, three yards, Alabama is marching down the field as the final Tennessee fans file out of the stadium. The majority of the fans left in the stadium are wearing crimson. They serenade us with the taunting Rammer Jammer Yellowhammer cheer.

Hey Vols!
Hey Vols!
Hey Vols!
We just beat the hell out of you!
Rammer Jammer, Yellowhammer, give 'em hell, Alabama!

For the first time in his coaching career, Fulmer has lost consecutive games to the Crimson Tide. Last year the score was 41–17, this year it's 29–9. Neither game has been remotely close by the fourth quarter. The players leave the field slowly, somberly, lifting their heads up to look into the stadium seats. The last, best chance to save the season has been lost. A ragtag bunch of Tennessee fans remain above the tunnel, children begging for wristbands, older fans with orange pom-poms draped low, the orange-and-white fronds limp in the cool night air.

Inside the locker room the downtrodden players immediately deposit their helmets into a yellow bin. The white helmets with orange power T's clang together as they land, the only sound in the locker room.

Fulmer's pregame notes have been swept off the dry-erase board. He stands now in the center of the brand-new locker room. His voice is hoarse and, for the first time, I'm struck by how out of place he looks, humble and plain-spoken, in this brand-new and fancy locker room, which the university has just spent $15 million refurbishing.

"Keep your heads up . . . in the first half you gave yourselves a chance," Fulmer says. His voice catches. "We've got four games left, every game is winnable. Now I want you to hear me now and understand what I'm saying, every . . . game . . . is . . . winnable. We're even."

He's not moving as he speaks. The words of encouragement seem meant for him as much as anyone in the room. "We gotta keep the faith, get bowl-eligible . . . don't blame the officials or anyone else." Finally, he closes. "I appreciate your effort tonight. One knee."

After Fulmer leads them in a quiet prayer, the players disperse to their lockers and begin to undress. Mike Hamilton is standing near the front of the locker room. Yet another nationally televised game has ended in failure. Hamilton shakes my hand and his grip is extremely firm, painful even. I've shaken Hamilton's hand lots of times and his grip has never been this powerful before. "Boy, the fans were nasty out there tonight," Hamilton says to one of the men standing next to him. "Nasty." His eyes are large and round, as if he's just seen a ghost.

The managers are stripping the jerseys off the pads now, and Fulmer walks just a few steps and sits down on the edge of one of the beige training tables in the center of the locker room. No one is near him and no one is speaking to him and his face is focused on the ground. He's slowly rubbing his knees. Eventually he stands, moves across the locker room, and puts his arm around the shoulder of top recruit Tajh Boyd. A circle of recruits stand in the corner of the locker room near Boyd, and Fulmer reaches out and rests his arms on their shoulders.

For all the world it appears that the recruits are the only thing in the room keeping him from falling over.

CHAPTER 17

DUELING FULMERS

I CAN'T MAKE UP MY MIND about whether Phil Fulmer should be fired. In the week after the Alabama game I sit for hours reading threads about Fulmer on Volquest and other message boards. Most message board posters have made their decisions. I can't.

My mind is frozen, moving at a glacial pace. One moment I'm convinced Coach Fulmer has to go, another I'm convinced it's imperative that he stay. In an effort to figure out what the decision would be if it were mine to make, I do what they taught us in law school: examine both sides of the issue. Of course, in law school you went with the side that paid you the best. Now, for better or worse, I am completely a free agent, a Vol fan divided against himself. Because it's more painful, first I construct an argument for why Fulmer must go:

• **Fulmer Must Go**

Since 1998 Phil Fulmer has not won an SEC title. This 10-year span is one of the longest droughts in the history of Tennessee football. The only longer span without an SEC championship was

1970 through 1984. The Vols have not been ranked in the top 10 at the end of the season since 2001, and it appears likely that the Vols won't be ranked at all by the end of the 2008 season. Put it this way: How many other teams in the SEC would offer Fulmer their head coaching position if Tennessee fired him?

The answer is zero.

Lately Fulmer has been defending his losses by saying, "We didn't get dumb overnight." Maybe not. But did the rest of the SEC get smarter? In a globalized world, Fulmer is incredibly local— having grown up in Tennessee, played at Tennessee, and coached at Tennessee. No other SEC school is coached by a man who is a graduate of his own team's school, much less one who grew up in its home state. Is Fulmer a regional relic from a time before the coaching of college football became a national business?

Tennessee football is big business, with tens of millions of dollars a year in revenue and a huge footprint of influence. Effectively, Tennessee football is a corporation based in Knoxville that exports its product via television and the Internet, and its apparel to all corners of the globe. Would we expect any other global business to limit its CEO to people who had previously worked for the corporation or lived in the same state where the corporation was based? No way.

In keeping Phillip Fulmer as head coach, Tennessee is fighting a losing battle. At long last, we've entered the mercenary era of college football coaches. It isn't important whether your coach has a shared history with the state or the fans; what's important is whether he wins games. College football is the ultimate bottom-line business, and the Vols have been losing ground to their competitors ever since the 2001 team walked off the Georgia Dome field a loser.

Since the turn of the century a new era of coaches has emerged in the SEC. Urban Meyer, Nick Saban, and Mark Richt all have winning records against Fulmer. They happen to head up Tennessee's biggest rivals. None of these men has ties to their schools. All are younger than Fulmer. And all are paid handsomely to win. Richt has been at Georgia for only seven seasons, and he's already won two SEC titles. Meyer has been at Florida for just three full seasons and has already won an SEC and a national title. Phil Fulmer has had 10 seasons to prove he can still win an SEC championship and he hasn't been able to equal what Florida and Georgia have done.

I don't dislike Coach Fulmer, and I know his players love him, but he can't match these coaches anymore. The game has passed him by. Tennessee has given Fulmer more than adequate time to demonstrate he's still got what it takes to helm a dominant football team. And he hasn't done it. Period. It's time for him to go.

Then I flip the coin and think about the reasons for keeping Fulmer on.

• **Keep Fulmer**

Only one coach has ever been better than Coach Fulmer in the history of the University of Tennessee and they named the football stadium after him. General Robert Neyland went 173-31-12 in his 21-year career at Tennessee. Right now Phil Fulmer is 150-50. Winning 150 games at a school is extremely rare. In fact, Tennessee is the only school in modern history to have two coaches win 150 games. In 3 years or so, Fulmer could pass General Neyland to become the winningest coach in UT history.

What's more, Fulmer is sixth all-time in SEC victories with 96. Steve Spurrier has 100 and is in fourth place all-time. Depending on how much longer he coaches and how much longer Spurrier coaches, Fulmer could move into second place all-time behind Bear Bryant. As if that weren't enough, Phil Fulmer is a former UT player and assistant coach, and has been head coach for 16 years. In all of the SEC no other coach has lasted more than 10 years.

While it's true that Fulmer has not won an SEC title since 1998, UT has competed in the SEC title game three times this decade—in 2001, 2004, and 2007. Only the 2001 loss to LSU was an upset. That loss came the week after one of the biggest wins in UT football history—a road win at Florida as a double-digit underdog—and cost the Vols the opportunity to play for a national championship against Miami. The other two games Tennessee lost to superior teams. In 2004 Tennessee lost 38–28 to a 13-0 Auburn team—the last team to go 9-0 in the SEC. Tennessee was playing with a third-string quarterback, Rick Clausen, after two true freshmen, Erik Ainge and Brent Schaeffer, were lost for the season to injury. Anyone would be hard-pressed to suggest that Tennessee should have won this game. Last season, 2007, Tennessee lost a close game to the eventual national champion, LSU, after leading until only 8 minutes remained in the fourth quarter. Few would argue that Tennessee was better than LSU last season. Yet the Vols came very close to claiming the SEC title, just 10 months ago.

So in his last three opportunities to play for the SEC championship, Phil Fulmer has faced two of the three or four strongest teams to emerge from the SEC West since the SEC began divisional play in 1992. That's just tough luck.

What's more, in the 16-year history of the SEC championship game, a time that corresponds with Fulmer's tenure, Tennessee, with five appearances, trails only Florida with eight. Thus far in the 2000s Fulmer has taken UT to the championship game every 3 years. With two top-10 programs in the same division, Georgia and Florida, how many coaches in America could do better? Consider that Florida has only been to the SEC championship game twice in the 2000s and Georgia has been three times (with one of those trips being a tiebreaker over the Vols). No one is currently dominating the SEC East, although Georgia has won two of the three times they've advanced to the championship game this decade and Florida has won the SEC title both times they've advanced as well.

If UT fans are truly convinced that Georgia's Mark Richt and Florida's Urban Meyer are great coaches, I wonder who they believe Tennessee can hire to do better than equal the performances of these men?

Talent-wise the Fulmer era has produced more NFL players than any other period in Vol history. At the end of the 2007 season, Tennessee had more players on NFL rosters than any other program in the SEC. Virtually every season Fulmer has managed to produce a very highly rated recruiting class. He does this despite the fact that unlike many schools in the SEC, Tennessee has to recruit nationally in order to compete for championships. In fact, 85 percent of the athletes on scholarship at UT are from out of state. This necessitates a great deal of travel (one of the reasons Tennessee has the highest recruiting budget in the country) that many coaches in the SEC don't have to do. As if that weren't enough, Coach Fulmer is going to bring in another stellar recruiting class in 2009; currently this class has 21 verbal commitments and is ranked #7 in the country. If someone were to replace Fulmer he'd not only have to be a great coach, he'd also have to bring in more talented players than any other SEC school. That's a difficult proposition to manage.

Tennessee has hired 20 coaches in the history of the program. Fulmer has done better than all but one in total number of wins and is the only other coach to have won a consensus national title. If given 3 more years to coach, Fulmer will likely be the winningest coach in UT history and will have, at worst, the third-most wins in SEC history. It's very likely that in two decades, no matter who has coached in those intervening years, Tennessee fans will look back on the Fulmer years with great fondness.

Finally, Fulmer is not going anywhere else. Many coaches today show no loyalty to their present employer and are constantly looking for the next job. That isn't the case with Coach Fulmer: He's no mercenary. He will be at Tennessee until he retires. Whether that will be sooner or later remains to be seen, but the idea that Tennessee is going to do much better than Fulmer is a mindless pursuit of fool's gold. Tennessee is coached by an extremely successful Tennessee native and graduate who played for the school and knows what it feels like to run through the T on game day. He deserves the right to end his tenure at Tennessee on his own terms.

When I finish this analysis, I am no closer to making my own decision about Fulmer's future. But I know that Mike Hamilton is getting very close. Fulmer needs to win against every other team left on the schedule. Only then, if the Vols can rebound from 3-5 to finish 7-5, is there a chance Fulmer will be back in 2009 for his 17th season.

CHAPTER 18

GOOD TIME CHARLIE AND THE FOOTBALL FUNERAL

AT 7 P.M. ON THURSDAY, OCTOBER 30, Vol truck driver Charlie Harris and I leave the parking lot behind the Neyland-Thompson Sports Complex with the helmets, jerseys, pads, medical supplies, braces, and sundry other property that the UT team needs to face its foe on Saturday. Our destination is Columbia, South Carolina, where the Vols will play the South Carolina Gamecocks for a nationally televised game. I'm sitting shotgun in the front seat of the UT big rig. Behind us are two bunk beds and behind us farther still in the trailer sits all of the UT football equipment. But now, just outside the sports complex, we're already confronting our first obstacle. "Look at this motherfucker blocking the road," says Harris, gesturing in front of us at a white pickup truck that has stopped, inexplicably, just outside the exit to the complex. "I'm going to have to hit the fucking curb," he says with a scratchy Southern accent that sounds like it should be accompanied by the jangling of ice in a glass of whiskey.

He hits the curb. Softly. And only with the front left tire.

Harris is a 65-year-old Vietnam veteran who has driven trucks for a living since 1968. He's clean-shaven, an orange UT baseball cap atop his white hair, jeans hanging loosely on his lean hips, white tennis shoes gently pumping the gas and then jabbing down on the brake. Harris has been the driver of the UT tractor-trailer since the university purchased it in 1999. His first game was the Fiesta Bowl in Tempe, Arizona, in which Tennessee played and lost against the University of Nebraska. In the past 10 years Harris has become an icon for the football team, known throughout the program as Good Time Charlie. "Coach Fulmer always tells me that if I don't get there they can't play the game," says Harris as we enter the interstate heading east.

Already this season Harris has driven all the way across the country for the UCLA game. During the return trip Harris was pulled over in Texas for going 75 in a 65-mile-an-hour zone. Harris apologized to the police officer. "I told him I was just trying to get back home and I felt really bad because my team lost. It was Texas, he understood." The officer let him go with a warning.

The UT big rig draws an awful lot of attention. The paint job on the truck's exterior is a re-creation of the Tennessee team storming onto the field as the band opens into the T, which cost $14,000. The trailer used to be plain white with an orange T on the side, but when Fulmer spotted the Auburn equipment truck at the SEC championship game in 2004, he realized Tennessee's paled in comparison and took action. Says Charlie, "I took him [Fulmer] and showed him Auburn's and he said, 'We can do better than this.' He walked around the truck with a notepad and when he was done he gave it to Frazier [equipment manager Roger Frazier] to get it done. Now the truck is sharp. Real sharp. People don't miss us."

Charlie winks at me. "Sometimes the girls even show me their boobies. It happens more often if we win. The girls are happier then. If we win, we'll see some boobies. Good boobies too. The young girls are the flashers, not the old ones."

When asked which school has the best-looking girls in the SEC, without skipping a beat Charlie replies, "LSU has some baby dolls. I like them. Florida girls are phony."

We're outside Knoxville and about 70 miles from Asheville when Charlie looks over at me. "Do you mind if I take my teeth out?" he asks. "They don't fit very well. You don't have to look at me, if you don't want."

I reassure him that neither of my dad's parents had their teeth, so I'm used to seeing people without teeth. Charlie explains that he knocked out his teeth in an accident unloading materials from the bed of his truck a few years ago but still doesn't like to take his teeth out in public.

"I represent the university when I'm driving the truck, see."

As part of that representation, Charlie has to be on his best behavior. On the last trip a Georgia fan called the university and accused Charlie of flipping him off and cursing at him. "I didn't do it, but some people are just mean and start rumors about you."

For the next hour and a half Charlie and I talk about UT football. Charlie grew up in Knoxville and has been a UT fan his whole life. So far, this year has been disappointing for him. How disappointing? "We talked about changing the pictures on the side of the truck because some of the players aren't on the team anymore. Like Jayson Swain is gone. [The now-graduated Swain is pictured making a touchdown catch on one side of the big rig.] But then the season's been bad, so we decided to wait one more year and do it next year when we're better."

I've never ridden in a big rig before and I'm enjoying the experience being up higher than everyone else on the road. Although I'm a bit nervous that at any moment we'll be hijacked by Alabama fans and forced to drive the big rig replete with Tennessee's equipment into a deep lake where we'll sink to the bottom and never be heard from again. While I'm ruminating upon a life spent on *Unsolved Mysteries* reruns, I notice that Charlie doesn't have a CB radio in the cab of the truck, so we can't call for help if we're hijacked.

"Do you not have a CB?" I ask.

Charlie glances over at me, sheepishly. "I took it out seven years ago," he says.

"Why?"

"Some of the truckers would call and say things like, 'Yeah, we kicked your ass,' after games that we lost. After a while that got pretty frustrating. So now I don't have one."

Charlie Harris estimates that he removed the CB during the 2002 season, right about the time Fulmer's losses became more substantial.

"I guarantee you that all the truckers are talking about us on there, though. They used to ask me for helmets and jerseys and stuff. Some of them would even follow me to the gas station, pull up beside me, and say, 'Got a helmet for me?' I had to tell them no. Now it's just easier to drive without one."

Charlie is interested in my first book, *Dixieland Delight,* and this new book because he is a published author as well. Charlie tells me that he self-published his book, *Trucking Through Time,* in 2003. The novel was about two truckers who become stranded in a Wyoming snowstorm. Convinced they're going to die, the truckers eventually climb out of their truck, only to realize they've time-traveled back to the 1800s. Then they have to find a way to survive and return to their truck.

Charlie wrote his book in longhand while he cared for his ailing mother. He says the book just poured out of him and that the best feeling of all was to arrive at truck stops and see his book for sale. "Once I saw my book for sale in a different state and, buddy, there is no better feeling in the world than that.

"I gave Coach Fulmer a copy and he read it. He came up to me and said, 'Charlie, I want to tell you, I was really impressed by your book.'"

Charlie launches into a series of stories about his military career. He was a marine on board a ship that almost stormed the beaches of Cuba during the Cuban missile crisis. "They told us nine out of ten of us would die and called us back at the last moment," he says. He later served two tours in Vietnam as a sergeant in the Marine Corps. When I mention this later to Tennessee officials, none of them had any idea. Probably because Harris is not that quick to talk about his experiences. "Man says he wasn't scared in 'Nam, he's either an idiot or a damn liar. It was terrifying."

Harris explains that UT football was a welcome connection to home while he was in Vietnam. A friend of his sent the *Knoxville News-Sentinel* sports page to him and he kept up with the UT football team that way. Often, when scores were announced, fights would break out among the Southern marines. "Guys fought like hell with each other when they found out their teams lost."

We're driving through the windy stretch of interstate where Tennessee turns into North Carolina, a road so curvy it's terrifying to drive in a normal car, much less a big rig. Harris is in the right-hand lane and we're caught behind another truck that is only going 40 miles an hour. An antsy Harris drives behind this big rig for about 5 miles. Finally he says, "Boy, it's hard to sit here going this slow. I have to go slow, though, because I'm driving the Tennessee truck and someone will report me if I pass him."

Trucks are not supposed to pass other trucks in the left lane on this part of the interstate. The penalty is a $500 fine. Several trucks go flying past us, rattling the cab of our big rig. Charlie drums his hand on the steering wheel, leans forward then back, cracks the window, fiddles with the thermostat, takes a drink of coffee, then speaks again. "If I weren't driving such a distinguished truck, it'd be a different story," he says.

Once he accepts that it's going to be slow going for a while, Charlie continues to talk about Vietnam. One night he and another man were sent out to a hill to watch for approaching Vietcong. They weren't supposed to draw attention to themselves, just count the number of soldiers who passed by them in the dark night. It was pitch-black and Harris says he was on one side of the trail and the other soldier was on the other. "He started yelling for me and I ran over to the other side of the trail and found him. He was not moving at all and he said all calm-like, 'There's an ape, right beside me.' He'd panicked and tried to throw a grenade at the ape, but he'd messed up and now we were afraid it was about to go off. We dove over and covered our heads for a few minutes and then when we finally stood up, that cave ape was standing beside us again."

I explain that I had no idea there were apes in Vietnam. "Oh yeah, tons of 'em," says Charlie. "They wouldn't hurt you, but they'd scare the hell out of you." But then, as quickly as he's told a funny story about life in Vietnam, Charlie gets serious.

"Vietnam taught me that some people are evil," he says. He tells me the story of a little girl who brought him breakfast every morning in a Vietnamese village where he was stationed. "She was the cutest little thing I'd ever seen, no more than six or seven. Just a beautiful little girl." He pauses and looks away, out into the mountains of North Carolina. We're now on I-26 and are headed south toward Spartanburg, South Carolina.

The Vietcong found out that the girl and her family had been friendly with the Americans, and when the Americans left there was no one to protect the family. "They raped the little girl and killed the family. Nailed the mom upside-down to the wall of their store. Now tell me this, Clay, how could people do this to their own people?"

We're silent in the big rig carrying the UT equipment to the game. After a time Charlie Harris breaks that silence.

"Do you know how I got the name Good Time Charlie?" he asks me.

I tell him I have no idea.

"You remember the song 'Good Time Charlie's Got the Blues'?"

I say I've never heard of it.

"Well, it was before your time. That was my CB handle on the road, Good Time Charlie."

Abruptly, as he's wont to do, Charlie shifts gears. "Did you know I'll be sixty-six on Sunday? I wish to hell I wasn't going to be sixty-six. That's old."

When asked how old he wishes he could be, he says, "Twenty-nine. That's the most wonderful age in the world. You just have no idea what you don't know, how much more you'll learn in the next ten to twenty years."

I tell Charlie I'm twenty-nine.

"Well, you're a lucky son of a gun then."

At a truck stop in Clifton, South Carolina, Charlie pulls in the big rig, parks, puts in his teeth, and begins to fill up with gas. Immediately, truck drivers materialize and begin to take photos of the big rig and speak to Charlie. He grins, shakes their hands, and poses for photographs. When we return to the road, Charlie is still high on the contact with fans.

"People treat me different when I'm driving this truck," he says. Then he launches into a story about the UT–Notre Dame game in 2005. "Notre Dame fans are the nicest, most welcoming fans in the whole world," he says. "When I pulled up at the stadium there was a cute girl in a little skirt there, and the Notre Dame stadium manager says, 'Take Charlie on a tour.' Buddy, that girl took me into the classrooms, where they eat, and everywhere. I was in orange head to toe, and everywhere I went they treated me with respect, like I was really something. Those are class people."

He sighs.

"This might be my last year driving the big rig, though. I'm not sure. I'm not as young as I used to be."

We drive on through the South Carolina night in silence for a time. We've come down out of the mountains now and we are in the flat country. Columbia is less than 60 miles away. Occasionally, in the overhanging lights from the interstate, we see a palm tree or two in the distance.

We talk about games lost and won, players come and gone, just two fans riding along a dark interstate with the UT football equipment keeping us company. Harris is fond of former Tennessee quarterbacks Condredge Holloway and Peyton Manning. But most of all he loves Coach Fulmer.

"Phil Fulmer is a damn fine man," he says. "You know how I know? His daughters. They treat everybody right, everybody like family. They're a good Christian family, see. Every time his daughters see me they come up and give me a hug. They don't have to do that. They don't have to know the old guy who drives the truck to the games. But they do. That's because of Vicky and Coach Fulmer. They raised them girls right. People talk about wins and losses. Shoot"—Charlie waves his right hand above the steering wheel—"I want to win too. After that UCLA game I was sick for a week. But lots of people win ballgames. Not everyone has a good family."

When we reach the outskirts of Columbia, Charlie hands me the directions.

"You're the navigator," he says, "you bring us to the hotel."

This is the first job I've had on the trip and I'm nervous that I'll mess it up. But we only have two exits to follow before we've arrived at the Holiday Inn and Suites on Two Notch Road. I've rendered my first actual assistance to the UT football team, and I feel a point of pride. An older black man is waiting outside in the parking lot for our arrival.

"You with Tennessee?" he asks when Charlie rolls down the window.

Charlie nods. When he rolls up the window he says, "Why do people see us driving this truck and the first question they ask is if we're with Tennessee?" It's as close to sarcasm as Charlie Harris gets.

As soon as we've parked he's made friends with the attendant, who, he learns, also served in Vietnam as a marine.

"Shit," says the attendant, "I was only nineteen then, didn't know any better than to go walk in a jungle with a machine gun."

For a time the two men talk alone while I attempt to take pictures of the big rig. And fail. It's cold and I forgot my coat: I'm shivering in the early-morning chill. Halloween has arrived. I'm suddenly very sad because I know my son will be dressing up and trick-or-treating for the first time this weekend, and I won't be there to see it. He's going as Darth Vader.

I come around the corner of the big rig. Charlie is pointing something out to the parking lot attendant about the truck. They're both smiling. "Good grief, boy," he says to me, "where is your coat?"

AT 4:30 P.M. ON Saturday the team buses load up to depart for South Carolina's stadium. For the first time all season players are required to wear suits to an away game. It's an odd move, designed, most likely, to try and break the karma from three consecutive road losses. I ride on Bus 3 alongside kicker Daniel Lincoln. I'm checking updates on my BlackBerry for Florida-Georgia because the bus only gets cable television. Florida scores to go up 14–3. Lincoln looks over. "Who's winning?" he asks.

"Florida," I say.

"Figures," says Lincoln.

Kickoff between South Carolina and Tennessee is set for 7 P.M. Eastern and will be televised to a live ESPN2 audience. The bus ride to the stadium is short and quiet; the players listen to their headphones and stare outside the windows. We're accompanied, as always, by an escort from the local police. When we reach South Carolina's Williams-Brice Stadium, a bevy of Volunteer fans wearing orange call out to each player as they pass through a small barricade.

Charlie has arrived earlier and pulled the body of the big rig down an entrance ramp to the stadium so that the managers can unload the equipment and prepare the locker room for the arrival of the team. The South Carolina locker room is spartan; stickers with the Volunteer players' numbers have been placed above wooden lockers, inside of which the players' jerseys hang on hooks. The carpet is worn and blue. The showers and urinals look like those in an old high school's locker room—the walls have been painted and repainted again for decades.

I head out onto the Williams-Brice field and watch the earliest UT players warm up. None of them is in his uniform yet, and they goof around as they get ready for the game. Offensive linemen compete to see who can throw the football farthest, while defensive linemen attempt to field punts that are soaring into the heavens off the foot of Britton Colquitt. The scent of barbecue and smoke filters from nearby tailgates and wafts over the field while music blares in the empty stadium—everything from Kanye West to Johnny Cash. It's warm, but a cool night is coming.

As the players mess around on the field several of the UT coaches, wide receivers coach Latrell Scott and running backs coach Stan Drayton among them, are sitting on the sideline in their suit coats. Near them is UT athletic director Mike Hamilton. Hamilton is still looking for a signature win to hang his hat on. This is the team's last opportunity for that win. Even at 3-5, Hamilton's hopeful that the Vols can win their final four, get to 7-5 and then win a bowl game to finish at 8-5. He needs this finish, he tells me, to justify keeping Coach Fulmer.

Hamilton, UT athletic director since 2003, and Fulmer have worked together as athletic department employees since 1992. That year Hamilton joined the Vols in the fund-raising arm of the athletic department and Fulmer became head coach. Currently Hamilton has a 5-year contract that will keep him at Tennessee until 2014. His salary as athletic director—$314,575—is little more than one-tenth what Phil Fulmer makes in a year. Yet Hamilton has been Fulmer's ostensible boss since 2003. Initially Hamilton took the top job with Fulmer's support. "I certainly think very highly of Mike Hamilton," Fulmer said in 2003 when Hamilton was hired. "It's great for Mike Hamilton, but it's also great for Tennessee."

Now, 5 years after he was hired, with Fulmer's fate in his hands, Hamilton sits down next to the UT coaches on the aluminum bench on the visitors' sideline of Williams-Brice Stadium. The afternoon light is beginning to fade and soon the assistant coaches leave and Hamilton sits alone on the sideline watching the field. He's wearing a gray suit and his arms are crossed in front of his chest. The juxtaposition of a suit with the football field is startling; the business meets the game. Hamilton sits alone for 10 minutes.

One of the most interesting and surprising realities of major collegiate athletics is how solitary many of the moments surrounding the intense competition are. The decision-makers, coaches and administrators, at the University of Tennessee are rarely accompanied by entourages. Often, like now, they are alone with their own thoughts, especially on the road.

Slowly the South Carolina fans are beginning to file into the stadium, and still Mike Hamilton sits and watches the field. Finally, he stands and walks past me. As he passes, I hear him softly singing along to the Stealers Wheel song blaring over the Williams-Brice loudspeakers.

"Clowns to the left of me, jokers to the right of me, here I am stuck in the middle with you," Hamilton sings softly. "Yes, I'm stuck in the middle with you, and I'm wondering what it is I should do."

In Mike Hamilton's wake, one of South Carolina's male cheerleaders approaches me as I sit on the team bench. The cheerleader is beefy, with forearms that are the same size as his biceps. He leans his barrel chest on the iron bleacher. "Which one is Eric Berry?" he asks. "I know he's number fourteen."

The UT players are not yet dressed in uniform. I scan the field for Berry. "He's not out here yet."

The male cheerleader nods. "I figure there's nobody on offense worth watching for," he says.

In a sentence he's summed up the 2008 campaign for the Vols thus far.

"We're not much better," he says, "no Duce on this team."

South Carolina fans still love former All-SEC running back Duce Staley, who, after starring at South Carolina and starting at tailback for the Philadelphia Eagles, now lives in Columbia and hosts a sports talk radio program. On Friday night, Halloween, I went out drinking in Five Points, the main bar district just off the Gamecock campus in downtown Columbia, with a couple of South Carolina fans. I was standing near the front of the bar when I saw a guy who I thought was dressed up as a fat Duce Staley, which, to be fair, is a genius costume.

So I pointed him out to my friend Drew Toney. "Hey, look, it's a guy dressed up as fat Duce Staley."

Drew stared at him for 10 seconds. "That's actually Duce Staley. He does sideline reporting for South Carolina now. God, everyone loves that guy."

And it's true; Staley is swarmed by South Carolina undergrads clamoring to buy him drinks.

Back on the field, the UT players are beginning to arrive in their gear. "It's awful quiet in here," says Arian Foster as he runs past me to get loose.

When the players leave the field to head back into the locker room, I jog back with them. Inside, the trainers and managers are distributing drinks, eyeblack, and paper shot glass–size cups of vitamin B-12 that they pump from a large container. A UT trainer, Alyson, is preparing the cups. When asked if the B-12 works, she says, "Oh yeah, it gives you a spurt of energy. I use it before I run."

Soon the team is gathered in metal folding chairs in front of a dry-erase board. Kickoff is approaching, and the mood is somber. Suddenly Vol senior linebacker Ellix Wilson breaks the pregame silence by standing and screaming, "It's my fucking senior year and I'm tired of this shit! Tired of it, man."

Wilson is a 5' 10", 5th-year senior from Memphis who is starting at middle linebacker for the Vols. He's also the younger brother of a member of the 1998 national championship team, wide receiver Cedrick Wilson.

Beside me, UT defensive end Robert Ayers sits alone at his locker, clad in full uniform, reading passages aloud from his white-covered Bible. Ellix Wilson's voice fades and silence holds for a few minutes. Then Vol sophomore Eric Berry stands.

"When I say, 'Killas,' y'all say, 'Killas,' and then when I say, 'Trained assassins,' y'all say, 'Trained assassins,' and then when I say, 'Want some,' y'all say, 'Gone get some.'"

Then Berry starts, "Killas!"

"Killas!" the team replies in unison.

"Trained assassins!" Berry chants.

"Trained assassins!"

"Want some," Berry leads.

"Gone get some!"

"Let's go bang a motherfucker, man!" Berry yells in conclusion.

The cheer seems to get the team fired up. I'm kind of fired up. Of course, I have no idea what it means. In fact, I've never felt whiter in my life. Later student manager Andrew Haag will confess, "I don't know what he was saying, either, but he's Eric Berry. He's so cool, he can do anything and it's cool."

Ellix Wilson stands in the center of his teammates wearing his number 35 white road jersey. He begins an emotional tirade that makes Bobby Knight seem monotone.

"Coach Clawson, get our motherfucking playmakers the ball," he begins, the whites of eyes large as he slaps himself in the chest with his hands. "I'm fuckin' sick of this shit. We got too many fuckin' good players at wide receiver and too many good running backs to do this shit! We all been talking about it. If they playing ten yards off G. Jones why we running one-yard passes? Let's get our playmakers the ball, Coach, and fucking score!"

He picks up his chair and slams it down.

"This shit is worse than five-six," he screams, spinning around and looking at all of his teammates. "This shit ain't Tennessee! We ain't lost but two damn players off last year's team!" He begins to cry. "I cry every night about losing. You may not see me cry, but I'm tired of fuckin' losing. This shit ain't Tennessee." He begins to cry harder now, tears streaming down his checks, slams his metal chair down again on the floor, and the echo carries across the silent locker room. Now he speaks once more, slower, choking on his tears. Each word declines in volume until the last, which is barely audible. "Man, I'm just tired of losing, this shit ain't cool."

No one touches Wilson. No one speaks to him. Coach Fulmer finally breaks the silence. "Everybody feels the same thing," he says. "Hell, it ain't Tennessee. Hell, it ain't us. I don't give a crap about what happens to me and my coaches. Well, I care, but I want y'all to have a good time, win. You've worked too hard not to. You're damn good kids. We're going to win and we're going to play Tennessee football!"

Now Fulmer pivots and scans his team. He angrily defends himself against his critics. "These bastards get mad at me when I don't go for it on fourth and one from the forty. We've won a lot of games playing field position and I'm not gonna stop."

The players are nodding their heads.

"Everyone out but the players and coaches while we read the Maxims," Fulmer says.

The student managers, medical staff, and I filter out of the locker room and stand in the South Carolina night. The buzz is all about Ellix's speech. "That's the best player speech I've ever seen," says one manager. Another pipes up with a sarcastic aside, "Rico [McCoy] gave a pretty badass speech at Florida . . . that turned out well." One of the women on the training staff says, "Ellix scared me."

With the fire coming out of the locker room I see no way this team can lose. I contemplate turning on my cell phone and telling everyone I know to bet their house on Tennessee's football team. Phil Fulmer may be able to lead this team to a bowl game yet.

The team bursts through the doors and the front line of the team stands just outside the locker room on a small concrete platform. From here they are visible to some of the fans in the South Carolina stadium, and the Gamecock faithful begin to rain down abuse on the players. But the team doesn't notice. Arian Foster, down in front, bobs his head and begins to dance. The rest of the team is bouncing now too, on the toes of their cleats, a roiling mass of yelping and pad-slamming, a fiery beast of a team, angrier than they have been all season.

The team files across a concrete walkway to a covered access area. The covering tarp only extends about 10 yards. Several of the players bang on the ceiling, and the covering billows in response to their punches. The players and nearby fans are yelling as the team waits to enter the field. Then, suddenly, the team shoots onto the grass into the building roar, and a crescendo of hate descends upon them.

"Bring it, motherfuckers, bring it!" screams Arian Foster, waving his arms above his head in the direction of the crowd.

At kickoff the entire sideline is jumping and shouting with more enthusiasm and adrenaline than I've seen this year. Tennessee's defense stops South Carolina on their first drive and momentum builds on the sideline. On UT's first offensive play Nick Stephens hits Lucas Taylor for over 20 yards and the Vol offense seems to have turned a corner. But then Stephens misses a couple of open receivers, including an egregious miss on a screen pass, and is sacked on third down. Tennessee punts.

South Carolina takes possession at their 18 and quarterback Stephen Garcia goes to work—hitting a series of nifty, and dangerous, passes back against the grain while scrambling. Ultimately he completes a 12-yard touchdown pass, and as quickly as Ellix Wilson's speech fired up the team, South Carolina has stolen the Vols' confidence. South Carolina fans scream their alternating "Game" and "Cocks" chant and the cock is crowing on the scoreboard. The stadium is a sea of white swirling towels. South Carolina leads 7–0.

Phil Fulmer's face is tightly drawn, his teeth exposed, creases opened up on his cheeks and on his forehead, as if he's just tasted something unbelievably sour. Fulmer makes this face when something is going wrong on the field. It's an involuntary reaction, one he often covers up by clapping his hands and chewing fiercely on his gum. Things get worse from here. With a decent drive going, Nick Stephens drops back to pass and throws his first interception in five games. A South Carolina defensive back swoops in, catches the ball, and streaks down the field in the opposite direction. He scores without being touched. It's 14–0 South Carolina.

Stephens storms to the sideline yelling at wide receivers coach Latrell Scott about what the route was supposed to be. Scott angrily motions that the route was supposed to be a curl and not a sideline out. Stephens kicks his foot into the ground. Fulmer grabs him by the arm, and within 30 seconds he's replaced Stephens and put Jonathan Crompton back in at quarterback. "Fast, fast," Fulmer yells to a wide-eyed Crompton, demanding that he get ready as rapidly as possible. Vince Kanipe, the UT policeman in charge of Fulmer and his wife, turns to me. "I have never seen him pull a quarterback that fast before," he says.

Former Tennessee quarterback Condredge Holloway consoles

Stephens on the sideline. A startled Jonathan Crompton, goat of the first four games of the season, returns for the first time since the fourth quarter against Auburn 5 weeks ago. He completes his first pass, but from there things go downhill. On third down he's blindsided and slammed to the ground—sacked. Fulmer winces and pulls off his baseball cap. No matter what the head coach tries, UT's offense just can't get it together.

Once more, the Vols call on their defense to make a game of it. And the defense responds, stopping South Carolina on a fourth and inches and regaining possession. For a moment the UT sideline comes alive with excitement, but on the first play after the defensive stop, Tennessee runs a screen pass. Backup tailback Lennon Creer catches Crompton's pass and fights for yardage, gaining just 1 yard. Then, as he falls to the ground, the ball squirts free, a fumble. Worse still, South Carolina picks up the football and returns it to the 4-yard line.

Along the sideline coaches scream for the defense, the same defense that just stopped South Carolina on fourth down, to return to the field. Members of the defense audibly groan as they rush back to the field. The defense is only on the field for one play—South Carolina and Steve Spurrier score on a quick slant pass. It's 21–0 Gamecocks in the second quarter and Williams-Brice Stadium is rocking. Fulmer covers up the pained look on his face by clapping as loudly as he can. Even 5 feet from him, his clapping makes no sound.

On the next drive, Crompton is sacked once more on third down. Vol lineman Anthony Parker, who doesn't believe man has yet walked on the moon, storms off the field and rips his helmet from his head. "Don't nobody know what the fuck is going on!" he yells. Crompton grabs Parker by the shoulder pad. "AP, that was the mic [middle linebacker]," he says, his wide eyes a jumble of confusion.

The half comes to a merciful end and the team jogs off into the face of delirious Gamecock fan screams. Tennessee has not lost to South Carolina in Columbia since 1992—the final season of the Johnny Majors era. Inside the locker room at halftime, the defense gathers in front of a dry-erase board in the rear of the locker room and defensive coordinator John Chavis arrives to coach them. The offense is meeting in the front of the locker room, out of sight from where the defense gathers. But the defensive players are focused on the offense anyway. "They ain't done shit all night," says one defender. "They awful," says another.

Chavis holds up his hands. "Don't talk about the offense," he says. "They're taking pop-tart wide receivers and blocking our linebackers with them. That's bullshit. Shit, throw their ass down and make some plays." He claps his hands and then steps in front of the dry-erase board and says, "We're not going to change much, but we got to fill this gap." He points to the dry-erase board.

Chavis coaches his defense for 3 or 4 minutes and then asks if there are any questions. A player says, "They know our signals, Coach." Chavis pauses and runs his hand back over the top of his black hair. "They changing their offense after we give them our look," the player says.

"Well, we'll have to do a better job hiding them [the signals]. But you've got to be able to see them. You've got to see."

Chavis turns and walks away to head back to the front of the locker room; then, as if he's suddenly remembered something, he returns to the team. "Ain't nobody fall yet, have they?" The players shake their heads. "Well, then let's ball till we fall," Chavis says. He claps his hands furiously and then he leaves the locker room.

After the players meet with their position coaches, Fulmer addresses the team. He points out that South Carolina was also down this same amount to Tennessee last year and almost found a way to come back and win in Knoxville. "Make it a game in the first five minutes," he says. "We got the ball and there's thirty minutes left. Let's go play like big boys now."

As the team heads back onto the field, Arian Foster walks along slapping hands with each of his offensive linemen. "We got this shit," he says, confidently, to each of his linemen in turn.

Back on the field, Nick Stephens, now reinstated at quarterback, hits wide receiver Austin Rogers for a 50-yard gain on the first play. Rogers is dragged down from behind and returns out of breath to the sideline. "Too slow," says a player beside me. "I'm sorry," Rogers says, apologizing for not scoring.

On the first play after the big gain, Stephens misses a diving Gerald Jones on a crossing pattern. The defense's frustration with the offense continues to boil. Defensive tackle Demonte Bolden screams, "Why you diving, you dumb fuck? You ain't got to dive. Always diving and shit, just catch the damn ball."

The Vols face a fourth and 3 and go for it. Stephens's pass falls incomplete, near no one at the South Carolina 20-yard line. Fulmer pulls off his hat and runs his hand slowly through his thinning hair. Once more the furrows on his cheeks appear. Gamecock fans are deafening in their cheers, and a South Carolina student near the UT sideline holds up a sign that reads EVERYONE SAYS PHIL IS NEXT 2 GO, the E, S, P, N, and 2 underlined for the television cameras. Even the opposing fans know that Phil Fulmer, down 21–0 to his archrival Steve Spurrier, is coaching for his job.

On the next series, Tennessee tries to go back to the Rogers pass, the same play that opened the second half for a big gain, but South Carolina is waiting for it and nearly intercepts. Tennessee's offense is so stagnant that Dave Clawson is calling plays like a teenager playing the Madden video game for the first time: He has one successful play and repeats it immediately.

On Friday at the hotel I happened to catch a replay of the UT-Vanderbilt game in 2005, the season the Vols finished 5-6. In that game the UT offensive line opened gaping holes for a then-redshirt freshman Arian Foster. Arian had over 100 yards rushing in the first half. UT went on to lose that game, but as I watched the replay I noticed how easily the offense moved the football. Now? When the Vols get a first down I want to do a cartwheel. So do tens of thousands of other UT fans—and the defense.

South Carolina kicks a field goal to go up 24–0.

At the beginning of the fourth quarter the Vols finally score a touchdown on an Arian Foster run—his first of the season. Last season, by contrast, Foster had 12 rushing touchdowns. Foster is on his way to rushing 14 times for 56 yards in this game. It is the most carries he has had since October 4.

UT's 2-point conversation fails, and in predictable fashion, South Carolina returns the ensuing kickoff back to the Vol 32. Then, like he has all season, Eric Berry provides the only highlight in an otherwise depressing game for Vol fans. Berry swoops in front of a Stephen Garcia pass and heads up the South Carolina sideline with the ball cradled under his arm. Cut off, he reverses field and angles all the way back across the entire field until he is in front of the UT sideline. I find myself running along beside him waving my right arm for Berry. For just a moment I think he has clear sailing to the end zone and I'm ecstatic, my heart inside my throat.

Later I'll watch this play on TV and catch myself on the television screen at the exact moment that Berry picks off the pass. I watch myself leap up into the air, pump my fist, the look of sheer joy inescapable. It's an odd feeling, seeing yourself as a fan, the innocence and purity of a fan's reaction when he doesn't know he's being watched. I pause the replay and look at my face onscreen, frozen in ecstasy. For that instant I see what I've looked like during Tennessee games for the past 23 years. In a season of losses, this is the only image of unbridled joy. It's why I care, why we all do: for transcendent moments just like these.

But on the field South Carolina's players have recovered and cut Berry off. Berry goes down at the USC 44 and a rush of energy overtakes the sideline. The Berry swell of momentum lasts just four plays. That's how long it takes the Vols to be stopped on fourth down at the South Carolina 35. Once more the defense trudges onto the field. On his way out to the field Vol defensive lineman Donald Langley sees me writing in my notebook on the sideline. He pauses and looks down at me. "You better not be writing no bad shit," he says.

Unfortunately, there ain't much good shit to write.

I'm shivering. It's freezing in the South Carolina night air and I wish I'd remembered my jacket. Behind me two elongated heaters warm the bench. The heaters reek of gas, and if you stand at the right angle you can see the warm air rippling in the sky, burning up and returning to normal temperature. Like the Volunteer season after every positive play.

We're about to be 3-6, 1-5 in the conference, and I feel like I'm partly to blame. Maybe I should have thrown myself on the field and made a tackle on the South Carolina interception earlier tonight, taken whatever social opprobrium resulted. Perhaps I should walk over to the bench and give a pep talk to the team.

Fans think they have all the answers. We don't. All of the players already know everything I could tell them. I have a front-row seat to the team's implosion, but I know they're playing hard. As wide receiver Gerald Jones so eloquently put it after the Georgia loss, "Shit just don't go right." Continuing the theme, Tennessee's Dennis Rogan fumbles a punt return and South Carolina converts a field goal to make the score 27–6.

Tennessee center Josh McNeil is standing on the sideline next to Mike Hamilton when the ball is fumbled. Later he will tell me, "I was standing beside him and I didn't even want to look him in the face because I knew what he was thinking. I wanted to grab him and say, 'It isn't Coach Fulmer's fault. It's our fault. All our fault.'"

Coach Fulmer is still clapping, almost as if he realizes the die is cast—his career at Tennessee is over—and he wants to get in as many moments of coaching as he possibly can. He's not quitting, no matter what. Fulmer gathers the kickoff team around him, and I can't help but think of the futile nobility of coaching with every ounce of your soul to the final moment, trying to correct mistakes that you won't be around to see remedied. He keeps clapping, tapping their helmets in an effort to encourage his team. Above us the fog is coming down and settling in the upper reaches of Williams-Brice. There are only a few faint traces of orange remaining in the stadium.

I feel like I've aged a decade since that kickoff exactly 2 months ago on September 1 in California. I exhale my breath into the cold night air and wonder what my son thought of his first Halloween back in Nashville. The final moments tick off the clock, and the team jogs, ghostlike, through the falling fog and brightly lit field to the tunnel and visitors' locker room. A reporter runs up to Mike Hamilton, who is running alongside the team, to ask him a question about Fulmer's fate. He waves off the reporter. "Not now," he says.

INSIDE THE LOCKER ROOM the players drop their helmets in large bins and begin to strip off their jerseys and pads. It's warm in the locker room, but it smells of sweat and dirt and grime and cleats covered in dead grass. Like defeat. A few curses pepper the silence, and a couple of chairs scrape across the worn carpet. The players gather around, and Phil Fulmer instructs his players to drop to one knee and take the hand of the man beside them. In the prayer he asks his team for the courage to overcome obstacles that they don't understand. Then he stands.

Fulmer purses his lips and stares out at the locker room.

"I damn well appreciate the fight," he says. "I think, from what I saw, the seniors backed up their comments."

Vol defensive tackle Demonte Bolden begins to curse from his middle locker. "I'm sick of this shit. Y'all say we don't want to lose and then we still fuckin' lose. Shit . . . I'm a senior."

Phil Fulmer walks over to Bolden and places his hand gently on the back of Bolden's neck. He leans over and speaks to him so that no one else can hear. In the silence the managers continue stripping the Tennessee jerseys off the pads. The pads, unadorned, are stacked one after another on large metal rods.

Tennessee defensive coordinator John Chavis hugs offensive coordinator Dave Clawson in a tender embrace. Chavis throws his arm over Clawson's shoulder, and Clawson appears shocked, as if he's just been blindsided by a car he did not see. "I want you to know whatever happens, we're in this together," Chavis says.

Clawson blinks in the bright light of the locker room. "I appreciate that," he says.

Starting quarterback Nick Stephens approaches Chavis. "I'm sorry for the offense," he says.

"You don't have to apologize for anything," Chavis says.

On the other side of the locker room, Bolden continues to rant. Fulmer takes him into the alcove of the dressing room and places both of his arms on Bolden's shoulders. He speaks to him for a few moments and soon Bolden returns. When he does so, he is silent.

Coach Fulmer leaves the locker room for his press conference, but he doesn't make it far. In the exposed hallway between the locker room and the interview room, he runs into his youngest daughter, Allison, and embraces her. Fulmer is not crying, but his daughter is. Both of her arms are locked around her father. A few South Carolina stadium staff members stand in the hallway outside Williams-Brice Stadium, but give the two a wide berth. As his daughter cries, Fulmer, ever the consoler, always the clapper, lightly pats her on the back. He is speaking so softly to her that it appears he is saying nothing at all.

Inside the postgame press conference Fulmer is surrounded by 15 media members of varying ages. He stands at the front of the small room and the bright lights of the cameras go on, and Fulmer is immobile. In the rear of the room, Mike Hamilton, face expressionless, stands with his arms crossed in front of his chest. Fulmer's answers are soft and barely register in the quiet room. "The frustration of the offensive team right now, on a scale of one to ten, is probably a ten," he says. The reporters ask Fulmer if his program is slipping and whether he can solve the problems. Fulmer quietly says he can, that he's done it before and he deserves a chance to do so again, but his answers barely register in the somber room.

When Fulmer leaves the press conference, I walk outside to the big-rig truck that is parked on the sidewalk. Charlie Harris and I have to wait until the team leaves before we can get the truck back down to the trailer parked in the rampart outside the visiting dressing room.

Charlie has the truck running, heat cranked up high, and has brought me a postgame meal—fried chicken wrapped in napkins. We listen to the postgame radio show, during which the South Carolina announcers focus on the fact that Tennessee has just lost at Williams-Brice for the first time since 1992—a loss that precipitated the firing of Johnny Majors. They've also just announced that Duce Staley won't be joining them for the postgame show because he's nursing an illness. Right . . .

Outside the truck a few South Carolina fans pass by and taunt us. "It's a long drive back to Knoxville," they call. This, of course, is true whether we'd won or lost. Charlie shakes his head. "Most fans are pretty good, but some of them . . ." He shakes his head again and doesn't finish the sentence.

It's 11:30 P.M. and in half an hour Charlie Harris will be 66 years old. "I'm going to go say bye to my friends," he says. He climbs down the three steps to the ground and walks across the parking lot to the smattering of Volunteer fans still waiting on the team members to emerge from the locker room.

Among those friends that Charlie Harris will speak with is Coach Phillip Fulmer. As he leaves the locker room and makes the slow walk to the bus, Fulmer sees Charlie. "Be safe, Charlie," Fulmer says, "be safe."

The UT team buses pull out; they are going to the airport where the players will catch a charter flight back to Knoxville. In their wake only the big rig and the managers remain from Tennessee. All of the fans are gone, and the lights are turning off over the field. The managers have already packed up much of the football equipment and are now eating a postgame meal, barbecue and fried chicken, out of Styrofoam containers.

Charlie knows all the managers by name and claims, "One of the best things about this job is that you get to spend four years with all the managers . . . well, some of them five."

In fact, it could be as many as seven, as student manager Nick Trail informs me. "I've been here six but I'm getting a master's degree. But we've had one go for seven years to get a bachelor's. He graduated with 150 hours of credit, he just didn't want to leave Tennessee football."

The managers spend the next hour loading the truck. When they arrive back in Knoxville they'll unload all the materials, wash the jerseys, prepare the pads and helmets, and get ready for practice that evening. Charlie Harris, eyes drooping, leans over to me as the clock passes midnight. "I'm not tired," he says, "but this is one of those nights when I could be tired."

I tell him I'll stay awake with him, and he nods.

At 12:31 we climb into the cabin of the big rig and Charlie pulls forward through the gates of Williams-Brice Stadium. Hitting the road again seems to reenergize him. The streets of Columbia are empty and he commences a story immediately.

"Back in 2001 I had to go through a weigh station in Florida. It was on the way to Gainesville. I pulled up and the guy there said, 'What do you have in the truck?'

"I said, 'What do you think I've got in the truck? I've got football equipment.'

"He said, 'How much equipment do you have?'

"I said, 'Enough equipment to whip your team's ass.'

"His supervisor waved me through. Then, on the way back, he was working the other side. I pulled up grinning at him and he just said, 'Awww, hell,' and waved me through."

Charlie cackles.

We're on the interstate now and driving at a good rate of speed through the darkness. After a half hour, Charlie pulls off and buys a full container of coffee. "I'm not that tired, I just need some coffee to make sure I don't get tired," he explains. The truck stop is empty other than two women working the counter. Charlie buys me a Sunkist and a Payday candy bar. "Have you ladies seen my truck?" he asks.

Back on the road, Charlie tells me about the only time he ever got a flat tire on the way to a game. He was driving down to Gainesville with a manager asleep in the compartment behind him. "I'd been telling him how dangerous going on the road in the SEC could be and when he heard the tire explode he shot up in bed and said, 'What happened?' I said, 'Hell, the Gators just shot out one of our tires. I told you we were in hostile territory.' Buddy, you should have seen him then, he went diving to the ground and crawled to the window. It took him a long time to live that one down." Charlie hoots as he slaps the wheel in front of him.

We're silent for a time and then a glum Charlie turns to me. "I don't believe we're going to see any titties tonight," he says solemnly.

We drive on through the night, higher and higher into the dark North Carolina mountains, just me and Charlie and the detritus of a defeated football team. After a little while I say, "Happy birthday, Charlie," and he beams.

"Well, thanks," he says, "I'm glad you remembered."

Somewhere in the winding roads between North Carolina and Tennessee I fall asleep. Not for long, but long enough to realize how tired I am when I wake back up. The road is empty and Charlie is still beside me.

"Some of these sonsabitches drive with their brights on all the time," he says, as if our conversation has never ceased.

We arrive back in Knoxville at 4:50 in the morning on Sunday. Charlie parks the big rig at the UT football complex and we wait for the managers' bus to return. It has been almost 58 hours since we left the Neyland-Thompson complex on Thursday evening. No cars pass. There is no sound.

"Did you know," Charlie says, "that I used to have a UT orange hat with GOOD TIME CHARLIE written in red lettering on the hat? I left that hat at the Waffle House and when I went back to get it, it was already gone. I don't blame them for taking it, but it was a good hat. We won with that hat."

A friend arrives to pick Charlie up, and for the next half hour I'm alone at the UT football complex with the pads, the helmets, and the UT big rig. I lie down in the back of the truck and stare up at the ceiling.

Finally, from way down the road, comes the sound of the managers' bus returning to the football complex. The bus parks and student manager Nick Trail trudges down the stairs. "This is why night road games are horrible," he says.

I say good-bye, get in my own car, leave Knoxville, and drive through the darkest of night and on into the breaking of dawn. For the entire drive all I can think is: I went to a football game and came back from a funeral.

CHAPTER 19

THE FUTURE

IT'S 3 IN THE MORNING IN the middle of the week, and I can't sleep. The house is silent. It's cold and dark outside, the winter of fan discontent. I tiptoe down the stairs, wearing only my boxers and an old 1998 SEC Back-to-Back Champion T-shirt with holes under both arms that I won't allow my wife to throw away. Downstairs, I turn on the computer and log onto Volquest.com. Several hundred other UT football obsessives, their screen names scattered across the top of the message board, are also up late reading about the team.

I immerse myself in reading threads about the Vols. I've come to grips with the fact that of all the seasons in the history of Tennessee football to follow my favorite team with unlimited access, I've picked the worst one in the program's 110-year history. This season has been as painful as any I can ever remember. We've lost to our biggest rivals by double digits. We've won just one SEC football game out of six.

Many Saturdays I've come home from the games, often in the dead of night, and sat down on my couch to rewatch the losses on my DVR. I've watched all the games twice, except for the UCLA game. I just couldn't bring myself to watch it again. The UCLA recording sat in the DVR lineup for over a month. Once I clicked Play and watched the pregame analysis. I only lasted until ESPN's Mark May predicted that Arian Foster would rush for 150 yards. Then I had to turn off the television and erase the DVR recording. College football sadomasochism has its limits.

Now I'm trying to take solace in recruiting. I lose track of time scrolling through highlight tapes of high school seniors who have committed to my Vols. I'm convinced that if I just watch enough highlight tapes I can divine the future of my team, of my coach, of our seasons to come.

While I'm watching, my wife comes downstairs. I don't hear her. Basking in the flickering light of my computer screen, I don't see her, either. She stands in the doorway of my office, and when she speaks she startles me.

"What," she asks, "are you doing up this late?"

I jump, then reach up and turn off the sound of the highlight films.

"Nothing," I say.

"Are you looking at porn?"

"No."

I feel guilty, more embarrassed than if I had been caught looking at Internet porn. My fan obsession, when not being shared with other fan obsessives, doesn't seem very dignified. "Recruiting videos," I say softly.

"Recruiting videos?" She comes to my side of the desk, stretches, yawns, leans over, and looks at my laptop screen. On the screen is a video of Tajh Boyd, the quarterback recruit with Coach Fulmer in the Alabama locker room, playing at Phoebus High in Hampton, Virginia. The silent highlight video flashes in front of both of our faces. There is no other light in the house, and for once, my Tennessee football obsession has arrived at a perfect metaphorical moment: It's all we can both see.

Lara yawns again.

"So he's supposed to be a good quarterback?" she asks.

"Yes," I say, "maybe the next quarterback at Tennessee."

She yawns again and doesn't say it, but I can tell she's thinking: "So this is the player who is going to keep you up late at night. This is the guy who will bring ruination or ecstasy to my husband's fall weekends."

Early in our relationship Lara worried about my football obsession. She wondered why I would scream at the television screen during games, slam doors after losses, and occasionally disappear for a half hour to stew over my team's defeat. Later, when we talked about having children, she worried that all family outings during the fall would be circumscribed by the Tennessee Volunteer football schedule. Eventually she decided she liked me enough to put up with my obsession. But on nights like these, when I should be in bed but the Volunteers are calling, I'm truly embarrassed by how much I care.

"Why are you watching his film?" she asks.

I start to speak, reconsider, catch my words in my mouth, taste them, and realize how unpalatable they're going to be to someone who isn't also a diehard fan. "Because I'm trying to see how good he is," I say.

"Coaches do that, right?"

Her question hangs unanswered. My wife is far too logical to ever be obsessed with a team, too level-headed to permit a group of people she doesn't know to dictate her emotions. She smiles down at me, shakes her head. She leaves me then, walks back to the door of my office, and asks me one final question: "Is there ever anything that could happen in a Tennessee game that would make you not watch the next one?"

The question floors me. I realize that while I obsess about the results, torture myself on every play, and root for men and boys I don't know at all, in the end, no matter what happens, whether I watch the game from the sideline or my upstairs lounge, I'm always going to be back for the game the next Saturday.

"No," I say.

"Then deal with it, Clay, deal with it."

CHAPTER 20

"I LOVE PHILLIP BUT . . ."

ON THE AFTERNOON OF SUNDAY, NOVEMBER 2, 2008, Mike Hamilton phones Volunteer coach Phillip Fulmer on his cell. Hamilton asks Fulmer to meet him in his office at Stokely Athletic Center. The two never meet on Sundays. Fulmer arrives and they talk for an hour, sitting across from each other at Hamilton's brown conference table. On the floor of the office lay pictures waiting to be hung commemorating great wins, including the 1998 national championship game, from Volunteer football seasons past. During their conversation, Hamilton lets Fulmer know that he's being fired. At long last, the eight people, four inside the university, including the university president, and four major boosters from outside the university, whom Hamilton has trusted most in his analysis, are all in agreement: Phil Fulmer has to go.

Their common refrain is, "I love Phillip but . . ."

Although Fulmer is not surprised by Hamilton's decision, he does not take it sitting down. Later, Fulmer will describe how he argued to keep his job. "I said, 'Mike, this is when we hunker down and go to war and fight. You know, if you've lost ten percent of the people coming to the games, they'll come back if you win.' And I felt like I deserved, with the length of time I'd been there and all that I'd accomplished, that I needed a year to get it fixed and then make a decision if it didn't work."

On his drive home after meeting with Mike Hamilton, Fulmer reflects upon the change in athletic directors at Tennessee, from his old coach Doug Dickey, whom he trusted intimately, to the more business-minded Mike Hamilton. "I liked Coach Dickey being there because I knew what was expected and so on, what he expected of me," Fulmer will say later. "He didn't mind one bit coming over there and having a conversation about football or the team or anything. I don't know that I ever didn't trust Mike . . . necessarily. He was just different. Much more corporate, much more. Having not played ever, it would be very difficult for him to understand our world, having been from the development world where you stroke the boosters rather than Coach Dickey being a coach. He [Coach Dickey] understood those problems and how to make a stand and how to be tough, if you needed to be tough."

Fulmer telephones Thunder Thornton from his car. "Well," Fulmer says, "he finally did it."

At the end of the meeting Fulmer says he asked for just one thing. "I said, let me break the news to the team and the coaches prior to anything being announced. I think the news was out before I even left the building. It was really upsetting to me."

The news officially breaks on Monday morning. Just short of 16 years to the day after he received the head coaching job, Phillip Fulmer's career at Tennessee is over.

FULMER HAS ALWAYS REMINDED me of my own dad. They're both Tennessee men, born within 6 years of each other in small towns. Phil Fulmer was born in 1950 in Winchester and my dad was born in 1944 in Goodlettsville. Each man responds to success and failure, victory and loss, with a quiet and innate optimism.

Both men are tall—my dad is 6' 3" and Fulmer is 6' 1"—and broad-shouldered. Each man was an athlete. Both are quick to smile, gentle in a way that belies their size. In Little League my dad always gravitated to the kids who weren't any good, who didn't have fathers who came to practice to help them. Other dads focused on winning, and my dad wanted to win too, but he was always more proud of a mediocre kid on our team fouling a pitch off than he was that we'd won. "It was a good swing," he would tell the boy's mother.

Similarly, ever the optimist, Coach Fulmer always stands on the sideline clapping vigorously in the face of adversity. After losses Fulmer focuses on how close Tennessee was to victory: his players were always little more than one play away from winning, even if they weren't. The Tennessee football players are his boys, even when they do things Fulmer doesn't approve of. To fans and players alike, you always get the sense that he considers his team to be his family.

Even my father's and Fulmer's voices sound a bit similar; they are Southern, they speak slowly, elongate their vowels, and occasionally pause in mid-speech to decide which word should come next. They use words like *fixin'* and *heck* and *daddy* and *supper,* words foreign to people in other parts of the country. With one look at Phil Fulmer and my dad, anyone can tell they are from the South before they even open their mouths.

Both men continue to be religious in a time when the popularity of religion is at an all-time low. My dad always leads us in grace at his house no matter who the company is. At the end of games Coach Fulmer gathers his players, instructs them to take a knee, and leads them in prayer. Both men are decent and honest men, not given to show. Artifice and sarcasm never found them.

But most important, both men are selfless in a way in which many fathers aren't selfless today. Whenever my dad behaves charitably, he never makes a show of it. Instead he makes it seem like the most natural behavior in the world. As a kid, I remember going to minor league baseball games with very old men and my dad. Often the older man was a friend from church or an old friend of my then-deceased grandfather's.

Invariably my dad, by then a grown man for decades, addressed these men as "Mister" and responded to all their questions by saying "no, sir" and "yes, sir." We picked them up at church and drove downtown and watched the games with them, and all the while I never really understood why they were with us. My dad took the time to ensure that these men had a good seat and had what they needed to eat, and he occasionally leaned over and discussed a confusing call as if he was trying to unpack exactly what happened as well.

From a distance Phil Fulmer has always struck me as the same kind of man. And during this season, which I've had the good fortune to spend up close and personal with the Vols, I've heard dozens of stories of his generosity from everyone who surrounds the program, most of them people who aren't particularly well connected, people whom Fulmer didn't have anything to gain by impressing. From helping to get people into graduate school after football, assisting them in finding jobs associated with the UT football team, or never refusing to pose for a photo or sign an autograph for a fan, Coach Fulmer is accessible and welcoming to every single person he encounters. In an age when college football coaches have become, all too often, inaccessible and unwelcoming, convinced of their own genius and dismissive of their fans, Fulmer is a throwback to a different era.

In May 1998 Fulmer received a letter from a newly formed nonprofit, the Jason Foundation, located in suburban Nashville. The Jason Foundation is the brainchild of Clark Flatt, who created it in response to a horrible tragedy, the suicide of his son Jason Flatt in July 1997. In the wake of his son's suicide, Clark Flatt became aware of the prevalence of teenage suicide, learning that over 100 teenagers kill themselves each week. According to the Jason Foundation, "More teenagers and young adults die from suicide than from cancer, heart disease, AIDS, birth defects, stroke, pneumonia and influenza, and chronic lung disease combined." But in order to get the message out, they needed someone in the state of Tennessee who could draw attention to the issue. A teenage volunteer suggested the foundation contact Phillip Fulmer. Flatt sent the letter, expecting, at best, a form letter in response explaining that Fulmer appreciated the letter but was too busy to take on the burden of assisting a newly formed nonprofit. Ten days later his phone rang. It was Phillip Fulmer.

Fulmer invited Flatt and four teenage volunteers to Knoxville to meet with him. After the 184-mile drive, Flatt sat down in Fulmer's office and immediately began his sales pitch: "Let me tell you why youth suicide—" Fulmer raised his hand. "You don't have to sell me on anything, just tell me what I can do to help you." Fulmer threw his body and soul behind the foundation, raising money through charity dinners, hosting a charity golf outing each summer, and donating his own money to the cause. But that wasn't enough for Fulmer. When Flatt provided him with the phone numbers of teenagers struggling with depression, Fulmer called the youngsters himself. He did this for almost 10 years before anyone in the national media found out.

That first year Flatt met Fulmer at a UT event on West End Avenue in downtown Nashville. Fulmer signed autographs for a few hours and then left with Flatt. The two crossed a busy West End Avenue only to see a UT fan in a maintenance outfit, probably a janitor, rush to the door across the street. The fan spied Fulmer on the other side of the street and called out, "Hey, Coach!" and waved. Without prompting Fulmer walked back across the busy street, shook the fan's hand, posed for a photo, and signed two footballs. When they were finished he turned to Flatt. "I don't worry about when they want to meet me," Fulmer said. "I worry about the day when they don't."

Fulmer is now the national spokesperson for a foundation that has grown from one father's crusade to 83 offices in 30 states. "He's talked to tens of thousands of people for us," says Flatt. Fulmer also persuaded the American Football Coaches Association to partner with the Jason Foundation. "Thanks to him we have access to pretty much every college football coach in America," continues Flatt. "They all know our message now."

When I left the South to go to college, I found reassurance in being able to turn on the television and see Coach Fulmer on the sideline every weekend. No matter where I was when the television came on Saturday, Coach Fulmer was there. Tennessee was with him. And so, in some small measure, was my own dad. Phillip Fulmer wasn't just the head coach of the Tennessee football team, he was a symbolic father to every Tennessee football fan who grew up during his coaching tenure.

THE NEWS OF FULMER'S firing breaks on Monday morning, November 3, 2008. Tennessee center Josh McNeil wakes up later on Monday than normal because he has no classes on that day. His phone has 20 voicemails and 30 text messages. He turns on the television and the first thing he sees on ESPN is that Fulmer has been fired. He's in shock. McNeil speaks with his roommate, tight end Jeff Cottam, whose older brother Brad Cottam graduated the year before, and then with other players on the team. Neither McNeil nor his roommate wants to leave his apartment.

"It's almost like even though you've prepared yourself for it, you're still shocked when it happens. I couldn't believe it," McNeil says. "It wasn't right the way we found out from television, it flat-out wasn't right." Over and over in his head McNeil keeps thinking, "How did it come to this? Last year we were in the SEC championship game and then we beat Wisconsin in the bowl game and now this? How? How did this happen?"

Arian Foster is receiving treatment for a deep thigh bruise injury from the South Carolina game, watching television, when he sees the news break on ESPN. Immediately he feels responsible. He wonders whether he should have been more forceful about demanding carries, made a bigger show of not getting the ball enough, whether he could have done something, anything, to keep the season from blowing up around him. "I just felt like I didn't help the team as much as I could have. My heart was in it, but I don't know many preseason All-SEC backs that don't get the ball." Later still he says, "My grandfather used to say the older you get the farther you see down the road. I never really knew what he meant until now."

Foster's own difficulties with the season lead him to withdraw into himself. After 5 years of complete devotion to Tennessee football, his final season has turned disastrous. Players cope with the failure in different ways. Some blame the media, some blame the athletic department, some blame their coaches, some blame their teammates. Foster, a bruising back with a penchant for deep introspection, picks up a pen and writes this poem, entitled "Utopian Pie":

a place where the shade is not neglected by the sun,
take me there,
to the place where rivers run with thoughts,
where freedom isnt gold,
and where peace plays piano harmonious with war drums,
where rose petals grow wise and fall up,
take me there,
a place where the time is rhythmic and life sings hymns to itself,
a place where poetry is unspoken, and drank by the thirsty,
a place where blood was taboo and love was the law,
where the sea was the proof that the sun wasnt god,
we the water,
he the author,
write my story at the bottom of the universe's autumn,
take me there . . .

UT's coaching staff learns of Fulmer's firing in an equally startling way. Offensive coordinator Dave Clawson is at work in the film room when the news breaks on ESPN. This is the first he's heard of Fulmer's release. Clawson's family has only been in Knoxville since June. When he goes home that evening, his 9-year-old daughter will tell him that she heard of Coach Fulmer's firing from another student at her school. She has just one question for her dad. "How," she asks, "could anyone fire a man that nice?"

Later that Monday morning Mike Hamilton walks his prepared

statement over to Coach Fulmer's office to share it with him before the press conference, as he promised he would do in their Sunday meeting. He doesn't see Fulmer, nor does he have any idea what Fulmer will say at the press conference. Hamilton spends the rest of the day preparing for the press conference and making telephone calls to major donors to personally inform them of his decision.

In the early afternoon the coaching staff notifies the team of an afternoon meeting via text message. At 4 P.M., the team meets at the Neyland-Thompson Sports Complex, where only coaches and players are in the quiet room. Fulmer, furious that news broke before he could tell the team in person, arrives with his daughters and his wife. Many of the players are crying before he begins to speak; many are angry. Fulmer explains that football is big business and that business is the reason he's being fired. "It's not like it used to be here," he says. He tells the players not to feel responsible for the result. Some can't help it. "For the rest of my life, I'm going to have to deal with the fact that I was on the team that got him fired," McNeil says later. "Do you know how hard that is at a place like Tennessee? Where all the old players are family?"

Midway through his talk Coach Fulmer turns to his daughters and says, "I remember when you were so little the guys used to walk around with you on their shoulders." Fulmer breaks down then and begins to cry. His players join him. Everyone in orange is crying.

Phil Fulmer's relationship with his daughters has always humanized him to the players. "One minute he can be dog-cussing you for something you've done and the next minute one of his daughters shows up and he changes," says McNeil. "I used to tell Allison [Fulmer's youngest daughter], 'I'm going to keep you with me all during practice.' Coach Fulmer knew it too. Sometimes he'd see one of them coming and say, 'You just got lucky.' He couldn't stay mad in front of them."

Now their coach's connection with his daughters has brought the entire team to tears.

Fulmer's comment to his daughters resonates with his coaching staff as well. Says McNeil, "It's a cycle, some of them have kids now. Coach Cutcliffe's kids were here, Coach Adkins's kids are always here. It's one big family. Everybody's connected somehow. I wonder how many coaches know the equipment managers on a personal level."

Four months later, I'll ask Fulmer to describe how he felt at the moment of this meeting. Fulmer is quiet for a long time. Finally, he speaks: "When something you've given your youth to, your whole life to, and you have a couple of decisions by whoever, the powers that be, that made the decisions and they take all that away, it's really hard. Coaching at Tennessee had to come to an end sometime, three, four, five years, whatever it would have been, it would have been time to retire and move on. But it's just gut-wrenching, the whole thing was, trying to manage your own emotions and then you've got your children there who sacrificed a lot of their dad's time, again we had an unbelievable and great relationship, and your wife who has sacrificed a lot, that's the hard part. The girls growing up with the players . . . I'm getting emotional now and I still try not to go there and think about it; it's hard, it's a hard time."

After Fulmer and his family exit the room, the team learns that athletic director Mike Hamilton would like to meet with them as well. Rather than stay and hear what Hamilton has to say, the entire team departs together. They're furious with Hamilton and want him to know it. The players walk to Neyland Stadium and meet in their new $15 million locker room—the locker room so fancy that Phil Fulmer always seemed a bit incongruous inside. They talk about what their next move should be. Ultimately they decide that since Coach Fulmer has always been there for them when they need him, they'll be there for Fulmer when he needs them.

At 5 P.M., in the brand-new media center just off the football locker room, the press conference begins. It's packed; every news organization in the state has sent reporters. Many national broadcasters are there as well; ESPN breaks into their programming to carry the press conference live.

For his entire life Phil Fulmer has wanted to coach the University of Tennessee. Not only has he achieved that dream, he's taken a small state of 6 million people to the pinnacle of the nation's sporting glory in 1998. And now, less than 10 years after he won that national championship, the place he's loved all his life, the university he's called home for 34 out of his last 40 years, is letting him know that he's no longer needed or wanted. "It's like one day we told our daddy not to show up for dinner," says McNeil.

Wearing a black-and-gray-striped suit and an orange tie with a Tennessee pin on his left lapel, Fulmer enters the room and sits at the table alongside a nervous Hamilton, who later says he was thinking over and over to himself, "This is Tennessee on national television, this is Tennessee on national television," terrified that something might go very wrong. Fulmer's not wearing any hat and, suddenly, absent of his hat, he looks older and balder than he normally does. Slowly, Fulmer reads from what appears to be a handwritten script.

"As a young sophomore playing for Coach Dickey, that field outside is where I first got my jersey dirty playing in a big game for Tennessee. It was September 27, 1969, and I was nineteen years old. We were playing Auburn on television that day, something rare for Tennessee at that time, and we whipped a higher-ranked Auburn team. Tennessee football has been the focus of my professional life ever since."

Watching Coach Fulmer deliver his speech is like watching your dad cry. It's agonizing and uncomfortable as Fulmer chokes on several words.

"However, this 2008 season has not gone as well as anyone would like. That includes me, our coaches, our players, our administration, and our great fans. Many fans have been supportive, some have been angry, all of us are disappointed . . . Our Tennessee family is united in its goals but divided in the right path to get there. I love Tennessee too much to let her stay divided."

At this point Vicky Fulmer joins Coach Fulmer on the stand. She reaches out her left hand and rubs each of his shoulders as she passes him, just for an instant. Fulmer continues, "I love this university and hope everyone knows that beyond a shadow of a doubt. As I close I want to thank the Tennessee people for all the opportunities I have been given and earned here. I have been blessed to work hard at a job every day doing something that never felt like a job. I was doing something that I loved." Fulmer's voice cracks, and he seems on the verge of losing control as he says, "We will say thank you to everyone who loves the Vols."

Fulmer's remarks last no more than 7 minutes. He takes only a few questions, including one from a reporter who asks what it's like to see his players present for his press conference and what it means to him. Fulmer bites his upper lip, holds it there, mouth trembling for an instant. "That's what we're about," he says. "It's in the name of Saturday afternoon but it's not really about Saturday afternoon at all. It's the reason we all got into coaching. It's about having that relationship that we all have and I feel good about it. A lot of people don't ever get to experience that and I've had it for a long time."

Finally, asked to sum up his tenure at Tennessee, the old offensive lineman returns to the line of scrimmage once more.

"It's not about, you know, just your name on the plaque somewhere at all; it's more about being in the trenches and fighting out."

As soon as Fulmer answers the final question and Mike Hamilton takes back over the microphone, the entire Tennessee football team stands and exits the press conference. But not before senior wide receiver Josh Briscoe asks a rhetorical question of Hamilton: "Why has it become more important to make a dollar than to keep the Tennessee family and the Tennessee tradition that we've had for years?"

In 1990 Tennessee lost 9–6 to Alabama. I watched the game with my grandfather and cried. After the loss, he remonstrated me for the tears. "Men don't cry about football games," he said. I was 11 then. For 18 years I haven't shed a single tear over UT football. But today, as I watch the press conference, I cry, great heaving tears come rolling down my cheeks.

I'm not crying because I think it's unfair for Coach Fulmer to be forced out—his record hasn't been good enough of late. I'm crying for what we've lost and what I don't think we'll ever have again: a time when a college football team represented more than a business.

For months I've argued that there are two perfect questions to ask when assessing a coach. I've shared these questions with countless audiences when asked about the status of the Tennessee football program. I've puffed out my chest and spoken slowly so that everyone could comprehend my distilled brilliance. "The first thing to ask," I've said, "is how many other places would hire him? And the second question to ask is this: How ridiculous would you think it was if a major corporation said they were going to hire a new CEO but restricted their candidates to residents of a particular state or graduates of a particular school? Because UT football, like it or not, is a big business." Then I've waited for everyone in the audience to nod. The questions were poised to elicit understanding nods. My rhetorical questions implied that Phillip Fulmer was a remnant of a bygone era, a homegrown Tennessee boy who wouldn't be hired by anyone else; and that Tennessee football was a major national corporation, which we were running like a small nonprofit church in 1943.

Now, in this exact moment, I hate myself for asking these questions, for thinking myself so smart and worldly in their formulation. Because I hate the very basis of the questions. Like just about everyone in this day and age, I allowed my passion to be dictated by a cold and clinical dispassion. I sold my fandom to the corporate behemoths, willed the final ounce of my soul to a multinational corporation that existed solely to make money. Outsourced my own dad.

In the end Phil Fulmer represents the final capstone of the era when the SEC went national. He is the final man to be born in the state where he coached, the final head coach to be a graduate of his school. For better or worse, all of our football teams will be helmed by hired mercenaries now; a once-regional game has become the nation's pastime. CBS and ESPN have turned our teams into national behemoths. Yes, more people than ever before see our teams play from all four corners of the country—and beyond. But I'm afraid that's going to make the teams feel, paradoxically, further and further away from the way we experienced them in our youth. It used to be that the SEC solely belonged to the people of the South. No longer.

In the hours that follow e-mails trickle into my inbox from fans of every school in the SEC. All of them say virtually the same thing: "I hated Coach Fulmer and Tennessee, but I've never been sadder watching a press conference."

For once even the posters on Volquest are stunned, amazed that at long last the man they've blamed for Tennessee's futility is no longer at the head of the Volunteer family. Now that the Vol revolution is complete, many comment on how much Tennessee truly meant to Fulmer. Thousands of grown men confess to crying during the press conference. A few publicly second-guess their calling for his firing. After months of ridiculing his every decision, questioning his every move, UT fans have gotten what they wanted. But they are not gloating.

Later that day, my radio show co-host at 104.5, Chad Withrow, a Tennessee graduate, calls me and says, "If everyone could have seen this side of Fulmer all along, I don't think we would have ever fired him. Ever."

That night my dad calls me. "I listened on the radio," he says, "because I didn't think I could watch it on television."

FIVE DAYS LATER, TENNESSEE'S home game against Wyoming is a disaster. Thunder Thornton lines up alongside the Vol Walk wearing a 1998 national championship hat. He's had his own message embroidered on the back of the hat. FIRE HAMILTON, the hat says. "I did it for the team," he says.

I watch the game on TV with my dad in Nashville. We're both too emotionally drained to make the trip to Knoxville. It's the first time I've ever seen Tennessee run through the T and not gotten chills down my spine. For the first time in years I don't particularly care what happens. At this point the game is an afterthought.

Arian Foster is injured and doesn't play. Nick Stephens starts at quarterback and is picked off twice. The first interception is returned to the 4-yard line. Shortly thereafter Wyoming throws a touchdown pass. The second interception is returned for a touchdown. Just like that, Tennessee is behind 13–0 at the half. The crowd is stunned. What's more, it's homecoming. Tennesseans from across the state and country have descended on Knoxville to find a program in transition, the end of an era.

Jonathan Crompton replaces Stephens at quarterback and throws a touchdown pass to wide receiver Gerald Jones in the third quarter. The lead is sliced to 13–7. On fourth and 18 from the Wyoming 47-yard line with 1:43 remaining, Crompton throws an incomplete pass. Wyoming takes over on downs. Tennessee loses 13–7 to a Wyoming team that entered the game as a 27-point underdog with a record of 3-5. The Vols have put up just 219 yards of offense on 67 plays against one of the worst statistical defenses in the country.

Tennessee falls to 3-7, the worst record in the history of the Volunteer football program. There will be no bowl game.

At the end of the game, my dad stands up. "Well," he says, "we really let the rest of the SEC down today."

"The rest of the SEC doesn't care about us anymore," I say.

"I feel really bad for Coach Fulmer," replies my dad.

CHAPTER 21

THE LIST

THE LIST BEGINS WITH 30 NAMES. Mike Hamilton has long kept a list of potential replacement football coaches—an actual physical list of printed names that is fluid and constantly evolving. He edits and revises this list frequently—the coaching golden boy can have a bad season, a coach can sign a huge contract that takes him off the table, or a coach can go down for rules violations. In a world as cutthroat as college football, a coaching list should never be stale.

Hamilton keeps his list at home, away from prying eyes. He's never known when the list would come in handy, but in the wake of Phil Fulmer's firing suddenly the list is his holy grail. And gold, pure gold, for the trove of Tennessee fans who are watching every move, every hint of a move, and every rumored move to divine the name of the next head coach. Hamilton is aware of this obsession, and he's going to do his best to avoid reading intimate details about his search in the newspaper.

This is not Hamilton's first big hiring decision—in 2005 he hired Bruce Pearl, then a basketball coach at the University of Wisconsin-Milwaukee. Hamilton conducted his basketball interviews from a Chicago hotel room. He didn't leave and didn't permit anyone to contact him, to such an extent that the front desk didn't allow a pizza that he'd ordered to be delivered. Bruce Pearl's team, Wisconsin-Milwaukee, was in Chicago at the time playing the University of Illinois in the NCAA tournament. Hamilton considered going to watch the game but was afraid of drawing public attention to his interest in Pearl. He emerged from that search with a very successful hire and with few leaks.

But Hamilton knows that this search, for a football coach, will be much more complicated—Hamilton compares hiring a new basketball coach to turning around a motorboat in the river, and hiring a new football coach to turning an aircraft carrier. Never before has the University of Tennessee held a national coaching search for its football job, and Tennessee fans and the media that report on Tennessee are already fast on his heels.

At 5:30 A.M. on Thursday, November 6, 2 days before the homecoming game against Wyoming, Hamilton embarks on the first leg of his cloak-and-dagger scheme. He travels in a different car than his own (reporters have been known to follow the cars of athletic directors) to a Shoney's Restaurant off I-75. There he meets three other members of the athletic department, Gary Wyant, John Currie, and David Blackburn, changes cars, and the four of them take I-75 south en route to Atlanta, Georgia—a major metropolitan area into which they can rapidly disappear.

Hamilton has chosen to drive in a car because he knows that in the age of Internet message boards, zealous fans track all plane travel of everyone associated with UT football and eagerly dissect their movements online. Already Volquest has reached a fever pitch over the significance of several University of Tennessee plane trips to locations near rumored coaching candidates. But Mike Hamilton would never fly the UT planes; he's aware of the online flight trackers.

The four men from the UT athletic department arrive at an Atlanta hotel and meet Chuck Neinas, a consultant who will assist in the hiring search. Neinas, via his company Neinas Sports Services, is an expert in the black arts of the coaching search. In the world of college sports he might best be described as a "fixer." The university has hired him to initiate contact with potential candidates and their agents. He's an intermediary of the highest order whose résumé includes shepherding legislation through Congress as an executive with the NCAA, serving as commissioner of the Big 8 conference for a decade, and spending 17 years as the head of the College Football Association. By having Neinas make the initial contacts, Tennessee can avoid a public rejection if a coach isn't interested and keep the list of candidates virtually secret.

With Neinas already awaiting them, the four men from Tennessee check into a suite with a conference table and, beginning at 9 in the morning, spend the day poring over candidate biographies and discussing the pros and cons of each coach on Hamilton's list. They dissect the 30 names on Hamilton's list with the goal of cutting this initial list to 10 to 12 by the end of this first day.

When the group from Tennessee emerges from the hotel room and returns to their car for the trip back north to Knoxville on I-75, they have their list of a dozen names. Now the real nitty-gritty commences, the interview process. Over the next 3 to 4 days, Neinas will be making telephone calls to the representatives of each of these coaches to gauge their interest and find out whether they would be available to interview for the Tennessee job.

During this initial trip to Atlanta, even Hamilton's wife doesn't know where he is. But this doesn't mean he isn't recognized. At a Pilot gas station in northern Georgia, the foursome stops to fill up. As he walks through the gas station, Hamilton is stopped by a truck driver, a Vol fan. "Hey, you out getting us a coach yet?" the man asks.

Hamilton laughs nervously. "Not yet," he says.

CHAPTER 22

THE UPSIDE-DOWN BOWL

ON SATURDAY, NOVEMBER 22, Tennessee arrives to play Vanderbilt in Nashville. But most fans are more interested in the search for a new coach than in what happens on the field this week. Volquest is alive with coaching rumors. Everyone has a source. It's almost as if this football season has already ended. Threads relating to the coaching search fill the first page, while a stray discussion or two deals with the actual game at hand.

Volquest posters speculate about some of the biggest names in coaching. One day Tampa Bay Buccaneers coach Jon Gruden is in town to meet with Mike Hamilton. Another day former Pittsburgh Steelers coach Bill Cowher is golfing with Tennessee's top boosters. More vague rumors swirl about every successful coach in America. From Butch Davis at North Carolina to Mike Leach at Texas Tech, Troy Calhoun at Air Force, and Lane Kiffin in California, speculation runs rampant.

But only one man really knows the ins and outs of this search. And that's Mike Hamilton, who's here in Nashville for the game against Vanderbilt. As soon as the game ends, he will climb on a commercial flight out of Nashville and head off for another interview. But no one knows this . . . yet.

While speculation about his successor runs rampant, Coach Fulmer telephones Clark Flatt, head of the Jason Foundation, and says, "I'm not going to be as much of a use to you now that I'm not a head coach anymore. I wanted you to know I understand if you need to find a new national spokesperson." Flatt is floored. "I told him he'd always be our national spokesperson, that we weren't quitting on him." Fulmer is quiet on the other end of the line for a moment. "Thanks for sticking with me, Clark," he croaks.

CHARLIE HARRIS PULLS THE Vol big rig to a stop on Jess Neely Drive outside of Vanderbilt's football stadium. Now that Tennessee has lost to Wyoming, he knows this will be his final road trip of the year. The Vols will finish their season with a home game against Kentucky next week.

Many players, coaches, and team personnel are taking the loss of Coach Fulmer very hard. One of them in particular is graduate assistant and former UT cornerback Inky Johnson. Listed at 6', 170 pounds, Inky Johnson is and always was, in actuality, 5' 9" and 150 pounds. A slight young man with slim shoulders and deep-set eyes hidden inside large eye sockets, Inky was so small without pads and cleats that girls in Knoxville didn't believe him when he said he was on the football team. He didn't play football as a sophomore or a junior in high school because of injuries—an injured ankle as a sophomore and a broken clavicle as a junior. As a result, he was an unheralded recruit from a small Atlanta high school who did everything for his team, including kick field goals. He didn't even make his official visit to Tennessee until the spring of 2004, during basketball season.

Inky grew up a fan of the Georgia Bulldogs, but did not receive a scholarship offer from the team. When Tennessee offered him a free ride and a spot on the football team, he accepted immediately. Even still, Johnson was such an invisible recruit that when he was introduced to the UT media, several reporters actually asked him, "Do you really think you're ever going to get on the field?"

Johnson replied, "Yeah, and I'm gonna start."

He did start—as a sophomore against Alabama, and in the rest of the games in that horrid 2005 season, the 5-6 campaign that included a 28–24 loss to Vanderbilt. The next season Inky was entrenched as a starter at left cornerback when a 1-0 Tennessee team took the field against Air Force on September 9, 2006. Coming off a win over Cal-Berkeley in the season opener, Air Force's triple option offense befuddled the Tennessee defense.

"They were killing us," says Inky.

With 2 minutes left and the Vols clinging to a 31–24 lead, Air Force attempted an onside kick. The ball deflected off Inky Johnson's hands and Air Force recovered. Shortly thereafter the Vols were in a cover 3 defense when Air Force completed a swing pass to the sideline. Inky rushed forward to make the hit and the Air Force receiver shrunk to prepare for the impact. The force of Inky's tackle landed between his helmet and his right shoulder. The receiver went down on the Neyland Stadium turf and Inky collapsed to the ground and did not get back up. As the trainers rushed to check on him, Inky lay staring at the blue sky above him. He didn't believe he was seriously hurt, not even when the trainers lifted his right arm to the sky and he said he could feel nothing at all. They put him on the stretcher and carried him directly to the medical center. His dad and team chaplain James "Mitch" Mitchell rode in the ambulance with him.

"I hit that guy pretty good, huh?" Johnson asked during the ambulance ride.

"Yeah," his dad and Mitch agreed, "real good."

Upon arriving at the hospital and enduring a battery of tests, Johnson noticed the doctors speaking in a circle out of earshot. Left alone, he began to worry that his injury was more serious than he'd expected. When the doctors returned to speak to him, they said he had to undergo surgery immediately; his subclavian artery had burst and if they didn't begin operating immediately, the doctors might have to amputate his right arm.

Inky never flinched.

During his first surgery, the doctors successfully took an artery from Inky's thigh to replace the one he'd torn in his shoulder. But when he woke up, his doctors informed him that he'd also torn three nerves in his shoulder; the damage to his body had been more severe than even they had anticipated. He would never play football again.

But for the moment, football was the least of his worries; Inky Johnson was going to have to fight to keep his right arm. Inky's teammates and coaches visited him in his Knoxville hospital room en masse. The coaches took it hardest, especially defensive coordinator John Chavis. "Chief's [Chavis's] eyes watered up. It was the first time I ever saw him cry," says Inky.

Inky spent 1 week in the hospital and was then sent to Rochester, Minnesota, for further surgery. There doctors discovered that Inky had torn not just three but all five nerves in his shoulder, a devastating injury. The doctors were uncertain that Inky Johnson, the smallest man on the UT roster, a starter by his sophomore year, would ever be able to use his arm again. In the meantime, Inky needed to carry his right arm in a sling for every waking hour of the day.

"People only think about football, but a lot more got taken away from me," says Inky. "Simple things, things no one thinks about anymore. Dressing, tying my shoes, taking a shower, all of them took so much time." As if that weren't enough, Inky was right-handed, so he could no longer write. Tennessee provided him with voice recognition software to aid his writing, but the computer program was fickle and often malfunctioned. "It didn't get my accent," says Inky. Eventually he taught himself to write using his left hand.

Inky says he did his best to disguise how much his injury troubled him, how overwhelmed he was by his handicap. Only his roommates—three football players—and his parents had any idea how difficult things were for him. He talked to his parents often. "I don't know how I made it through the end of the day," he would say, cradling the phone with his left hand.

"Fans don't know about any of the risks. They only see you on Saturday and think they know you," he says 2 years later. He laughs, stares at me, through me. "They don't know what you go through, what you give up, the times you don't see your family. They want you for those three hours and then they don't want you anymore."

When asked whether he'd have played football if he'd known of the injury that would come, he's silent for a moment, then breaks into a large smile. "To be honest with you, I wouldn't have. People lie and say that they would have, but I wouldn't have." In the same breath Inky says that he loves football and his family at Tennessee. "There's just something," he says, "about running through that T."

In 2008 Inky graduated with a major in political science, and now he's a graduate assistant on the UT sideline, a link between the players and the coaches, a starter who never lost his job. On Saturday at Vanderbilt he's on the sideline, jacket bundled over his right arm in a sling, pacing up and down as Tennessee begins their game.

I remember when Inky Johnson was injured. I'd listened to the game on the radio in my bedroom and I was enraged that my Vols were letting an upstart military academy challenge them at home. I threw my pillow on the ground when Air Force scored to make it 31–24. I let loose a string of curses and slammed the bedroom door closed when Air Force recovered the onside kick, never even thought about the ball that skittered between Inky Johnson's fingers and changed his life forever.

I heard UT's radio announcer, Bob Kesling, say that Inky Johnson was injured on a pass play that ended in an Air Force completion, but my reaction was to curse and wait impatiently for the player to get off the field so the game could continue. I knew the name Inky Johnson only vaguely; he was just another player who could be replaced, not a star. Of course, I didn't know how badly he'd been injured, but I was already prepared for the game to recommence, one nearly anonymous name at defensive back replaced by another. Fans don't make time to care about every player on the football field, because, in the end, there is always another one coming.

Our lack of caring is a cruel and harsh reality that most fans never acknowledge, even if the players toiling on the field for free feel it. Thankfully for Inky, Coach Fulmer insisted that his connection to the team remain unbroken, first as a student assistant and later as a graduate assistant.

Now Inky's grappling with the chasm in Vol leadership. "It's crazy, man, I don't even know how it all happened. I still can't believe it. They did that man wrong."

TODAY THE COMMODORES ARE favored over Tennessee by 3.5 points. Never before in my life has Vanderbilt been favored to beat Tennessee. I arrive on a gray day in Nashville, a 2-mile commute from my downtown house to the stadium.

After a 5-0 start to the season, Vanderbilt head coach Bobby Johnson, a white-haired man who bears an uncanny resemblance to Steve Martin, was universally lauded as the best coach in the land. Vanderbilt climbed as high as #13 in the rankings and then began a tumble—losing four consecutive games to run their record back to 5-4. Needing just one win to guarantee their first bowl season since 1982, Vanderbilt choked on four consecutive occasions.

Enter Kentucky. Last week Vanderbilt won 31–24 in Lexington to get six wins and become bowl-eligible. Qualifying for a bowl has made Bobby Johnson the closest thing to a rock star that Vanderbilt has ever seen. The implacable Johnson has not allowed this success to alter his personality. He still rarely sees an adjective he trusts and grins slowly, almost ponderously, as if his mouth can't quite comprehend the direction in which his lips are moving.

Back in June I had the good fortune to share a private jet ride with Johnson. The two of us flew to and from Birmingham to play in a charity golf event at the exclusive Shoal Creek golf course. The plane was already coming to Nashville, and Birmingham's *Roundtable Radio* added me as an additional passenger because Johnson would be flying there anyway. I was happy to play in the event, and I received only one instruction from Lance and Ian of *Roundtable Radio:* "Whatever you do, Clay, don't curse. He doesn't like cursing."

So as Johnson and I sat across from each other on the 70-minute plane ride, knees almost touching on the five-seat airplane, I made a bit of small talk and did my best to keep from cursing. It's not that I'm a sailor on shore leave, but I was afraid that the fear of cursing would, paradoxically, make me more likely to curse. I spent the whole flight biting my tongue. On the way there it was pretty easy to keep control of my vocabulary. On the difficult Shoal Creek golf course, it was impossible. Thankfully Coach Johnson and I weren't paired together.

One of the perks of the tournament was that each participant received a nice piece of Nike luggage. A consolation prize, as if we needed one, for managing to complete one of the most beautiful and difficult courses in the South, a course so gorgeous that merely taking a divot felt like sacrilege.

On the way back, my cursing ban was put to the test. About halfway from Birmingham to Nashville, as we cruised several thousand feet high in the clear blue afternoon sky, I noticed that Bobby Johnson, heretofore completely focused on the newspaper in front of him, kept looking in my direction. His expression was one of studious attention, as if he'd looked deep into my soul and discovered the inner curse words percolating in my voice box. "Clay," he said, "can you get the pilot?"

I turned and tapped our pilot on the shoulder. The pilot turned around and lifted his headset.

"Coach Johnson needs you," I said.

When he had the pilot's attention, Johnson pointed out the window. "We've been leaking fuel for a while now," he said, delivering the line as calmly as if he'd just offered a first-grader a peanut butter and jelly sandwich. At that exact moment I knew that Vanderbilt was going to a bowl game this season. Bobby Johnson, tens of thousands of feet in the air, was unflappable as our plane leaked fuel. What's a fourth-down call to a guy like this?

I was not as calm as Johnson. I gripped the beige armrests and stared out the window at the fuel disappearing into the billowy white clouds. I wondered how long it would take to pass out when the plane plunged toward the ground. Meanwhile the fuel was clear, almost unnoticeable as it scampered into the distance.

"We know," the pilot said. "We'll be fine. We're going to refuel in Nashville."

At this point Johnson nodded and returned to his newspaper.

I sat across from him mouthing silent curse words over and over again.

For the remainder of our flight, Johnson did not bat an eye. Instead he read his newspaper. Occasionally he looked out the window to confirm that we were still leaking fuel, but he never said a word. When we landed, I practically leapt out of the plane and kissed the ground. Johnson was more concerned with prosaic matters. "Make sure," he said, addressing me, "that you get the right suitcase."

NOW JOHNSON IS ON the opposing sideline from my Tennessee Vols, whom Vandy is favored to beat for the first time in modern history. I'm sitting in the stands, surrounded by my buddies in the Vanderbilt student section, which is virtually empty because Vanderbilt gives its students the entire week off for Thanksgiving. The Vanderbilt football stadium is nowhere near full, and there are fewer UT fans than I've ever seen at a UT-Vandy game in Nashville. A few signs in support of Phil Fulmer dot the pockets of orange. It's freezing in the stands.

UT takes possession of the ball first, with Jonathan Crompton starting at quarterback again. He's been promoted after Nick Stephens's performance against Wyoming. On his first pass attempt, the second play of the game, Crompton drops back and throws a dart 5 yards to his right. The good news is the pass is caught. The bad news is the other team catches it. This interception will be the only pass attempt of the day for Crompton.

My friend Junaid groans beside me. "Did you ever believe," he asks, "that our offense would get so bad that we can't even complete a pass to the right team?"

Vandy doesn't score despite having great field position and so begins a football game that sets back offensive football by 60 years. It's awful. Neither team can complete a pass; in fact, Tennessee is playing this game as if the forward pass has been repealed for this week. With 7:03 remaining in the first quarter, UT redshirt freshman quarterback B. J. Coleman makes his first appearance of the season. He completes a pass, but it's called back for a penalty. Tennessee continues to pound the ball with the running game.

And by "pound the ball," I mean slowly move down the field at around 3 or 4 yards a clip. The first quarter is scoreless. But then in the second quarter UT flexes their muscle, 1933-style. My grandfather would have been impressed. The offense is so unimaginative that B. J. Coleman, slightly more mobile than a refrigerator, runs the quarterback draw not once, not twice, but three times out of four plays early in the second quarter. Buoyed by this offensive onslaught led by their slow-footed quarterback, Tennessee's Montario Hardesty scores from 8 yards out with 11:25 remaining in the quarter.

In most games a touchdown lead is not that significant. In this game the score might as well be 35–0. With 7:25 remaining in the half, Daniel Lincoln adds a field goal and then, mercifully, as he has done all season, defensive back Eric Berry makes a play worth celebrating.

Vandy's Chris Nickson drops back to pass but finds himself under pressure. Rather than take the sack, Nickson attempts to complete a pass over the middle in the direction of Eric Berry. Bad decision. Berry swoops in front of Vandy's receiver and snags the football. Forty-five yards later he's standing in the end zone and UT leads 17–0. The game is effectively over.

It's certainly over for Vandy's starting quarterback, Chris Nickson. In the final home game of his career, Nickson has one of his worst efforts at Vanderbilt. He finishes 1 of 5 passing for –4 yards with an interception returned for a touchdown. On the quarterback rating scale these numbers are known as "death." Junior quarterback McKenzi Adams replaces Nickson and promptly throws his own interception to Tennessee's Brent Vinson. UT adds another field goal. It's 20–0 at the half, and McKenzi Adams is probably busy texting Auburn quarterback Kodi Burns to see if Burns is interested in joining his boy band after graduation.

My friend Chad Messier, a Vandy season ticket holder and fellow Vandy Law alum, reacts with disgust. "This is just awful," he says, summing up the game in four succinct words.

As the UT team jogs off the field I see Inky Johnson running toward the tunnel, injured right arm hiked up under his orange jacket. He's grinning, lost in his own private joke or simply ecstatic to have a lead as he exits the field for the final halftime of a road game in his SEC career. His former roommate, Jerod Mayo, is soon to be named the NFL defensive rookie of the year. If Johnson is bitter about his career coming to a quick close, he never shows it.

The second half is more of the same, awful offense mixed with solid defensive play. With 11:07 remaining in the third quarter, Vandy kicks a field goal. Seven minutes later they intercept a B. J. Coleman pass and return it for a touchdown. The 'Dores have surged to within 10. For the final 19 minutes of the game, Tennessee will not attempt a pass. Instead they try four men at quarterback; Coleman is replaced once more by Crompton, and Eric Berry and Gerald Jones also run plays at quarterback after taking direct snaps from the center. In the end, Tennessee's quarterbacks will combine to share this stat line: 4 of 8 passing for 21 total yards. Two of the incompletions are intercepted, one for a touchdown. The Vols run the ball 51 times for 222 yards—an average of 4.4 yards a carry. The Dave Clawson offense that arrived in the late summer with such power and potential is officially dead. But the Vols win, 20–10.

After the final seconds of the game drip away in a light rain, I walk outside and stand in the afternoon chill beside the UT big rig, parked on Jess Neely Drive just outside the Vandy football stadium. After a time Charlie Harris comes out from the locker room. He sees me standing beside the big rig and beams.

"Clay," he says, "good to see you!"

A few days before, I'd gone to the local mall and purchased a new baseball cap for Charlie—a Tennessee coach's hat. I've had it stitched in red lettering on the back. GOOD TIME CHARLIE, it reads. I hand the hat to Charlie—a replacement for the one he lost 2 years ago at a South Carolina Waffle House. "Well, I'll be damned," he says, putting it on immediately.

He's brought his own gift for me, a golden bracelet with my wife's name on it. Charlie makes the bracelets in his spare time. "Now don't give it to her until Christmas," he says.

The bracelet is beautiful, delicate and bright in the fading afternoon light of a November Saturday. I cradle it in my hands. As we talk, three female Vandy fans walk past. "Go on and put the big rig back in the garage," they say, "we going bowling."

They stop to see what Charlie will say. Charlie beams at them. "You ladies cold, you want to see inside?" he asks.

Charlie and I had planned that I might ride with him to whatever bowl game UT qualified for. Now, after the Wyoming game, he won't be going anywhere in the big rig.

"I don't guess we'll be going bowling," Charlie says. He sighs. "I'm not sure if this is my last year or not, not sure if they'll want me back."

Charlie adjusts the brim of his new cap, pulls it down so that his eyes are shaded a bit. "This is a sharp hat," he says. "Hopefully we'll win some games with this one."

CHAPTER 23

MIKE HAMILTON
FINDS HIS MAN

ON THE THURSDAY OF THE OPEN week after the Wyoming loss, November 13, Hamilton hits the road again. Once more he meets his trio of search colleagues—all University of Tennessee athletic department employees—at a Shoney's. Their first interview is Lane Kiffin, the former coach of the Oakland Raiders who has previously been offensive coordinator and recruiting director at the University of Southern California. Kiffin is just 33 years old and 2 months removed from being fired by Al Davis, owner of the Oakland Raiders. Davis fired Kiffin on September 30, 2008, for violating the terms of his contract, but after watching Davis's crazy press conference, most observers, including Mike Hamilton, who has researched the affair, believe that Davis has lost touch with reality and that Kiffin did not violate his contract.

By the time Tennessee interviews him, Hamilton believes that Kiffin has already interviewed with or is a serious head coaching candidate at Syracuse, Washington, and Clemson. One of Hamilton's associates instructs Kiffin to fly to Atlanta, book a suite with a conference room attached, and wait there until the four Tennessee men arrive for the interview.

That Wednesday night Hamilton speaks with Kiffin for the first time, just to ensure that he's arrived in Atlanta okay. In the meantime, Kiffin has made his first and only error of the interview process. He's sent a FedEx package to Hamilton's home. The package, a collection of articles and notes about him that Kiffin wants Hamilton to see, arrives while Hamilton's wife, Beth, is hosting a group of women at her house. Hamilton receives a panicked phone call from his wife, who manages to hide the package in his home office. Later Hamilton will hear a rumor that FedEx delivered a package from Lane Kiffin to his house. But much to Hamilton's relief, the rumor will be shouted down by people who simply find it unbelievable. Who would be so dumb?

On Thursday, November 13, Hamilton conducts his first interview for the Tennessee job. The interview is scheduled to last 2 hours. Instead it lasts 4 hours. Kiffin regales the group with a detailed recruiting plan for Tennessee and with news that his father, Monte, the current Tampa Bay Buccaneers defensive coordinator, has a clause in his contract that would allow him to leave to coach alongside his son. Hamilton already knows this, having been informed of the clause by Kiffin's agent, Jimmy Sexton, but he's intrigued by the idea of bringing the best NFL defensive coordinator to the SEC.

Kiffin, light-brown-haired with a boyish face and a perpetual smirk hanging on the edges of his lips, is brash, passionate, energetic, and detail-oriented. Kiffin's rise to the top of the coaching ranks has been meteoric. A former college quarterback at Fresno State, Kiffin gave up his senior season to begin work as a student coach. In 1999 he accepted a coaching staff position at Colorado State and then a year later jumped to the NFL's Jacksonsville Jaguars. In 2001 Kiffin moved to USC to join newly hired Trojans coach Pete Carroll as the tight ends coach. Kiffin, a dogged recruiter, rapidly shot up the coaching ladder at USC. First he became a wide receivers coach, and then, in 2005, he ascended to the offensive coordinator position. Just as important, Pete Carroll named Kiffin his recruiting director. Helming an offense led by quarterback Matt Leinart, running backs Reggie Bush and LenDale White, and wide receivers Dwayne Jarrett and Steve Smith, Kiffin's offense ran roughshod over college football, averaging 49.1 points per game. The boy wonder, Kiffin, rode this job to the head coaching position of the NFL's Oakland Raiders. On January 23, 2007, Kiffin, just 31 years old, became the youngest coach in the NFL since 1946.

Hamilton is most impressed with Lane Kiffin's proven track record as a recruiter, and his plan to do the same at Tennessee. In 2002, Kiffin helped USC put together the number-13 recruiting class in the nation according to Rivals.com. By 2003 USC surged to the number-three class in the nation. Not to be outdone in 2004, USC locked down the number-one class in the country. With Kiffin taking over recruiting coordinator duties, the Trojans followed their first number-one class with the number-one-rated classes in 2005 and 2006. As if that weren't enough, USC's recruits have turned into great NFL players; from 2003 to 2008, no school in the country has had more first-round draft picks than the USC Trojans. At this interview Kiffin convinces Hamilton that he can replicate USC's success in nationwide recruiting at Tennessee, and that he can put together the best coaching staff in football, including his father, Monte.

Born on Leap Year Day, February 29, 1940, Monte Kiffin is a 68-year-old grizzled football veteran. Having worked as a head coach for 3 years at North Carolina State, Monte has been coaching defensive football since 1966. For the past 25 years Kiffin's been a defensive coach in the NFL, and his vaunted Tampa Cover 2 defense, predicated on leaving his safeties deep to keep from getting beat on the big play and leaving the middle of the field to roving big-play linebackers, is one of the most imitated defensive schemes in NFL history. He's the highest-paid defensive coordinator in the NFL under a multiyear contract to Tampa Bay for $2 million a year. And now, thanks to a contractual provision that allows him to leave and coach with his son, Lane Kiffin is telling Mike Hamilton he can bring his dad with him to Knoxville.

All four men leave impressed with Kiffin, but the interview process is just beginning. Early public speculation focuses on North Carolina coach Butch Davis as the leading candidate. Hamilton knows this is not the case but allows the rumor to grow because he believes it serves as a smoke screen to the actual search. The *Knoxville News-Sentinel* and many other newspapers, Internet sites, and assorted fan message boards will all breathlessly discuss Davis as the primary target. In reality Hamilton never interviews Davis for the job.

From Thursday, November 13, through Tuesday, November 25, Hamilton does interview half a dozen other candidates in four major metropolitan areas, including Dallas and Atlanta. Hamilton and colleagues travel via cars or commercial flights, though they are careful not to depart from Knoxville. Instead they leave from Nashville and Charlotte for direct flights to their destination cities. Generally the men travel on different flights and always in coach class seats, where Hamilton sits in the aisle and scans passing faces to watch for flickers of recognition. To draw less attention, he has switched his regular briefcase (which features a large orange power T) for a plain briefcase. He does the same with his Tennessee luggage. And while he does check his bags, he keeps his briefcase, with the coaching information, with him at all times. He reads nothing pertaining to the coaching search on the flight lest someone see what his papers say.

When asked which coaches he interviewed for Fulmer's job, Hamilton refuses to give a single name other than Lane Kiffin. But through a variety of other sources, I have pieced together a list that I believe to be accurate. I believe Hamilton met in person with Troy Calhoun of Air Force, Turner Gill of Buffalo, Brian Kelly of Cincinnati, and Gary Patterson of TCU, and conducted an interview over the phone with Mike Leach from Texas Tech. Hamilton was also scheduled to meet with Will Muschamp of Texas, but Muschamp signed a coach-in-waiting deal 4 days before his face-to-face interview with Hamilton. Per sources, Troy Calhoun of Air Force was the number-two choice.

In preparation for each of these interviews, the University of Tennessee books hotel rooms for the coaches. Hamilton has no public contact with any man, no walk down the hallway, no elevator ride, and certainly no public dinner. But one coach and his wife do stay for dinner with the group. The dinner arrives via room service and is enjoyed in a conference room, where not even a waiter is present.

Hamilton remains most impressed with his first interview, Lane Kiffin. As the search progresses, Hamilton telephones Kiffin: "How quickly can you be in Dallas?" he asks. The next day, on Monday, November 24, both men arrive in the city. Hamilton telephones Kiffin to check on his arrival and asks him to stop by his room if he gets a chance. Kiffin arrives at Hamilton's room and the two men visit for two and a half hours as the Green Bay Packers–New Orleans Saints *Monday Night Football* game plays on television. Kiffin doesn't leave until 1 in the morning.

The next morning, Tuesday, November 25, Kiffin officially interviews a second time for another two and a half hours. By this time Kiffin has put together a list of potential staff members that he believes he could bring with him to Tennessee. Among the names are Ed Orgeron, formerly the head coach at Ole Miss and currently the defensive line coach with the New Orleans Saints, and his father. Hamilton and the interview team are close to being sold on Kiffin as their hire.

A day later, on the Wednesday before Thanksgiving, ESPN reports that Tennessee has extended an offer to Lane Kiffin. This is inaccurate; the university has not yet offered him the job. Nevertheless, two members of the local Knoxville media commence a vigil outside Hamilton's office. When he leaves his office, Hamilton has to promise both reporters that he's going to the bathroom (there isn't one in his office) and not dodging them.

On the Friday after Thanksgiving Hamilton officially extends the offer to Kiffin and Kiffin accepts. As the Saturday morning paper arrives on doorsteps across the wide state of Tennessee for the final game of Phillip Fulmer's coaching career, the smiling face of Lane Kiffin stares up from the front page. The dawn of a new era has arrived in Knoxville.

CHAPTER 24

"ONE LAST TIME FOR TENNESSEE"

AS I ENTER THE MOUNTAINS OF East Tennessee, it begins to rain, a cold and biting rain that strips the air of fall and brings on winter. It's November 29, 2008, and the kickoff of Tennessee's final game against Kentucky is only hours away. Tennessee has won 23 in a row against the Cats and now, in Phil Fulmer's final game, he'll attempt to make it 24.

Somberly I park near the stadium and walk down James Agee Street until it meets University Boulevard, cross the street, and continue on Phillip Fulmer Way, the street outside Neyland Stadium, where in the late summer Tennessee won their home opener against UAB. That game was less than 3 months ago, only 78 days before, yet it seems as if a lifetime has passed. Then it was so hot and muggy that everyone in the stadium was drenched in sweat. Now a near-freezing rain falls down on all the fans standing on Phillip Fulmer Way as the orange-clad band passes.

I pull out my notepad and jot down notes. As I do so, an older Tennessee fan looks over at me. "You're the only person under thirty I've seen writing something down with an actual pen," he says. He grimaces and looks up at the sky, squints into the cold raindrops. "Things can change fast," he says.

The Vol Walk, six deep, a small file, proceeds slowly today. Coach Fulmer, red-eyed, walks with his wife, Vicky. This is the first time in over a decade Vicky has not perched at her usual spot at the top of Lake Loudon Boulevard greeting the team with hugs. As Coach Fulmer passes for the last time, fans, young and old, male and female, cry openly. Among them is Brock Lodge, the former male cheerleader who yearned to tackle David Palmer back in 1993. "I cried and my wife cried. Everyone was crying," he'll say later.

Kickoff is set for 6:30 P.M., just after sunset, but amidst the constant drizzle the sun has not been seen all day. I walk to the edge of the G-10 parking garage and look down into the Tennessee River. The fog is hanging low and deep, and the lights across the river are indistinct through the mist, shimmering on the distant shore. The weather befits the mood; the atmosphere outside Neyland Stadium is somber. The tailgates are quiet. Few people are grilling in the falling rain, and fewer people have shown up for this game than for any other so far this season.

Today is Senior Day, and underneath the stadium row after row of parents are lined up in the order in which their sons will be announced. As I pass the line, Arian Foster's dad, Carl, reaches out his hand and stops me.

"He made it," I say.

Mr. Foster grins. "He did that," he says.

Arian Foster is 174 yards short of the all-time rushing record. Absent a spectacular final game, he's going to finish his career behind Travis Henry, the battering-ram runner on the 1998 national championship team. Carl and I talk for a while and then I head up to the press box for the first time all season. The crush of media attention for Phil Fulmer's final game keeps me off the sideline for the game today.

The press box is packed, three rows of orange countertops filled with balding white men who make a living observing the team from a view that provides a much worse vantage point than a nice flat-screen television in front of your home couch. The press box towers high in the air, the players mere ants moving outside the glass-enclosed windows all the way down on the field. I've dressed for the elements, like a fan. I'm in three layers of shirts, two layers of pants, and three pairs of socks. Immediately I begin to sweat.

The only connection to the field outside is a small window to my right. It's pulled open so that a faint breeze wafts in, just enough to let us know that the weather outside is cold. Down below the roar of the fans rises as the band forms the T, but we can hardly hear a sound inside the press box. The crowd is much less than capacity, particularly the student section, where hardly anyone has bothered to show up on the Saturday after Thanksgiving. In front of the smallest crowd of the season, the announcer introduces each senior, who then walks onto the field alongside his parents and shakes Coach Fulmer's hand near mid-field.

The press box public address announcer comes on and informs us that anyone who cheers will be kicked out of the press box. This is a working body of professionals watching college kids play a game. This is serious business. No cheering.

Finally, after all the seniors are standing on the field with their parents, the announcer introduces Phil Fulmer, who had returned to the locker room a few minutes before. Fulmer, wearing an orange Tennessee jacket and an orange Tennessee cap, power T lined in white above the brim, jogs out holding his wife's hand and accompanied by his three daughters; his son-in-law, former player Robert Peace; and his only grandson, Joseph Phillip Peace, born just 3 months ago. As he nears the Vol sideline Fulmer raises his right hand for just a moment, a slow acknowledgment of the fans, and then, just as quickly, raises his left hand as well. It's a short wave, shy even. That's all. Phillip Fulmer has just completed his 204th jog onto the field as the head coach of the Tennessee Volunteers. It will be his last run through the T.

No one in the press box reacts.

Small televisions hang above the plate-glass windows. The UT-

Kentucky game is due to broadcast on ESPN2, but the game before it, Maryland–Boston College, has run over. As a result, it takes a little while for the telecast to be beamed into the press box. Once it begins I'm struck by a terrible realization: ESPN is a full 10 seconds behind the actual action on the field. The play begins, ends, and then we all look up and watch it begin and end for the rest of the television audience. I should have known that live sporting events are on a significant television delay, but I had no idea. All those times I've sat at home watching game-deciding plays, and they've already been decided.

The first half of the football game is as ugly as the weather. Time after time the announcer in the press box intones comments like, "Running back number three for two yards."

Jonathan Crompton is starting at quarterback for Tennessee. On the positive side, last week Crompton got his first career win as the starting quarterback in an SEC game. On the negative side, he attempted only one pass and it was intercepted. Today, he's the usual Crompton, strong-armed and inaccurate, scrambling in the pocket, never comfortable. But he has grown a beard. Since I'm a firm believer that men who grow beards get it done (BGID), I'm holding a small measure of hope for Crompton.

Kentucky's quarterback is Randall Cobb, a native of Alcoa, Tennessee, who spurned a scholarship offer from Tennessee because the Vols wanted to change his position from quarterback to defensive back. So far this year he has filled in admirably for Kentucky. But it's clear his arrival at quarterback was unexpected. Why? Because he's returning punts and staying on the field to play quarterback afterward. He leads Kentucky to an early field goal to take a 3–0 lead.

Tennessee misses a field goal and fails to move the ball on offense until the final drive of the first half. On third and goal, Crompton drops back and unleashes a pass that briefly assaults the speed of light. Not surprisingly, the pass is uncatchable. But a ref throws a pass interference flag, giving the Vols a first down at the 2. On a fourth and goal from inside the 1 with 2 seconds remaining in the half, Jonathan Crompton scores on a quarterback sneak and celebrates as if he's just won the Super Bowl. He's mobbed on the sideline by the team. After a year of futility the Tennessee football team's goals have boiled down to this: Don't let Phil Fulmer leave the field a final time as a loser. It's 7–3 Vols at the half, and the crowd exults as the team exits the field.

I head to the buffet to eat hot dogs and chili with the members of the media. John Adams, the short and portly lead columnist for the *Knoxville News-Sentinel*—a man who has sparred with Fulmer since calling for his ouster last year—is standing in line for free hot dogs beside me. "I am so glad this is the last time I'm going to have to watch this team play," he announces to the line.

The second half opens with a Tennessee offensive possession that features something no other opening drive has—a touchdown pass from Crompton to Denarius Moore. Sixty-three yards, the longest of the season.

Crompton's joy on the field is unabashed, pure; he high-steps across the field and pumps his right arm skyward, seeking, in a few seconds of joy, to erase the season that is so much different than he ever imagined it would be.

UT gets a stop and takes possession again. Moving with a precision heretofore unseen in the Dave Clawson offense, the Vols drive to the doorstep of the Kentucky goal line. On the second play of the fourth quarter the Vols score another touchdown to go up 21–3.

A stunned reporter rushes over to Tony Williams, a UT Sports Information employee sitting beside me, and asks, "This is the first time all season that Tennessee has scored touchdowns on three consecutive possessions, right?" Tony reviews the drive list for the season.

"Yep," he says. He shuts the stats and shakes his head. "We haven't scored enough touchdowns for that search to take very long," he says.

The Vols get a stop on defense and Arian Foster is back in now for the final carries of his career. As the final minutes of the Vols' season tick away, Foster darts left, cuts back across his body, steps right, and then falls forward for 3 yards. On second and goal from the Kentucky 3

Foster rushes for 1 yard, the last carry of his Tennessee career, his 650th run. All of these plays have netted him 2,964 yards rushing. In the end he finishes the game with 21 carries for 59 yards. His final 2008 stats show him with 131 carries for 570 yards and just one touchdown. Last season he rushed for 1,193 yards and 12 touchdowns.

I head down to the field for the final minutes of the game, which UT now leads 28–3. Kentucky drives the field and scores a touchdown in the pouring rain to set the final margin of 28–10.

On the final play of Phil Fulmer's Tennessee career, Jonathan Crompton takes a knee and then sprints to the sideline with the ball held in both hands—a game ball for Coach Phillip Fulmer on this, his 152nd and last victory.

John Chavis, tears hanging on the corners of his eyes, greets former UT offensive coordinator Randy Sanders, now the quarterbacks coach at Kentucky, and the two speak quietly. The Chavis defense finishes ranked third in the country, allowing just 14 touchdowns all season long.

Offensive coordinator Dave Clawson jogs out near midfield, where the team is gathering. Five months ago he moved his family from Richmond and arrived in Knoxville as the boy-wonder offensive coordinator who could become the next head coach of Tennessee. Though he had intended to spend the rest of his coaching career at Tennessee, his offense floundered, finishing the season ranked 115 out of 119 Division 1 football programs in total offense and 110 out of 119 in points per game at just 17.3. Last year's Tennessee offense, which returned nine starters, averaged 32.5 points per game. The complicated "Clawfense" is a bust. Now he and his wife and two children are set to move again; he won't be retained by Lane Kiffin.

The team prays at midfield and then two offensive linemen, number 78 Ramon Foster and number 75 Anthony Parker, raise a beaming and exultant Fulmer up onto their shoulders. Forty years after he arrived on Tennessee's campus as a 6' 1", 198-pound linebacker with dreams of becoming a dentist, Phil Fulmer exits Neyland Stadium born aloft by his players, a football clutched high above his head.

The locker room is packed, filled with many more people than at any point this season. Fulmer immediately takes note of this fact. "Guys, my family is here, so don't take off your britches," he says.

His players laugh as one.

For the fifth and final time of the 2008 season, the University of Tennessee football team sings in victory. Fulmer stands and yells, "I want them to hear, by gosh, how we treat the state of Kentucky." The team belts out the song, "We don't give a damn about the whole state of Kentucky . . . the whole state of Kentucky . . . the whole state of Kentucky . . . cause we're from Tennessee."

In the wake of the singing Fulmer praises his team and their potential. "Make those great decisions in the offseason not for anybody else, but for yourself, and your family," he says, bestowing on his players some final words of advice. "And remember those good times that you've had with your coaches while you've been here, particularly you upperclassmen . . . I appreciate you and we're going to be watching you every minute of the way. I'm going to take a knee with you one last time and count our blessings." And then he prays.

"We ask you to be with these young men as they continue their journey in the football world, in the academic world, in growing into young men and greater husbands and fathers. We ask you to be with each of us as coaches as we go on to other journeys and maybe different than sports or football, but know that every minute of the way that we want to walk forward in your light each and every day. We ask you to be with us as we travel and continue to be with these young men. In Christ's name we pray, amen."

The team stands and begins to file away from Coach Fulmer, who is left standing in the center of the locker room. Vicky Fulmer, wearing an orange sweater and white khaki pants, auburn hair bobbed in a ponytail, embraces her police escort, Vince Kanipe. Her eyes are red, tears in their corners. "I just keep telling myself that there are so many people with much worse obstacles to face than us," she says. Behind her Coach Fulmer raises his voice for the final time as the head man at the University of Tennessee. "One more time," he says, voice catching, "Tennessee on three."

"Tennessee," the team calls.

And after 34 years, the Phillip Fulmer era is over at the University of Tennessee.

IN HIS OWN PRESS conference immediately before Fulmer's, Kentucky coach Rich Brooks lashes out at Fulmer's firing: "I think it's a tragedy. I think it's a sad commentary on the coaching profession. Phillip Fulmer is a quality act, an outstanding coach with a huge, huge winning record; a Hall-of-Fame record . . . I'm sure he'll be inducted into the College Football Hall of Fame. It's a crime to see people like that forced out of the profession."

Later, the entire Fulmer family attends Tennessee's postgame press conference adjacent to the locker room in Neyland Stadium. Fulmer's three daughters hold orange-and-white rose bouquets. Occasionally they dab their eyes with white tissues. But their father has passed the point of crying. Now he's looking forward.

As Fulmer enters the press conference room to sit at the elevated table above the crush of media, he receives a standing ovation. Fulmer smiles. "Might be a first from the media," he says. Then he gives his statement. "To end up with one hundred more wins than we've had losses is a really great accomplishment. I've never really brought that up, but that's not done every day. I'm grateful, very, very grateful. Things change. Times change. Sometimes life's not always the way you want it to be. I've accepted that."

Few of the reporters' questions focus on the Kentucky game; all focus on Fulmer, who attempts to deflect many of the more personal ones. He touches on his own firing, on the end of an era in SEC football: "This world that we've created in college football, I've seen the best of it and I've seen the worst of it," Fulmer says. Finally, he's asked whether football defines him as a person. "Football's what I do, it's not what I am," he says. "I'm more proud of my family and being a father and a husband and how well they've done and I'm looking forward to enjoying some time with them here for a little bit . . . maybe, if somebody [another team] don't call." He laughs, leaves open the possibility that he'll accept another coaching job, and leaves the stage to hug his daughters.

After the press conference, Phil Fulmer and Vicky stand together just outside the locker room. Josh McNeil is the final player to leave the locker room that night. McNeil reaches out and rubs his coach's neck. "I love you, Coach," he says.

Offensive coordinator Dave Clawson walks back to the football office in the cold rain. Later, as he lies in bed late at night staring at the ceiling, he will focus on two plays that he wishes he could change from this season. The first is Arian Foster's fumble at the 6-yard line against UCLA. "Score there and we go up twenty-one–seven, win that game, and everything is different," he says. The second is the end-zone fumble against Auburn. Change those two plays, beat Wyoming (which Clawson believes they would have done absent the firing), and the team finishes 8-4. Not only does the university retain Fulmer, but he'd receive a guaranteed contract extension for reaching eight wins.

Arian Foster takes a solitary walk around Neyland Stadium after the game is over. In less than a month he'll be in Arizona training for the NFL. After a disappointing senior season, Foster, who received a second-round grade following his junior season, will go undrafted, eventually signing a free-agent deal with the Houston Texans. But now, after 5 years at Tennessee, he's trying to grasp that his collegiate career has ended. He's angry—not just about this season, during which he feels he was never utilized enough, but also about all the criticisms, all the praise, all the fans' love and hate, all the early-morning workouts and football games, the last 5 years of his life. The freshman who arrived from San Diego 4 years ago believing that he would win a couple of Heisman trophies will have to make do with becoming the second-leading rusher in University of Tennessee history. Had he known how 2008 was going to turn out, he would never have returned for his final college season.

Arian Foster's mother is also coming to grips with the end of her son's Tennessee career. After fighting countless battles on Internet message boards, she posts a good-bye message on Volquest.

"I have a sense of wanting it to be over. I think pretty much everyone has that feeling, so I don't think I'm all that different," Bernadette will write later. "But I also know that nothing will replace how I felt sitting in the stands and watching my son run through the T. It's been a fun experience for our family. We've met a lot of really, really great people over the last four or five years. We've made friends we will keep for a lifetime. I will always have a love for Tennessee that will not be replaced.

"Over the course of Arian's time here, I became a fan. I didn't intend to do that and I didn't think that it would happen. But it did. It's hard not to fall in love with all the tradition, the pageantry, the sights and sounds and smells that I still experience when I close my eyes. The people we took to games and watching their reaction was exciting and moving. I'll never forget the first time that I took my mom to a game and they released the eagle and he flew all around the stadium and when I looked at her, she was all teared up. I will always regret that my dad did not live to see his grandson do it, as he died the spring of Arian's redshirt freshman year. But he knew it was coming and that was exciting and a source of pride for him.

"I will always be a Tennessee fan. It'll just be a little different for me when Arian leaves. A little sad. A little empty. But I'll still be a fan."

OUTSIDE ON THE FIELD the rain is still falling and the lights are still on inside the near-empty stadium. Only a camera crew from Lexington, Kentucky, lingers. A cute brown-haired girl stands on the edge of the field, attempting to get her introduction correct for the local news. She makes a couple of errors and stomps her right foot in the wet grass. I walk past these newscasters and out onto the Neyland Stadium turf. A season that began in the California sunshine has just ended in late November's Tennessee rain.

I take a deep breath and look around the stadium, stare up into the empty stands as they climb into the sky, and let the raindrops hit me in the face. I sink down and feel the wet grass on my palms. It's altogether possible I'll never be on the field at Neyland Stadium again, and even after a 5-7 campaign, I don't want my season with my team to end.

So for a few moments I stare ahead into the far goal line, where fog and mist swirl in the stadium lights. I close my eyes and imagine all the ghosts of my Tennessee football past spilling onto the field at once. I'm every age I've ever been and every age I'll ever be, and the sensation of football time in Tennessee is constant and exhilarating.

It's been only 90 days since the season began, but it feels like much longer to the players. "Like ten damn years," says Josh McNeil. "I thought it would never end. Never," Arian Foster says emphatically. "Infinity," says Jonathan Crompton. Asked the same question, Phil Fulmer laughs softly to himself. "It felt like forever," he said, "forever."

Alas, the 2008 season has ended, and now I have to climb back out of my fan's fantasy camp and come back to real life. I'm a different kind of fan than my grandfather, Richard Fox, was in his old age. Maybe that's because I've never played for the University of Tennessee, never fallen on the Neyland Stadium grass and been injured like he and Inky Johnson were. Never been booed in my home stadium like Jonathan Crompton or come back for a fifth season at Tennessee when I could have taken money and gone pro like Arian Foster. Never been carried off the field like Phillip Fulmer after my 152nd career win. But I've felt each of these moments. Felt them so deeply, in a way that only another fan can understand. Maybe one day my son will feel it all too. Maybe he already does.

Many times this fall, as I've given Fox his first bottle of the early morning, he's pushed away the bottle and stood on the beige couch in our living room. He's stared into the corner, bounced up and down, and grinned at the distant wall. When I've turned and looked at where he's grinning, there's been nothing there for him to see. He did this often, and he always smiled. After a time I've stopped turning my head.

Because I've decided that babies can see things no one else can. And I'm convinced he's looking at the great-grandfather he was named after.

There was a day when it meant something to be from a particular place in the country; Fulmer's Tennessee was unique. Now that day has passed. The mercenary era of SEC football is here. It's time for younger men, men near my own age, to lead a team through the T and into a new dawn of football. I'm sad about Coach Fulmer going, but the reality is we don't live in Phil Fulmer and my dad's Tennessee anymore.

As I walk back to my dry car for my drive to Nashville, where my wife and son will be sleeping when I arrive home, a fellow Vol fan recognizes me in the rain-drenched shadows of Neyland Stadium.

"Hey, Clay," he calls.

I pause. We're the same age, two Vol fans going home late after the game. He's carrying a souvenir cup in his hand, and his breath billows out in front of him when he speaks.

"How you think Lane Kiffin's going to do against Florida?" he asks.

I grin.

Somewhere, somehow, it's always football time in Tennessee.

CHAPTER 25

SPRING FOOTBALL'S EVE

ON A BRIGHT AND SUNNY DAY in mid-March, three and a half months after UT football's 2008 season ended, a construction crew is remodeling Phillip Fulmer's house. Fulmer initially began the expensive renovation so he could better host recruits. "We started before they fired me," he explains, looking over the expanse of his 50-acre property. His blue eyes gaze out over the small creek that runs through the land and on across a bright green field cut short by a line of pine trees.

Fulmer walks around the stone walkway that surrounds the main house, an airy lodge with brown siding and tall picture windows. As he walks he greets each of the construction workers by name. On the outdoor deck he stops and speaks to the stonemason. "Jim, I caught four big ones last week. Well, they weren't real big, but I was pretty happy."

"You ever fly-fish?" asks Jim, an older man, in his sixties, who holds a trowel full of Spackle in one hand and a stone in the other.

"Oh, yeah," says Fulmer, "I love to fly-fish."

Phil Fulmer lives in the quiet suburb of Maryville, Tennessee, the same home he's lived in for the past 15 years. A street dead-ends at his property, where a yellow sign warns trespassers they've entered a private road. Twenty yards past the sign, an orange-and-white mailbox in the shape of a Tennessee football helmet gives the first clue as to who might live at the end of the road. There are no gates and no visible cameras, just three different buildings, a main house, a barn/storage unit, and another building Vicky Fulmer refers to as "Boys' Town."

Fulmer and I stand in the sunshine looking at a placard hanging on the stone facade wall of the Boys' Town building. The placard, a gift from booster Thunder Thornton, bears the text of the Theodore Roosevelt quote that appears at the beginning of this book. The inscription at the top of the placard reads:

PHILLIP FULMER
"A True Champion of the Arena"
Your friend,
Thunder (1997)

Fulmer opens the door to Boys' Town.

A Tennessee placemat sits above the hardwood floor where we enter. Fulmer, wearing a blue sports jacket, khaki pants, and a salmon-colored button-down shirt, ushers me inside. The walls are blanketed with photographs of Tennessee football players past and present. A large flat-screen television, the only thing other than pictures hanging on the walls, rises above a pool table with an orange-felt finish. Fulmer leads me around the room. "I picked all the pictures on the stairwell," he says. "Up top is a letter that Tom Osborne [Nebraska head football coach until 1998] wrote me after he beat our butt in the Orange Bowl. It was his last game coaching, and he congratulated me on getting there and said I'd get a national championship one day. I got one the next year. It meant a lot."

There is not a spare inch of wall space on the stairwell. Next to me Fulmer looks at the dozens of pictures, a photo of former quarterback Casey Clausen diving for a pylon against Alabama; Fulmer posing with Peyton Manning, Joey Kent, and Leonard Little on the Neyland Stadium turf; the front page of the *Knoxville News-Sentinel* after the 1998 Florida game, bearing the headline "Vols Do It!" and Fulmer holding the national championship BCS crystal trophy in 1998. "The rest of the room," he gestures around the downstairs walls, "somebody else, a decorator, did them; some of those I might not have picked."

Fulmer takes off his sports jacket and sits on a leather sofa, stained light red. The blinds are pulled to protect us from the bright afternoon sunlight. To his immediate left is a side table with a UT orange-and-white lamp, and a bookmarked copy of Tony Dungy's bestselling memoir *Quiet Strength* sits in front of him on an ottoman. On the wall behind his head are five photographs: a picture of Peyton Manning at the NFL draft holding up his number 18 Colts jersey, a picture of the UT student section in celebration, Fulmer hugging his wife Vicky and one of his daughters on the sideline, the team running through the T, and a Kentucky football player being driven into the ground by former UT defensive tackle John Henderson. Fulmer flexes a bit, stretches out his large hands, and rests them on his knees. On his right hand the 1998 national championship ring catches a bit of light, glistens.

"You gonna write a good book about us or a bad book?" he asks.

It's been 91 days since Phil Fulmer's final game, the victory over Kentucky. "Most coaches get run out of town; I got carried off the field," he says. In the immediate aftermath of the Kentucky game, Fulmer said he'd give himself 6 months to think about his situation before he made any decisions. He's halfway to that point, antsy to move on to something new, but still consumed by how his time at Tennessee ended. According to Fulmer, even rival SEC coaches were surprised by his firing.

"I had several call me when all this happened saying, 'What in the hell is going on?'"

I ask which coaches called. Fulmer grins.

"Naw, I can't tell you who."

Fulmer also received a personal letter from President George W. Bush in the wake of his firing. "It was just a very supportive little note on White House stationary. It was good."

The week after his final game at Tennessee, Fulmer traveled to

Atlanta to watch Florida and Alabama play in the SEC championship game. "I sat in a box with some wonderful Alabama people."

Fulmer looks up at the ceiling, runs his hands over his knees, and laughs. "When I walked into the Morgan Keegan box it was like the room turned to ice. They [Alabama fans] didn't know I was coming, and I didn't know they were going to be there either, but after a few minutes we introduced ourselves and really had a great time together." Asked who he was pulling for, Fulmer smiles again. "You know, they won't believe it, but I was kind of pulling for Alabama," he says. "I was surprised how well Florida played; they really had improved."

From the SEC championship game, Fulmer traveled with his family to the College Football Hall of Fame banquet in New York City. "Ordinarily I'd be there for one or two days at the most because of recruiting, but we stayed almost five days there, had a good time. You know, it's just getting away." Then Fulmer and his wife and youngest daughter traveled to Washington, D.C., and spent five days in the nation's capital.

Fulmer tells me he's been approached about his interest in running for office in Tennessee. "Just recently, actually. Probably as a Republican, that's beside the point really, because it's whoever the best guy is ordinarily. But the other day I told a good friend of mine that's in politics, being in politics might be the only thing that's worse than coaching as far as having to deal with people and their expectations. I don't think I would, you never say never . . . Vicky and I have discussed it, and she wasn't that excited about it."

Presently, Fulmer is a partner in business development with Northshore Management, a business run by former Vol football player Mike West. "They'd like me to stay on there and not coach again. I like it. We'll see."

But Fulmer still believes he may coach again. "I'm getting ready for the next job. I've talked to some people if they [those openings] come about. It will be hard, you know. But it might be exciting too. I won't have quite the emotional attachment, maybe. Fifty-eight is young in the world today. As long as I enjoy it."

But no matter how much he talks about the future, Fulmer can't help but circle back to the end of his tenure at Tennessee. "I never thought it [the firing] would happen. I still don't know exactly what happened," he says. "Picture this in the last twelve months: We play LSU for the conference championship until the final couple of minutes, won the bowl game for our tenth win [a victory over Wisconsin in the Outback Bowl], I'm inducted into the Knoxville Hall of Fame, got a new contract, won my one hundred and fiftieth game, and got fired in the same year. It doesn't add up."

Fulmer ticks each of these accomplishments off on his fingers as he says them. A pinky represents his firing, and he leaves his pinky extended in my direction for a moment. He pauses now, as if lost in thought, takes a drink from a bottle of water, slowly screws the top back on, and grips his knees with his large hands.

"There must have been something I missed somewhere in the relationship point, whatever the right word is, to make a decision like that. Mike Hamilton gave in when traditionally, we fight. We fight for what we believe in and obviously he didn't believe in me, that I could do what I'd done for fourteen of the sixteen full years I'd been there. He wasn't willing to fight for me."

Fulmer contrasts this lack of support with what he received as a young head coach from then-president Joe Johnston and athletic director Doug Dickey. "In 1994, we started one and three. And the amount of support from those guys was incredible. They fought for me. We got that straightened out, finished eight and four, and won the bowl game. It laid the foundation for the SEC championships and the national championship. You're going to have adversity. It's how you respond and who's in your corner."

Hamilton's and the university's lack of loyalty is especially difficult for Fulmer, an old offensive lineman who has always prided loyalty above all traits, to accept. "When things get tough, I work harder, get tougher." Like with the offense in 2008. "Our offense, we'd come to work on Sunday and try to figure out what you can do to fix it, and it's just like you'd go to practice and you'd do things better and then you'd go back to games and you'd do them worse. It was almost like, and you hate to say it, but there was this black cloud following you around and if it can happen bad to you, it happens bad to that team.

"Arian's fumble going in [against UCLA], Arian's fumble coming out against Auburn, I mean that doesn't happen; this is a college football team. He's taken ten thousand of those handoffs, counting all the practice time, and then against Florida you get down to the one-yard line, two-yard line, and you don't get any points from it, twice. You've got a chance to go in twenty–thirteen or maybe even tied up. It was miserable, it was miserable for everybody including the fans."

He takes a deep breath and another drink from his water bottle. Fulmer never believed the players would have such difficulty grasping Dave Clawson's offense.

"My mistake, again I've said all along everything begins with me, is I gave in too much. I was going to, and fully intended to, marry the [offensive] systems, but then he's gotta make the play call with just twenty-five seconds to decide, and I gave him [Dave Clawson] too much. And the system's good and sound, and Dave had been very successful and everything, but it just didn't work. The time, the players, I don't know how to say this exactly, whether it was UCLA and Auburn and they didn't buy in [to the offense] or it was later and we didn't execute. It was me and Greg Adkins [from the old offensive staff], and the new coaches are all good coaches and they knew the new system, and we [Fulmer and Adkins] knew the old system so I just couldn't get it fixed at midseason. Now, the coaches all knew what we were teaching, but it didn't click with the players. It just wasn't working. I still don't know why it didn't.

"You know, I could have made a tough decision and fired Dave and taken over myself which, if he'd have been obstinate or the system hadn't been sound or he hadn't been a good teacher, I would have done that. But I couldn't lay my head on the pillow just throwing him out there to the world, still never believing necessarily that we were going to lose all those games and it would cost me my job and other people's jobs too."

The reality is, however, that Fulmer lost his job for losing to inferior teams. Asked what his expectations were entering the season, he says, "I think there's no reason that you don't win eight or nine of those ballgames. That's the truth. Auburn's a crappy team that year, we just happened to play crappy. UCLA, I mean we score going in [when Arian Foster fumbled with the Vols leading 14–7] and it may have been thirty-five–seven, they'd probably quit. Wyoming? I mean, that was a joke. My team was drained after the firing; it was unbelievably difficult just getting them out there."

Tomorrow, on March 10, 2009, Tennessee begins spring football practice with a new coach, Lane Kiffin. I ask Fulmer what he thinks of being replaced by Kiffin. "Well, that's not my place to make a judgment, I don't know him. And I don't know, you know, guy won five games? I'd won one hundred and fifty." Fulmer laughs, shakes his head, and repeats, "It's not my place."

He continues, "We got a good team coming back, I'll say that. They should be good, the schedule's better."

On the day of his hiring Kiffin said he wanted to speak to Fulmer at some point in the future. "At this point, yeah, he has reached out to me, and I'll sit down with him at some point," says Fulmer. Asked whether he has an opinion of Kiffin's public comments about Urban Meyer and the Florida Gators cheating and other SEC controversies he's stirred up since his hiring, Fulmer abruptly stands and strides across the room, ponderous footfalls echoing on the hardwood floors. For a moment I believe he's leaving, cutting our interview short. The door opens behind me, the bathroom door. "I don't know him, and I don't really care to comment on any of that and I don't know what context it came out of." He pauses at the bathroom door for a moment, contemplates silence, then speaks anew. "It's either immaturity at the very least or poor judgment at the very worst."

Since his firing, Fulmer, a regular visitor at all sorts of Vol athletic events during his tenure, has attended only one Tennessee game: Lady Vol basketball coach Pat Summitt's 1,000th win against Georgia in Knoxville's Thompson-Boling Arena. "I took Vicky back to watch Pat's one thousandth win and we're in the box and everything's great, and all of a sudden they crank up 'Rocky Top' and she gets emotional. Which I understand. It was hard, really hard. And it's still hard on my girls, it's been hard on my friends, a lot of Tennessee people because it was such a surprise."

His eyes tear up at this point, and he pauses to collect himself. He looks down at the hardwood floor in front of him, lightly lifts his feet, an old offensive lineman looking for his best foot placement, and drops them back down to the ground.

"It's tough," he says, choking on the word *tough*.

"You can love a university, but the university can't love you back. It's just bricks and mortar."

On September 5, 2009, Tennessee kicks off against Western Kentucky. For the first time in twenty-nine seasons, Phil Fulmer will not be on the Tennessee sideline. I ask him if he'll be in the stadium. "I don't know where I'll be," he says.

ON APRIL 18, 2009, 51,488 Tennessee fans, the second-largest crowd to ever watch an orange-and-white game—the annual intrasquad scrimmage that signals the end of spring practice—gather in Neyland Stadium for the public debut of the Lane Kiffin era.

Before kickoff on a bright and sunny spring day without a cloud in the sky, Phil Fulmer strides to midfield to be acknowledged as the recipient of the 44th annual Knoxville Quarterback Club's General Robert R. Neyland Trophy, delivered earlier that morning at a Knoxville banquet. The award has been given each year to one of the top coaches in college football. Florida State's Bobby Bowden, Michigan's Lloyd Carr, Alabama's Bear Bryant, and Auburn's Pat Dye are among the past winners. Now, a little more than five months after leaving the field on his players' shoulders, Fulmer is back on the Neyland Stadium turf.

Before he's even been introduced by the public address announcer, the entire stadium crowd comes to its feet and begins to cheer as its members see Fulmer and his family striding across the Neyland Stadium turf. Fulmer, wearing a black suit, white shirt, and blue tie, the first time he hasn't been wearing orange at Neyland Stadium in over three decades, raises his hand to acknowledge the cheering Vol fans. The public address announcer's words of acknowledgment are inaudible over the cheering. Already having been presented the award that morning, Fulmer does not speak to the crowd now. At a press conference earlier, he reflected on what returning to Tennessee is like for him: "I'm a Tennessee guy, from start to finish," Fulmer said. "Certainly, I'll continue to support Tennessee football, always."

Now, as the team prepares to run onto the field as a prelude to the 2009 football campaign, Phil Fulmer slides off toward the exit, quietly heading for the Lettermen's Lounge.

That same day Mike Hamilton appears at a news conference to discuss the Tennessee athletic department budget. Football, the engine of Vol athletic commerce, fell $2.2 million short of projections for the 2007–2008 budget, $1 million short of ticket sale projections, and $1.2 million short for not making a bowl game. The athletic department is hopeful it will not have to dip into its reserve fund to cover the expenses for its $87.5 million budget.

As the spring game commences on the field, inevitable comparisons between the two eras of Tennessee football begin. Brock Lodge, male cheerleader who dreamed of tackling David Palmer in 1993, assuages his four-year-old son's disappointment over the lack of popcorn available at the game. "Phil Fulmer always had popcorn," his son Tripp says. "Lane Kiffin needs to work on the popcorn."

After the game, in which the first team offense will ultimately defeat the first team defense 41–23, Vol big rig driver Charlie Harris, who is ill and watched the game on television, calls me. "It's going to be exciting," he says, "but I don't think Lane Kiffin will know my name."

ACKNOWLEDGMENTS

I WROTE THIS BOOK FROM MY home office, and my son Fox was never far away. About half the time, I wrote with my door closed. As I typed away, I'd hear Fox running around on the lower level of our house, squealing, yelping, and making mischief. Often he'd walk into my office, wobble around my desk, lift his arms, and come sit in Dad's lap while I worked. Occasionally he struck the keyboard. He's a writer in training already. Sometimes, when the door was closed, he'd slide one of his toy cars under the door to get my attention. Then I knew it was time for Daddy to take a break from writing.

Writing a book from home with an infant could have only happened if my parents were making a serious run at greatest grandparents in the world. Tremendous thanks to my parents Norm and Liz Travis for all of their help. And, of course, thanks to my wife Lara for putting up with her husband being out of town all fall and for the mood swings of a fan in the wake of losses. It's taken a while, but I think she's a bona fide Tennessee fan now. I knew I had her hooked when she forwarded me an article this spring about Bryce Brown, the nation's consensus top player, committing to play football for Tennessee. "Thought you might want to see this," she wrote. If only she'd known her husband was watching the webcast of the announcement while on the radio in Birmingham, Alabama.

I wasn't 100 percent sure whether I wanted to dive back into another book about SEC football. Finally my agent, Byrd Leavell, a rock star of the first order, gave me a verbal slapping. "They aren't asking you to write a book about mold; they're asking you to write a book about your favorite team in the world." Well put.

My editor, Kate Hamill, is truly one of the best editors on earth. I'm tremendously fortunate to have her looking over what I write. The book is immeasurably stronger for her comments and suggestions. Even if, occasionally, I felt like a freshman playing for Bobby Knight when I read her editorial critiques penned on the manuscript.

Thanks to all the good folks at It Books, including Milan Bozic, who did a hell of a job designing the book jacket, and production editor Nancy Tan.

Thanks to everyone at the University of Tennessee who helped make this book possible. In particular, tremendous thanks to Tiffany Carpenter, who was extraordinary in setting up access and events; Tony Williams at the UT Sports Information Department's office, who was unbelievably helpful and responsive to all sorts of questions, like how many people dressed for the UCLA game, which I believe I asked 14 times; Bruce Warwick; and countless other members of the athletic department staff. I find it hard to believe there's a more responsive group anywhere.

My sincere thanks to everyone who spent time answering my questions and responding to the follow-ups that ensued: Phillip Fulmer, Mike Hamilton, Arian Foster, Bernadette Foster, Carl Foster, Josh McNeil, Jonathan Crompton, Charlie Harris, Thunder Thornton, Bill Stokely, Andrew Haag and the Tennessee student managers, Inky Johnson, Roger Frazier, Vince Kanipe, Dave Clawson, Mark Nagi, Brent Hubbs, Walter Slater, Professor Ed Hirt, and Max and Joy Haught. The list on a book like this is truly legion and inevitably I'm leaving someone out.

I've had the good fortune to make a living doing something that I truly love over the past several years. Thanks to everyone at CBSSports .com who gave me a shot with the ClayNation column several years ago, to the crew at Deadspin.com, and to my new home at FanHouse.com. Writing online is an immensely rewarding experience. So much so that occasionally when I finished a chapter of this book, I wanted to click publish and wait to hear what people thought. I've had to wait a while, but I hope you've enjoyed the story.

Also thanks to the great people at Counsel On Call, who allow me to practice law with great flexibility and feel a bit better about signing off on the law school student loan checks. I also appreciate all the help from the fine folks at 104.5 the Zone in Nashville and my co-host Chad Withrow.

Most important, thanks to the readers. From the moment I started writing on the Internet, 99 percent of the e-mails I've gotten from y'all have been positive, constructive, and encouraging. I can't thank you all, but I can thank one of you, which is what I'm going to do. So thanks to Scott Griffin.

When all was said and done, I wanted to write as honest a story about the fan experience, the player experience, the coach experience, the administrative experience, and the life experience of a Tennessee football season as I possibly could. I hope I've managed that. Now I just want September 5, 2009, to get here as soon as possible.